The Tenth Harbinger

Genesis 11:1-9
(the extrapolated original version)

1 - And the whole land was of one government, and of one ruler.

2 - And it came to pass, as they journeyed from the east, that they found a plain in the land of Shinar; and they dwelt there.

3 - And they said one to another, "Come, let us make brick, and burn them thoroughly." And they had brick for stone, and they had slime for mortar.

4 - And they said, "Come, let us build us a city and a tower, whose top [may reach] unto heaven; and let us make us a name, lest we be scattered abroad upon the face of the whole earth."

5 - And the LORD came down to see the city and the tower, which the children of men had built.

6 - And the LORD said, "Behold, the people are one, and they have one government; and now nothing will be restrained from them, which they have imagined to do.

7 - Come, let us go down, and there disrupt their government, that they may not follow their ruler's commands."

8 - So the LORD scattered them abroad from thence upon the face of all the earth: and they stopped building the city.

9 - Therefore the name of the place is called Babylon [city of religious towers]. And the LORD disrupted the government of the empire: and from thence did the LORD scatter them abroad upon the face of all the land

The Tenth Harbinger

America's Exact Role in World History and Triple Destiny Revealed

Watchman Bob

TheTenthHarbinger.com

Cover Design by Estela Jia Ceyril Redulla

ISBN-13: 978-1493795758
ISBN-10: 1493795759

Dedication

This book is dedicated to the Lord, who has blessed the world with a few truly wonderful, rare and brave souls who, for the sake of knowing the Truth, are willing and able to suspend the beliefs about their country and their religion with which they have been indoctrinated all their lives long enough to consider, with open minds and hearts, ideas that may challenge those convictions they take for granted. Those Spirit-led believers are the only ones we can trust to show us the way to the Kingdom of Heaven.

Contents

Introduction

"If the watchman sees the sword coming and does not blow the trumpet, and the people are not warned, and the sword comes and takes away any person from among them, that person is taken away in his iniquity; but his blood I will require at the watchman's hand." (Ezekiel 33:6)

When this watchman first read *The Harbinger* by Jonathan Cahn[1], like most Bible expositors and prophecy teachers, he was astonished by the clarity of its insights into the prophetic Scriptures. And he was mesmerized by the undeniable way in which it connected the details of an obscure, 2,850-year-old passage of prophetic Scripture (Isaiah 9:10) with specific current events and, very possibly, events in the near future of the United States of America.

In 2011, when *The Harbinger* was first published, it quickly made the *New York Times* Best Seller list and remained there for an amazing (for a religious book) 52 weeks. Then, in 2012 and 2013, *The Isaiah 9:10 Judgment* DVD, based on *The Harbinger* and featuring Jonathan Cahn as its narrator, was the number-one selling Christian DVD in the world. Various notable Christian ministers, Bible prophecy teachers and U.S. government leaders have referred to *The Harbinger* with superlatives like "astonishing," "stunning," and "mind-blowing."

In *The Harbinger* author Cahn reveals, in a captivating, vivid, narrative style, that the September 11, 2001, destruction of the World Trade Center in New York City was precisely predicted, in explicit detail, in the Isaiah 9:10 prophecy by nine harbingers or signs of terrible things to come. And by astutely linking the Isaiah 9:10 prophecy with the prophetic implications of the *Shemitah*—the practice of Ancient Israel of allowing the land to lie fallow every seventh year, as commanded by the Lord (cf. Leviticus 25:2-4)—*The Harbinger* also reveals how the economic collapse of 2008 and perhaps a much greater catastrophe to come on the U.S.A. in 2015 are accurately foretold in the ancient Hebrew Scriptures (the "Old Testament").

1

But, however intriguingly insightful and startlingly revelatory *The Harbinger* is, as this watchman reached the end of the book, he sensed that something was missing. It left him hanging. Although it hints at the possible, even probable destruction of the United States of America as a political nation in the same way the Northern Kingdom of Israel (the immediate subject of the Isaiah 9:10 prophecy) was destroyed by the Assyrians in 722 B.C., *The Harbinger* stops short of stating that, according to Bible prophecy, the U.S.A. will actually be destroyed as a political and/or physical nation.

In Chapter 20—"Things to Come"—the main character Nouriel, who speaks in the first person throughout the story, asks the prophet, the one who had been revealing the meanings of the nine harbingers to Nouriel, what happens next to America. The prophet replies that, as long as the U.S.A. does not turn back to God, there will be intermittent disasters intended to get the nation's attention. And if America continues to refuse to heed the warnings, all of God's favor—prosperity, protection and peace—will be withdrawn and the fall of the U.S.A., which was foreshadowed by 9/11, will occur.

Through his narrative, Cahn goes on to explain that the verses following Isaiah 9:10 predict the total destruction of Israel and, by projection, the "American empire" (note his use of the term "empire" in referring to the U.S.A.). Verses other than verse 10 that he references from Isaiah chapter 9 foretell the total political (verses 11 and 12), spiritual (verse 18) and physical (verse 19) destruction of ancient Israel and (again by projection) modern America. (Note that verses 18 through 21, although speaking figuratively of the people being destroyed by the fire of wickedness, also foretell their "devouring" one another and the land being "burned up.")

However, when pressed by Nouriel to tell him if the "American empire" will definitely be destroyed, as Israel was, the prophet applies the admonition of the Lord to His people Israel to the U.S.A.: *"If My people who are called by My name will humble themselves, and pray and seek My face, and turn from their wicked ways, then I will hear from heaven, and will forgive their sin and heal their land."* (2 Chronicles 7:14)

So, *The Harbinger's* final conclusion as to whether or not the United States of America will, according to Bible prophecy, definitely be destroyed by descendants of the ancient Assyrians (modern-day Middle Eastern Muslims) is contingent on whether or not the people of the U.S.A. repent of their "spirit of defiance," fully change their course and "return to God" (cf. pages 218, 219 and 221).

The Correct End of the Story?

It is very difficult to honestly deny the uncanny accuracy of the nine harbingers of Isaiah 9:10 in predicting not only the demise and destruction of ancient Israel but their amazing specificity in foretelling the 9/11/2001 destruction of the World Trade Center towers, the arrogance and defiance of America's leaders in proclaiming, without first turning to the Lord, "We will rebuild!"[2] and the collapse of the previously strong U.S. economy during the Bush and Obama administrations. But, does the final conclusion of *The Harbinger* as to America's future really concur with the Bible?

This watchman/commentator has been diligently studying and declaring the present-day implications of the prophetic Scriptures for many years, and he has found no such indecisiveness and equivocation there. In fact, there are over 250 verses of Scripture and about 60 specific indicators in the Bible that tell those who have "ears that hear" **exactly** what both the immediate (within the next few years) and final destinies of the United States of America are. What's more, there was a very important item that was discovered, in an amazing way, in the rubble of the fallen World Trade Center towers that links the Isaiah 9:10 prophecy to all those other passages of Scripture in confirming the destiny of the U.S.A. And that item is the **Tenth Harbinger**—the key to completing the prophetic message of the first nine harbingers explicated by Jonathan Cahn.

One may wonder why, if the Tenth Harbinger is so important in understanding the Biblical identity and destiny of America, it was totally omitted from Jonathan Cahn's book. Cahn was not unaware of it, because he mentioned it incidentally in *The Isaiah 9:10 Judgment* DVD. But he placed no significant importance on it—certainly not as much as he placed on the first nine harbingers. Nor is Cahn's overlooking the Tenth Harbinger because it does not exist or is insignificant. It does indeed exist and is of critical, life and death importance in warning Americans what is coming **very soon** on our nation so that we can do what we **must do** to be saved. So why has the Tenth Harbinger been ignored, not only by Cahn, but by virtually all Bible scholars, expositors and prophecy teachers?

Consequences

The reason this watchman believes that most Bible prophecy teachers, especially U.S. prophecy teachers, refuse to acknowledge the Tenth Harbinger given to us by the Lord is because its implications are just too inflammatory and threatening to the status quo of their American "churchianity." If they openly acknowledge and teach the Truth about the Tenth Harbinger, their profitable ministries, jobs and book sales will probably quickly come to a halt. This watchman knows that to be a very real probability because he has experienced some pretty severe repercussions, including losing his job, his 30-year career, and alienating most of his "friends" and family members because he has, for over ten years, been declaring in every way that he can—in person, through correspondence, a newsletter, a commentary on the Bible's book of Revelation[3], a website[4] and a blog[5]—the warning of the Tenth Harbinger.

Another Witness

However, this watchman is greatly encouraged to continue proclaiming the true and complete message about the identity and destiny of the United States of America in Bible prophecy—before it is too late for those precious souls who are willing to listen to the warning—because another witness to the Truth (cf. 2 Corinthians 13:1) has bravely stepped forward. His name is James F. Fitzgerald. Just last year (2013), two years after *The Harbinger* was published, Fitzgerald published his eye-opening book *The 9/11 Prophecy*[6]. In *The 9/11 Prophecy*, Fitzgerald takes the warning of *The Harbinger* a giant step farther by connecting the Isaiah 9:10 prophecy with the *"End of the Age"* (Matthew 24:3) prophecies of last book of the Bible, the Revelation of the Lord, and correctly, unequivocally (unlike Jonathan Cahn), at least partially discerning the destiny of the "American empire" and its *"great city"* (Revelation 18:10), New York City, in those prophecies. He also correctly observes that we are, at the present time, in the *"generation"* (Matthew 24:34) during which all the prophesied cataclysmic events that will destroy this present, dark and evil world, especially the United States of America, and usher in the wonderful "world to come" will be fulfilled. (cf. Matthew 24, Mark 13, Luke 21, Hebrews 2:5 and Revelation 1:1-5)

The Whole Truth and Our Response to It

Nevertheless, although James Fitzgerald is closer to correctly discerning the Biblical identity and destiny of the U.S.A., by also, like Jonathan Cahn, overlooking the Tenth Harbinger, he fails to connect the dots which complete the picture—he fails to see that the prophecies of Isaiah 9, Matthew 24, Mark 13, Luke 21, 2 Thessalonians 2, and the book of Revelation are linked to hundreds of other passages of prophetic Scripture to reveal the **exact** identity of America, her role in Bible prophecy and the **three ways** (one political and two physical) in which the United States of America will be destroyed. Therefore, both Cahn and Fitzgerald fail to correctly recognize what the Lord commands His people in America to do in preparation for the awesome, terrible or wonderful (depending on one's point of view) events of the "beginnings of sorrows" (Mark 13:8), the "Great Tribulation" (Matthew 24:21; Revelation 7:14) and the "Day of the Lord" (2 Peter 3:10; cf. Revelation 6:17) very soon to come, and leave them in real danger of being sucked, by the "great deception" (Matthew 24:24; 2 Thessalonians 2:11) that will accompany those tremendously trying times, into the clutches of the "lawless one" and perishing (2 Thessalonians 2:9-10).

And why do both Cahn and Fitzgerald fail to recognize the Tenth Harbinger? One reason is that they, like the vast majority of other American Christians, do not understand the true spiritual, religious foundation on which the United States of America was built and continues to function.

So, it is the fervent prayer of this watchman that those of you who read *The Tenth Harbinger* will have the courage to at least temporarily set aside your preconditioned traditions, allegiances and understandings about the history and the role in the world of the United States of America, and honestly open your minds and hearts to what God's sure Word of prophecy **really** reveals about the identity and destiny of America. You may be infuriated or you may be terrified by the contents of this book, but I assure you that you will not be bored; it will "rattle your cage" and you will have to get way out of your comfort zone to honestly, with an open mind evaluate the veracity of what is written here. But, please allow this watchman to assure you, from his own experience, that if you do have the honesty and the courage to face up to the Truth about what is happening and what will soon happen in the world, especially the U.S.A., what our Heavenly Father tells us to do about it and take it to heart and act on it in obedience, you will be able to face whatever comes. And you will be able to face the future not only with the confidence and peace of knowing exactly what to expect and how to deal with it, but with the thrilling joy of anticipating the end of this dark, rapidly deteriorating world and entering into the incomprehensibly wonderful Paradise of the Lord. Just be sure to read **all the way through** this book, through last chapter— **"In The End, there's GOOD NEWS!"**

What You Get

Here's what to anticipate from *The Tenth Harbinger* :

- *The Harbinger* and *The 9/11 Prophecy* will be reviewed, pointing out their revelatory insights as well as their flaws.
- The calling of a third witness, Watchman Bob, to testify to the **exact** identity and destiny of the United States of America will be described.
- A thorough, Biblical explanation of "True Christianity" will be given.
- The historical spiritual roots and present religion of the United States of America will be closely examined, revealing whether or not the U.S.A. is truly a "Christian nation."
- The true Biblical identity and destiny of America will be irrefutably proven.
- The Tenth Harbinger will be explained, confirming that it foretells the future of the U.S.A. just as accurately as do the first nine harbingers, as revealed in *The Harbinger.*
- A quasi-fictional, End Times narrative will be given, revealing how, according to current events in the light of Bible prophecy, things may go in the world and in the U.S.A. during the "Final Seven Years."

- What the Lord commands His people in America to do to not only survive, but to achieve a glorious victory during the coming time of great testing and trouble will be explained.
- The true, gloriously happy end of the story for the Lord's Overcomers will be told.

"You shall know the truth, and the truth shall make you free."
(John 8:32)

Watchman Bob
November 2013
Updated April 2014

Chapter 1

The Harbinger: Insightful but Incomplete

⁸The Lord sent a word against Jacob, And it has fallen on Israel.

⁹All the people will know—Ephraim and the inhabitant of Samaria—who say in pride and arrogance of heart:

¹⁰*"***The bricks have fallen down, but we will rebuild with hewn stones; the sycamores are cut down, but we will replace them with cedars.***"*

¹¹Therefore the LORD shall set up the adversaries of Rezin against him, and spur his enemies on,

¹²the Syrians before and the Philistines behind; and they shall devour Israel with an open mouth. For all this His anger is not turned away, but His hand is stretched out still.

¹³For the people do not turn to Him who strikes them, nor do they seek the LORD of hosts.

¹⁴Therefore the LORD will cut off head and tail from Israel, palm branch and bulrush in one day.

¹⁵The elder and honorable, he is the head; the prophet who teaches lies, he is the tail.

¹⁶For the leaders of this people cause them to err, and those who are led by them are destroyed.

¹⁷Therefore the Lord will have no joy in their young men, nor have mercy on their fatherless and widows; for everyone is a hypocrite and an evildoer, and every mouth speaks folly. For all this His anger is not turned away, but His hand is stretched out still.

¹⁸For wickedness burns as the fire; it shall devour the briers and thorns, and kindle in the thickets of the forest; they shall mount up like rising smoke.

¹⁹Through the wrath of the LORD of hosts the land is burned up, and the people shall be as fuel for the fire; no man shall spare his brother.

²⁰And he shall snatch on the right hand and be hungry; he shall devour on the left hand and not be satisfied; every man shall eat the flesh of his own arm.
(Isaiah 9:8-20)

In *The Harbinger, The Isaiah 9:10 Judgment* DVD, and in many speeches and television interviews, Jonathan Cahn, in an extraordinarily perspicacious, eye-opening way, explains how nine events in the destruction of the Northern Kingdom of Israel (also identified by the name of its principal tribe Ephraim and capital city Samaria) foretold, with amazing specificity and accuracy, the destruction, more than 2,700 years later, of the World Trade Center towers on September 11, 2001. Let us briefly review the history surrounding the fall of Israel and how the Isaiah 9:10 prophecy was fulfilled in Israel's destruction, then see, as explained by Cahn, how that prophecy applies with equal or even greater precision to the destruction of the World Trade Center. Finally, we will explain how, by overlooking the Tenth Harbinger, Cahn has unfortunately, even tragically, neglected to correctly tell the Biblical "end of the story."

Israel's Demise and Destruction Prophesied

The Hebrew prophet Isaiah began to utter his predictions in about 754 B.C.[1] During the following years, the first nine events in the destruction of the northern kingdom of Israel, as foretold by Isaiah (which, thanks to Jonathan Cahn, we now know were harbingers of disaster in a future "kingdom"—the United States of America) occurred.

Historical Background Brief [2]

Throughout her history the Lord had been warning His nation Israel of the severe consequences of not keeping His commandments—especially the second and third of the Ten Commandments—to not get involved in idolatry (cf. Exodus 20:3-4; Deuteronomy 6:14-15). But after Jeroboam of the tribe of Ephraim led the ten northern tribes of Israel to secede from the union of all twelve tribes in 931 B.C. and was made king of the new Northern Kingdom of Israel, he established two royal idolatrous worship centers—at Dan, in the northern part of the kingdom, and at Bethel, at the southern extremity of the kingdom. Dan and Bethel had long been steeped in idolatrous, pagan, cultic traditions. Jeroboam also established shrines throughout the kingdom staffed by non-

Levitical priests. (The Lord had designated only Levites to serve as priests in Israel—cf. Numbers 3:6-10.) Then, for the next 200+ years of Israel's (Ephraim's) history, **every one** of the eighteen kings who followed Jeroboam, to one extent or another, continued the idolatrous practices established by him. Therefore, at various times throughout her history, the Lord, true to His Word, brought other kingdoms against Israel to punish her. Also, the chronicles of the kings of Israel record a history of treachery, assassinations and violent deaths.

Jeroboam's reign was punctuated by conflicts with the Southern Kingdom (Judah, the "House of David"), in most of which Judah prevailed. In about 911 B.C. the forces of Abijah, King of Judah, dealt the forces of Jeroboam a crushing defeat, pushing the border of the Southern Kingdom about nine miles north into Israel. Jeroboam died shortly afterward. Then, Jeroboam's son, Nadab, who succeeded his father as king of Israel, soon found himself at war with the Philistines. But while the Israelite army was besieging the Philistine city of Gibbethon, Nadab was assassinated by his successor Baasha (1 Kings 15:27). In 895 B.C. Baasha's Israel was attacked from the northeast by the army of Ben-hadad of Aram (Syria), who gained control of most of eastern Galilee (1 Kings 15:20; 2 Chronicles 16:4). In 885 B.C. Baasha's son Elah succeeded his father as king of Israel, and was immediately forced by the threatening Philistines to resume Israel's war with Philistia. However, in the second year of his reign, Elah was assassinated and replaced as king by Omri (1 Kings 16:16). For the next six years, Omri was engaged in a civil war with a would-be usurper to his throne, Tibni, but finally prevailed. Then, Omri went on the offensive and managed to expand the borders of the kingdom through purchasing land, treaties with the surrounding kingdoms, and intermarriage between his children and those of other kings.

Omri's son Ahab, who succeeded him, married the idolatrous, pagan daughter of the king of Tyre, Jezebel, so he had plenty of encouragement to perpetuate the idolatrous ways of Israel, establishing the Canaanite/Phoenician god Baal as the principal deity worshipped in Israel. Also, after he became king, Ahab continued the land acquisition program of his father, but in doing so, he threatened to encroach on the land east of the Sea of Chinnereth (later called the Sea of Galilee) controlled by Aram-Damascus. A coalition of Aramaic (Syrian) kings, led by another Ben-hadad (a royal title rather than a name), responded by invading Israel and besieging Samaria. But, because they were disorganized, the Syrians were not able to sustain their control over Israel (1 Kings 20:1-22). And when Ahab mustered his forces and attacked the Syrian army, he won a decisive victory and gained a treaty with and generous trade concessions from Ben-hadad (1 Kings 20:23-34). However, three years later, in 853 B.C., Damascus challenged Israel again, and Ahab was killed in battle near the Transjordan city of Ramoth-gilead.

Ahaziah, Ahab's son, then became the king of Israel. However, like his parents, he was a worshipper of Baal. And when he inquired of Baal-Zebub as to his fate when he sustained injuries from a fall, the Lord instructed the prophet Elijah to tell the king that he would die, which he did, and the king died. Ahaziah's brother Jehoram (Joram) became king in his place. (1 Kings 22:51-2 Kings 1:17). However, Jehu, the commander of Israel's army, who had been on guard against the Syrians at Ramoth-gilead, was anointed by a messenger from the prophet Elisha to be the king of Israel and told to slay all of Ahab's family, including his wife Jezebel and Joram, because of their idolatry and murders of the true prophets of the Lord. And, in a real bloodbath, that is what Jehu did. He also killed all the priests of Baal and destroyed their idols and places of worship. However, he continued the idolatrous practices of Jeroboam, and the Lord brought the army of Syria, now led by its new king Hazael, against Israel, and various parts of the kingdom were taken, diminishing its size and power. (2 Kings 9:1-10:33)

And so it went throughout the history of Israel: idolatry, treachery, violent deaths and destruction caused by wars, exactly as warned by the Lord and foretold by His prophets. But, through it all, the kings of Israel managed, to a large extent, to maintain the cohesiveness of the kingdom—until **the breach** occurred.

Ominous Precursors of Disaster to Come—the Assyrian Threat and Invasion

Prior to the reigns of Omri and Ahab, the kingdom of Assyria, with its capital at Nineveh (which was founded by Nimrod), 200 miles directly northeast of Samaria, was a relatively insignificant kingdom. However, during the reign of Omri over Israel, the king of Assyria Asshurnasirpal II started expanding his kingdom to the west until his armies reached the northeastern corner of the Amurru (Mediterranean) Sea, then started advancing down the coast, extorting heavy tribute from the cities of Phoenicia—Arvad, Byblos, Tyre and Sidon. Asshurnasirpal's son, Shalmaneser III, continued his father's aggression when he became King of Assyria in 859 B.C.

So, during the armistice between Ahab and Ben-hadad, they banded their armies together with those of nine other kings of the Levant and engaged the army of Shalmaneser in western Syria, at Qarqar. That was in 853 B.C., the year of Ahab's death (which occurred later that year). The allied forces won a decisive battle, and, although Shalmaneser continued to make forays into eastern Syria and other areas, it was years until the Assyrian army returned to the coast.

Finally, in 841 B.C., Shalmaneser carried out a successful military campaign that took him all the way through Damascus and northern Israel to Mount Carmel on the coast of the Great Sea (the Mediterranean), then up the Phoenician coast through Tyre and Sidon to the Dog River, just south of Byblos. On this foray, Salmaneser's army plundered and destroyed numerous cities (cf. Hosea 10:14) and he exacted tribute from Israel and Tyre. However, he then withdrew to Syria where, for many years, the Assyrians were occupied with their expanding empire in places far removed from Israel.

The First Harbinger—a "Breach in the Wall" of Israel's National Security

"Therefore this iniquity shall be to you like ***a breach*** *ready to fall, a bulge in a high wall, whose breaking comes suddenly, in an instant."* (Isaiah 30:13)

Almost a century after Shalmaneser's invasion of Israel, Tiglath-pileser III, king of the greatly expanded, much more powerful Assyrian Empire, led his army into the western states. His method of conquest was different from his predecessors: Rather than simply exact tribute and submission from local kings, Tiglath-pileser placed governors over their territories and, if resisted, exiled the upper classes to other parts of the empire. That way, he could use the newly annexed provinces as stepping stones for further conquests.

In 743 B.C., the Assyrian army engaged the army of a coalition of western states led by King Azariah of Judah. The Assyrians won the battle, and the defeated kings, including King Menahem of Israel (2 Kings 15:19-20)[3], were forced to pay heavy tribute to Tiglath-pileser.

Eight years later, when Tiglath-pileser was engaged in other campaigns, Pekah, who had replaced Menahem as king of Israel, joined forces with Rezin, king of Damascus, in an effort to build a coalition powerful enough to fight the Assyrians. When Ahaz, king of Judah, refused to join their coalition, Pekah and Rezin enlisted the help of the Edomites and attacked Judah. Judah was also attacked from the southwest by the Philistines. (2 Kings 16:5-8; 2 Chronicles 28:5-18). Although the armies of Pekah, Rezin, the Edomites and the Philistines inflicted heavy damage on Judah, the kingdom was not destroyed and Ahaz continued as king. And when he appealed to the king of Assyria for help, although Tiglath-pilezer did not come to Judah's aid, his attention was drawn to the unrest in that part of his empire and he promptly responded.

In 734 B.C. the Assyrians conquered Philistia. The following year, after key cities in Phoenicia were conquered by the Assyrians, **the wall of Israel's security was breached**, numerous cities in the northern and Transjordan (Gilead) parts of Israel fell to the Assyrians (2 Kings 15:29), and many of Israel's inhabitants were taken captive and exiled to other parts of the Assyrian Empire. In 732 B.C., the Assyrian army defeated the army of Rezin and conquered Damascus. Also that year, Pekah was assassinated by Hoshea who assumed the throne of Israel (2 Kings 15:30). It was the practice of Tiblath-pilezer to allow some of the states he conquered, if they did not rebel and continued to pay the tribute he demanded, to keep their present governments. And so, although she had lost her independent sovereignty, Israel, with Hoshea as her king, was allowed to continue to exist.

Prophetic Implications for the United States of America

On September 11, 2001, a massive "**breach**" was blown in the seemingly invincible "**wall**" of America's national security. Not just one, but four giant, commercial airliners were inexplicably[4] not intercepted by the U.S.A.'s vaunted air defense system before they crashed—two into the World Trade Center towers, one into the Pentagon, and the fourth, apparently headed for the nation's capital, into a field in Pennsylvania.

What links this unprecedented invasion of and destruction in America with the invasion of Israel by the forces of Tiblath-pilezer, as prophesied by Isaiah? First, the symbolic significance of the targets of the attacks (the center of world commerce and the centers of the U.S.A.'s government and defense) links precisely the 9/11 attack with many passages of Scripture that foretell the future destruction of America. Second, the ones who hijacked the planes and the ones behind the attack (al-Qaeda) were descendants of and from the same part of the world (the Near East) as those who have, throughout history, hated and longed for the destruction of Israel. Third, the ones who are prophesied to attack Israel in the Gog-Magog War (Ezekiel 38) and who are prophesied to destroy the United States of America are from the same part of the Near East that was occupied by the Assyrian Empire. All these Scriptural prophetic connections between the Assyrian attacks on Israel, the 9/11 attack, and future attacks on both Israel and America will be explained in detail in the following chapters of this book.

The Second Harbinger—Assyrian Terrorism

"And they [the Assyrians] shall come against you with chariots, wagons, and war-horses, with a horde of people. They shall array against you buckler, shield, and helmet all around. I will delegate judgment to them, and they shall judge you according to their judgments. I will set my jealousy against you, and they shall deal furiously with you; they shall remove your nose and your ears, and your remnant shall fall by the sword; they shall take your sons and your daughters, and your remnant shall be devoured by fire. They shall also strip you of your clothes and take away your beautiful jewelry." (Isaiah 23:24-26)

15

According to Cahn, the Assyrians were the original terrorists, striking great fear in the hearts of their enemies, brutally torturing and mutilating those they captured. They very effectively used terror tactics as psychological warfare in intimidating those they came against in war, and to "keep in line" any captives who showed rebellious tendencies. And their terror techniques were often brutal—as examples, killing every living human and animal in a conquered city, burning them alive, or taking them captive and using them as human shields in the next conflict.[5]

The prophetic implications of the Second Harbinger for the 9/11 attack on America are obvious: The capital of Assyria was Nineveh, in what is now northern Iraq. And the Assyrian Empire encompassed territories that are now terrorist-sponsoring, Arabic, Muslim nations, including Iraq, Syria, Lebanon, Jordan, northern Saudi Arabia and Egypt, plus the Gaza Strip (ancient Philistia). Osama bin Laden, the founder of the terrorist organization al-Qaeda and al-Qaeda's leader at the time of its operatives' 9/11 attack, was a Saudi Arabian Sunni Muslim. Also, remember that Tiglath-pilezer's method of conquest was often to export captives from the conquered lands to other parts of the empire and to move governors and others from Assyria and other parts of the empire into the conquered territories. So, the populations in all those countries were mixed. Therefore, it is not inconceivable that the 9/11 terrorists were descendants—certainly in their determination to terrorize and conquer those who differed from them in nationality and religion—of those Assyrians who conquered Israel.

The Third Harbinger—The "Fallen Bricks"

"The bricks have fallen . . ." (Isaiah 9:10)

Sun-dried mud or clay bricks, or bricks made with a mixture of mud and other materials, were often used to build houses, walls and other structures in the ancient Near East.[6] The principal task of the Israeli slaves, before they were liberated from Egypt, was making bricks (Exodus 5:18-19). Archaeologists have discovered massive brick walls in Israel dating to the eighth century B.C.— the time period of the Assyrian invasions of Israel.[7] These are probably the "fallen bricks" to which the Isaiah 9:10 prophecy was referring.

In the same way the bricks in Israel fell during the Assyrian invasions and attacks on Israel, the "bricks" of the World Trade Center fell when the "Assyrian" terrorists attacked it on 9/11/2001.

The Fourth Harbinger—The Tower

*"The bricks have fallen down, but **we will rebuild**..." (Isaiah 9:10)*

In *The Harbinger* (page 66), Jonathan Cahn points out that the English translation of the Greek Septuagint version of Isaiah 9:10 reads, *"The bricks are fallen down ... but come ... let us build for ourselves a **tower**."* Cahn also notes, correctly, that Israel's attitude of arrogant defiance of the Lord did not change after being attacked by the Assyrians in 732 B.C., and that it manifested the same spirit as that of those who built the Tower of Babel (cf. Genesis 11:4; Isaiah 9:9). Throughout her history, Israel had been warned about the consequences of being proud hearted ... that it was solely by the Lord's "power and the strength of [His] hand," not by theirs, that they prevailed over their enemies or accomplished anything (cf. Deuteronomy 8:17; Jeremiah 50:32). Yet, even after being subjugated by the Assyrians, rather than repenting and turning to the Lord for their salvation, Israel proudly proclaimed, "We will rebuild with hewn stones [incomparably stronger and more durable than mud bricks]!" Or, if the Septuagint version is correct, they were declaring, exactly as did the ancient followers of Nimrod, in effect, "We will build a tower that cannot be destroyed!"

Incredibly, after the 9/11 attack on the World Trade Center, America's leaders responded with **exactly the same words** as those prophesied by Isaiah—*"We will rebuild!"* On 9/11, the same day the World Trade Center fell, the mayor of New York City proclaimed, *"We will rebuild!"* On September 12, a U.S. senator from New York proclaimed on the Senate floor, *"We will rebuild!"* On September 14, a New York state senator proclaimed, *"We will rebuild!"* On September 20, the President of the United States proclaimed, *"We will rebuild* New York City." On August 8, 2006, during a fifth anniversary of the destruction of the World Trade Center memorial ceremony, the governor of New York proclaimed, *"We will rebuild!"*

17

But not only did the leaders of the U.S. respond to the attack and destruction with the same words, but in **the same spirit of arrogance and defiance** as prophesied by Isaiah. The day after the attack, on January 12, 2001, an American senator proclaimed, in referring to rebuilding the World Trade Center towers, "I believe one of the first things we should commit to . . . is to . . . show the world that we are not afraid—**we are defiant!**" Then, on January 2, 2002, New York City's mayor proclaimed, *"We will rebuild,* renew, and remain the capital of the free world!" (Note that he referred to New York City as the "capital of the free world.")[8]

So, quotes reflecting Americas' leaders' arrogance and defiance following the fall of the World Trade Center towers are easy to find. However, quotes expressing their contrition of heart and crying out to the Lord for His protection and deliverance, especially in the Name of Jesus (the true Christian response to calamity), are virtually impossible to find. Those kinds of quotes are even difficult to find in the Christian community. In a survey of responses to 9/11 of ten well-known Christian leaders—writers, pastors and leaders of various Christian organizations—published in *Christianity Today*, only two mentioned sin and the need for repentance and only two suggested turning to God in reliance on Him rather than on self. Most spoke of changes that need to be made (with no mention of repentance and no reference to the Lord): "forgive," "pursue justice," "local church revivals," "speaking truth to power," "a national spiritual awakening," "creating a Christian counter culture," "ensuring that goodness prevails," and so forth.[9]

The Fifth Harbinger—The Hewn Stones

"The bricks have fallen down, but we will rebuild with **hewn stones***..."*
(Isaiah 9:10)

"Hewn stones" (Hebrew: *gaziyth*) refers to stones quarried or cut out of rock and shaped and smoothed by tools.[10] King Solomon had 80,000 "hewers of stone" (New International Version: *"stonecutters"*) cutting stones out of mountain rock to build the Temple in Jerusalem (1 Kings 5:15). After coming out of Egypt, Israel was commanded by the Lord to **not** build the altar on which they sacrificed burnt offerings of hewn stones, *"for if you use your tool on it, you*

have profaned it" (Exodus 20:25). Perhaps it was this command, to not arrogantly deny the provision of the Lord by resorting solely to the works of their own hands, to which Isaiah was referring in his prophecy.

Amazingly, not only was Isaiah's prophecy concerning the words *("we will rebuild")* and the arrogant, defiant spirit in which they would be proclaimed precisely fulfilled by America's leaders after the 9/11 disaster, but the exact material prophesied to be used in the reconstruction was placed, in the same spirit, at Ground Zero as the symbolic cornerstone of the new Freedom Tower of the World Trade Center just before construction on that tower began. In fact, at the dedication of the massive stone, the governor of New York confidently proclaimed,

> On September 11th 2001, this nation was challenged; attacked by those who sought to shake our faith in that freedom, our confidence in democracy. They sought to deny us those unalienable rights, so wisely, bravely and boldly proclaimed by our forefathers so many years ago. They attacked us to break our spirit. . . .

> How badly our enemies underestimated the resiliency of this city and the resolve of these United States. How badly our enemies underestimated the power and endurance of freedom. In less than three years, we have more than just plans on paper—we place here today the cornerstone, the foundation of a new tower…a new soaring tribute that will climb 1,776 feet high—marking the year of our nation's birth and proudly declaring our steadfast allegiance to freedom. . . .

> Today we take 20 tons of Adirondack granite—the bedrock of our State—and place it as the foundation, the bedrock, of this new symbol of American strength and confidence. Today, we lay the cornerstone for a new symbol of this City and this country, and of our resolve to triumph in the face of terror.

> Today we build the Freedom Tower.

Today, we, the heirs of that revolutionary **spirit of defiance**, lay this cornerstone and unmistakably signal to the world the unwavering strength of this nation. . . .[11]

Note the tone of the above proclamation. Was it one of contrition and soul-searching—asking the Almighty what had gone wrong with this "Christian" nation to make it so unexpectedly and tragically vulnerable to the 9/11 attack? Was it one of appealing to the Lord for His mercy and grace in protecting America from further devastating attacks? No, the governor's speech reflected just the opposite spirit, exactly as prophesied by Isaiah, did it not?

The Sixth and Seventh Harbingers—Sycamores Cut Down and Replaced with Cedars

"The bricks have fallen down, but we will rebuild with hewn stones; **the sycamores are cut down, but we will replace them with cedars.**" (Isaiah 9:10)

The prophet uses a second example of Israel's prideful intractability to emphasize his point. Just as hewn stones were prophesied to replace fallen bricks, cedars were prophesied to replace sycamores.

During biblical times sycamore trees (a variety of fig) were native to and common in Israel . . . growing mostly in the lowlands. They were valuable for the fruit they produced (cf. Judges 9:8). However, because their wood was soft and porous, it was not preferred as a building material.[12] Although most of the wood of cedar trees had to be imported from Lebanon, because it was beautiful, aromatic, strong and durable, it was the most the most highly favored building material in Israel, as it was throughout the Near East.[13] Solomon built most of the Temple and its furniture of cedar (cf. 1 Kings 5-10).

It is not certain whether the Assyrian invaders actually cut down the sycamores in Israel and the Hebrews replaced them with Cedars, or if Isaiah was just using the illustration of replacing what was native to Israel with what was foreign as figurative of the Ephraimites' arrogant defiance of the Lord. But **it is certain** that

20

the prophecy applies in a literal way to the 9/11 destruction of the World Trade Center.

On 9/11, as the towers were falling, a steel I-beam from the North Tower struck and uprooted a giant, lone, 70-year-old **sycamore tree** which had grown at the corner of Ground Zero! And that sycamore became a symbol of the 9/11 attack. On September 11, 2005—the fourth anniversary of the attack—a huge, sprawling, bronze sculpture of the trunk and roots of the sycamore, which had been placed in the Trinity Church courtyard at the head of Wall Street, was dedicated.[14]

But that is not all. On November 22, 2003, a tree, called the Tree of Hope, was planted in the spot where the sycamore had been uprooted; but it was not a sycamore . . . it was a Norway spruce—a tree of the same family (Pinaceae) of evergreen conifer trees as the cedars of Lebanon![15]

The Eighth Harbinger—The National Vow of Defiance

"The bricks have fallen, but we will rebuild with dressed stones; the sycamores have been cut down, but we will put cedars in their place." (spoken by a national leader in Washington D.C. on the third anniversary of 9/11)

Incredibly, when the conifer tree was planted in the place of the sycamore, every element of the Isaiah 9:10 prophecy (the arrogant, defiant proclamation "We will rebuild," the fallen bricks replaced with the hewn stone, and the "cut down" sycamore replaced with the "cedar" tree) had been specifically and literally fulfilled during and after the September 11, 2001, attack on the World Trade Center. But, there are implications of the prophecy for the nation as a whole, rather than just the World Trade Center.

As is explained in *The Harbinger* (page 105), Isaiah's prophecy was not limited to part of the Northern Kingdom of Israel, but as words that would be spoken by the leaders of the kingdom from its capital, Samaria, regarding the kingdom as a whole. And exactly the same occurred in the United States of America following the attack on the World Trade Center.

Many of the proclamations following the 9/11 attack involved the entire U.S.A., not just the World Trade Center or New York

City. For example, as has already been noted, on July 4, 2004, at the ceremony dedicating the cornerstone of the Freedom Tower, the governor of New York declared, "Today, we, the heirs of that revolutionary spirit of defiance, lay this cornerstone and unmistakably signal to the world the unwavering strength of **this nation**." And numerous proclamations based on Isaiah 9:10 regarding America were from the nation's capital, Washington, D.C., from national leaders. For example, on the third anniversary of the 9/11 attack, just two months after the governor's proclamation, the Democratic candidate for Vice President of the U.S. that election year and a member of the Senate, speaking in the nation's capital to a congressional caucus gathering, defiantly, at the beginning of his speech, quoted part of the Isaiah 9:10 prophecy as "the Lord's word to get us through"—"The bricks have fallen, but we will rebuild with dressed stones; the sycamores have been cut down, but we will put cedars in their place." Then, during his speech, the V.P. candidate made other references to the 9/11 tragedy and the Isaiah 9:10 prophecy, the implications of which he generalized to the U.S. as a nation (e.g., "Walk with me through this day. And you will see that while those bricks fell and the sycamores [were] cut down, our people are making those cedars rise.").[16]

The Ninth Harbinger—The Pronouncement of Judgment on the Nation

All day they twist my words; all their thoughts are against me for evil." (Psalm 56:5)

Obviously, what none of those leaders who used the Isaiah 9:10 prophecy as a rallying cry realized was that it was intended as a pronouncement of judgment on those who uttered it. Little did the leaders of Israel, after the first invasion of the Assyrians in 743 B.C., foresee that their words and the spirit of arrogant defiance and self-reliance in which they were spoken would, 18 years later, bring on a third attack by the forces of Shalmaneser, the king of Assyria following the reign of Tiglath-pilezer, that would not just oppress and reduce to indentured servitude Israel, but totally destroy the kingdom.

After the second invasion and the conquest of Israel by the Assyrians in 732 B.C., King Hoshea, in defiance of the Lord, continued the idolatrous ways of all his predecessors beginning with the first king of the Northern Kingdom of Israel, Jeroboam. So, the Lord prompted Shalmaneser to make Hosea his vassal and exact additional tribute money from him. But, Hoshea remained unrepentant and, during the sixth year of his reign, he made a foolish error that led to the total destruction of Israel. He failed to pay the tribute demanded of him by Shalmaneser and appealed to So, the king of Egypt, for help against the Assyrians. But Hoshea did not receive the help he requested from Egypt and, during the seventh year of his reign, he was imprisoned by Shalmaneser. Then Samaria was besieged by the Assyrian army for three years and, in 722 B.C., fell to the Assyrians. Then, as they had done with other kingdoms they conquered who had continued to resist them, the Assyrians dismantled Israel, took many of the kingdom's citizens (especially the nobility) captive and deported them to remote places, and brought in people from other places to replace them. And that was the end of the Northern Kingdom of Israel—all because of their stubborn, arrogant, unrepentant rebellion against the Lord their God. (2 Kings 17:1-6; 18:9-12).

And in exactly the same way that Israel's leaders pronounced judgment on their kingdom by proclaiming the words prophesied by Isaiah, America's leaders, by proclaiming Isaiah 9:10 from the nation's capital, have unwittingly pronounced judgment on the United States of America. The day after the 9/11 attack, the U.S. Congress issued a joint resolution expressing the official national response to the catastrophe. And the U.S. Senate majority leader presented the resolution with these words:

> I know that there is only the smallest measure of inspiration that can be taken from this devastation, but there is a passage in the Bible from Isaiah that I think speaks to all of us at times like this
> . . .
>
> The bricks have fallen down, but **we will rebuild** with dressed stone; the fig trees have been felled, but we will replace them with cedars.

That is what we will do. **We will rebuild** and we will recover. The people of America will stand together because the people of America have always stood together, and those of us who are privileged to serve this great nation will stand with you.[17]

The *Schemitah*—God's Schedule of the Execution of His Judgment on the Nation

"Then God blessed the seventh day and sanctified it . . . [T]he seventh day is the Sabbath of the LORD your God . . . Work shall be done for six days, but the seventh day shall be a holy day for you, a Sabbath of rest to the LORD. Whoever does any work on it shall be put to death . . . If you buy a Hebrew servant, he shall serve six years; and in the seventh he shall go out free and pay nothing . . . **Six years you shall sow your land and gather in its produce, but the seventh year you shall let it rest and lie fallow** *. . ."* (Genesis 2:3; Exodus 20:10; 21:2; 23:10-11; 35:2)

God is not arbitrary and unpredictable. He runs His creation on schedule. And that schedule is based on the number seven and multiples of seven. From the time Israel was established as a nation, the Lord's people were commanded to live their lives according to His schedule (not theirs)—the seventh day Sabbath, the seventh year release of servants and debts, lepers quarantined for seven days before being examined, seven Feasts of the Lord, seven Sabbaths from the Feast of First Fruits until Shavuot ("Pentecost"), the Feast of Trumpets (which is a rehearsal of the coming Resurrection and Day of Judgment at the beginning of the Seventh Millennium) on the first day of Tishri—the seventh month on the Hebrew calendar—and so forth. And there were severe consequences, appropriate to the violation, for those who did keep the appointments set by the Lord according to His calendar.

For example, from the time the children of Israel entered and occupied the Promised Land until the Southern Kingdom (Judah) was destroyed and its citizens who survived being killed were taken captive to Babylon (490 years), they did not obey the Lord's command to allow their land to lie fallow every seventh year. So, as prophesied (cf. 2 Chronicles 36:20-21), they were subjected to the destruction of their kingdom and servitude in Babylon, estranged from their homeland and close relationship with the Lord, for 70 years—one year for every *Schemitah* (seventh year of rest for the land)[18] they failed to keep.

And, as Jonathan Cahn has astutely observed and brought to our attention in *The Harbinger* (Chapter 17), since 9/11 the executions of the judgment of the Lord on America seem to be operating according to the *Schemitah* schedule.

During the **seventh** anniversary week of the attack on the World Trade Center, the week of September 7-13, 2008, the "Great Recession"—the collapse of the global economy—began with the collapse of Fannie Mae and Freddie Mac—government-sponsored mortgage lenders—then Lehman Brothers, one of the world's leading financial firms. During the ensuing days, financial institutions and individual investors all over the world went bankrupt, and the global economy bottomed out on September 29. Some of those U.S. firms (e.g., Fannie Mae and Freddie Mac) were bailed out by the government, in effect cancelling their debts *(Schemitah)*; others (e.g., Lehman Brothers and thousands of investors) lost everything which, like the Northern and Southern Kingdoms of Israel losing their land and being taken captive, settled their debt to the Lord (punitive *Schemitah*).

But, other than the economic collapse of 2008 occurring during the seventh anniversary week of 9/11, there are other amazing "coincidences" which seem to confirm that the Great Recession did not occur randomly, but was indeed brought on by the Lord according to His *Schemitah* schedule. September 29, 2008, the day the stock market crashed and the economy bottomed out, "just happened to occur" on Elul 29 on the Hebrew calendar, the eve of Tishri 1—the Day of Judgment.[19] But, as Cahn points out in *The Harbinger* (page 167), the economic collapse did not happen overnight. The entire previous year, beginning with the financial crash of Northern Rock, Britain's fifth largest mortage lender, on September 13, 2007, was marred with increasing numbers of loan failures, foreclosures and failing credit markets. And what date was September 13, 2007, on the Hebrew calendar? It "just happened to be" Elul 29. What's more, from the next day, Tishri 1 (the Day of Judgment), until Elul 29 the next year (the day the economy crashed), "just happened to be" a *Schemitah* year on the Hebrew calendar! But that is still not all…. The previous greatest stock market crash in Wall Street history occurred seven years earlier, on September 17, 2001, six days after 9/11. And what was September 17, 2001, on the Hebrew calendar? It "just happened to be" Elul 29, the last day of the *Schemitah* year that preceded Elul 29 of the *Schemitah* year exactly seven years later (on the Hebrew calendar), when the stock market crashed in 2008!

Are all these dates that seem to connect the 9/11 attack on the World Trade Center with the economic collapses of 2001 and 2008, exactly according to God's *Schemitah* schedule, just coincidences? As if to confirm that they are not, on February 24, 2009, the newly-elected President of the United States, in his first address as President to a joint session of Congress and to the American people, proclaimed, confidently and defiantly, concerning the floundering economy, *"We will rebuild!"*[20]—exactly the same words spoken by the leaders of New York City, New York State, the leaders of the U.S. Congress, and the previous President of the United States . . . and exactly the same words prophesied by Isaiah to result in the total destruction of Israel.

What is Next?

If indeed the economic collapse of 2008 was a punitive *Schemitah* of the Lord—a scheduled execution of His judgment on America—it begs the question: What will happen at the next seventh year *Schemitah* in 2015? In *The Harbinger* (page 222), Jonathan Cahn leaves the answer to that question open-ended. He states, through *The Harbinger's* prophet, that the destiny of America (which Cahn considers basically a Christian nation) depends on whether or not the Lord's people in this nation believe and act on God's promise to His people Israel:

> *If My people who are called by My name will humble themselves, and pray and seek My face, and turn from their wicked ways, then I will hear from heaven, and will forgive their sin and heal their land.* (2Chronicles7:14)

But is, according to the Bible, the soon-coming (perhaps as early as 2015) total destruction of America really contingent on the response of the Lord's people in the U.S.A., or is it inevitable? Did Jonathan Cahn overlook a key to understanding the ultimate destiny of America? If you really want to know the answers to those questions, keep reading, because the Truth will be told—clearly, exactly and irrefutably according to the Word of God.

Chapter 2

A Second Witness: *The 9/11 Prophecy*

*"By the mouth of **two** or three witnesses every word shall be established."*
(2 Corinthians 13:1)

Jonathan's Cahn's startlingly eye-opening book *The Harbinger*, published in 2011, is an amazingly insightful, well-documented witness of the fulfillment of the Isaiah 9:10 prophecy in the destruction of the World Trade Center on September 11, 2001. Plus, it plausibly presents the prophetic implications of the recurring seventh-year *Schemitah* in foretelling the economic crash of 2008 and probable future catastrophes to befall the United States of America.

But, just this year (2013), another compelling witness has come forward who, by connecting the Isaiah 9:10 prophecy with other Bible prophecies regarding America, particularly those of Revelation 18, has taken us a significant step forward in understanding the ultimate destiny of the U.S.A. That witness is James F. Fitzgerald with his book *The 9/11 Prophecy*.[1]

Accepting God's Call

"Here am I! Send me." (Isaiah 6:8)

In *The 9/11 Prophecy*, Fitzgerald uses an autobiographical style in describing how, through a lifetime of experiences, he has been brought by the Lord to an understanding of America's destiny, as revealed in the Bible. And, in *The 9/11 Prophecy*, he describes how the Lord used him to forewarn New York City of the attack on the World Trade Center.

Fitzgerald is also the author of the video production, *The WatchWORD Bible*.[2] After five years of labor-intensive work in producing *The WatchWORD Bible*, in May 1999 the first four video books—the four Gospels (Matthew, Mark, Luke and John)—were completed. But then, although it was out of sequence, Fitzgerald was convinced that he and his team needed to jump to the the last

29

book of the Bible and produce *The Video Book of Revelation*. And that decision was proven to be providential, because the Lord used *The Video Book of Revelation* to warn New York City of the attack on the World Trade Center (although, as with the Isaiah 9:10 prophecy, the warning was unheeded).

Because of all the symbolic imagery in the 22 chapters of the Bible's book of Revelation, producing it as a video book was a monumental task. But Fitzgerald and his team, against all odds, managed to get it done in about a year. And then, something else remarkable happened: In June 2000—the first year of the new millennium, before all the uncertainties and trepidation of Y2K had dissipated—*The Video Book of Revelation* was accepted to be shown at that year's New York International Independent Film and Video Festival.

But even more remarkable than the acceptance of *The Video Book of Revelation* at such a prestigious event, where mainly secular films and videos were showcased, was the prophetic significance of its showing in foretelling the destruction of the World Trade Center in the same city fourteen months later. In developing the video book, Fitzgerald did a thorough study of Revelation. And, when reviewing *The Video Book of Revelation* just before he and his team took it to New York City, he was particularly struck by a statement in chapter 18: *"This is the greatest city ever"* (CEV). In context, verses 17 and 18 state,

> *For in one hour such great riches came to nothing. Every shipmaster, all who travel by ship, sailors, and as many as trade on the sea, stood at a distance and cried out when they saw the smoke of her burning, saying, "What is like this great city?"* (NKJV)

And Fitzgerald began to wonder if there was some connection between the prophecies in Revelation 18 concerning modern Babylon the Great and New York City which considers itself the greatest city in the world. On close examination of the text, he discovered that Revelation 18, in foretelling the destiny of Babylon the Great, exactly describes New York City.

So, before *The Video Book of Revelation* premiered in New York City, its author became convinced that it prophesied a future destruction of that "greatest city ever," in a very short period of time ("one hour"). And he was also convinced that *The Video Book of Revelation* was not intended by the Lord to be simply a compelling video rendition of Revelation, but was a prophetic warning of future disaster. He also reasoned, if the showing of *The Video Book of Revelation*, specifically Chapter 18, was truly prophetic of a catastrophe that would strike New York City, to not be disconnected from the prophecy, the disaster must occur in the near future. Fitzgerald also reasoned, because the disaster was prophesied to occur in a very short period of time, to strike a specific target, and its smoke could be seen from far away, that it must be caused by a terrorist attack. Finally, he concluded that New York City must be a "type" of Babylon rather than the actual Babylon the Great because, according to Revelation 18, Babylon the Great will be totally destroyed; but, according to other chapters in the book of Revelation, that would not occur soon after the year 2000 because numerous other prophecies that could not possibly be fulfilled soon after the turn of the millennium must first be fulfilled.

So, producing *The Video Book of Revelation* took on incomparably more significance and was transformed from simply a video book project to a prophetic watchman's mission in the mind of Fitzgerald. And, with some trepidation because of the possibility that other members of his production team would think he had lost his mind, but convinced that he needed to add action to his convictions for them to be confirmed as more than just "vain imaginations," he immediately gathered his team and explained everything he believed the Lord had shown him. And, to his surprise, no one on the team, including his wife Betty, "argued or had issue with anything I said."[3]

Sounding the Alarm and New York City's Response

"The great day of the LORD is near . . . a day of trumpet and alarm . . . against the high towers." (Zephaniah 1:14, 16)

On July 7, the date of the festival's grand opening, the display booth for promotion of *The Video Book of Revelation* had been set up in Madison Square Garden, in the heart of New York City. And, after the event started, all evening, for several hours, a member of the team, dressed like John the Baptist, cried out *"Repent! The king-dom of heaven is near!"* and *"Turn back to God!"*[4] Meanwhile, Fitzger-ald and others on the team were praying that the Lord would have mercy on New York City. Then, Saturday, July 7, the video book was highlighted on the Madison Square Garden marquee and pro-moted through news releases sent to papers and radio stations. And its world premier showing was that night.

In *The 9/11 Prophecy*, Fitzgerald writes that sounding the alarm of impending doom at the grand opening evoked very little positive response—most ignored it and some were annoyed. And most who came by the display, apparently oblivious to its message, paid no attention to it. The response to the showing of *The Video Book of Revelation* was somewhat more encouraging. Although it was a small audience of 100 or so (including some family friends, a for-mer pastor and a ministry colleague) who attended the premier, and some who were invited did not attend, the video was given a stand-ing ovation by those who were there. The net effect of the film and video festival experience on Fitzgerald was an increased sense of foreboding that New York City, in its self-absorbed complacen-cy, was indeed ripe for the judgment of the Lord.[5]

Confirming New York City as a Type of Babylon the Great

"I will raise and cause to come up against Babylon an assembly of great nations from the north country." (Jeremiah 50:9)

During the months following the New York International Inde-pendent Film and Video Festival, although he was occupied with completing the video book New Testament, the identity of Babylon the Great of Revelation 18 was never far from Fitzgerald's thoughts and was frequently the topic of his Bible studies, particu-larly the prophecies of Isaiah and Jeremiah. Prior to the festival, he had noticed that Revelation 18's description of Babylon was re-markably similar to that of New York City, in three aspects:

- *"All the kings of the earth [have] committed fornication and lived luxuriously with her."* (Revelation 18:9). New York City is the headquarters of global politics (the United Nations).

And, to a large extent, it is through doing business with the U.S.A. and the support of the U.S. government that virtually all nations' leaders remain in power and maintain their luxurious wealth.

- *"And the merchants of the earth will weep and mourn over her, for no one buys their merchandise anymore."* (Revelation 18:11) The headquarters of world commerce (the World Trade Center) is in New York City. Also, the world's largest stock market (the New York Stock Exchange) and the center of global finance (Wall Street) are located in New York City.

- *"What is like this great city?"* (Revelation 18:18) The CEV version states, *"This is the greatest city ever."* In many aspects, New York City—in its standard of living, commerce, culture and influence on the rest of the world—is indeed, and by its own self-assessment, the *"greatest city ever."*

Also, reflecting on the national sins of greed (e.g., hoarding of wealth through the financial markets), immorality (e.g., approval of homosexuality), murder (e.g., abortions), and idolatry (e.g., worship of celebrities), reinforced Fitzgerald's perception of New York City, where those sins are concentrated and unbridled, as a type of Babylon.

Next, during the festival, the obliviousness of those who attended the grand opening to the warnings of impending catastrophe and the lack of interest in the showing of *The Video Book of Revelation*, plus his studies of Scripture during the months following the festival, continued to heighten Fitzgerald's sense of foreboding concerning what he anticipated to be a coming Muslim terrorist attack on New York City, just as Babylon was prophesied to be attacked.

Finally, all of Fitzgerald's apprehensive perceptions of New York City as a type of Babylon the Great were confirmed when the towers of the World Trade Center were destroyed in almost precisely "one hour" (Revelation 18:10, 17, 19) by descendants of those from the *"north country"* (Jeremiah 50:9; 51:27, 28), and the *"smoke of her burning"* could be seen from the sea, many miles away (Revelation 18:17-18).

Lack of Repentance: A Precursor of National Judgment

"They blasphemed the God of heaven because of their pains and their sores, and did not repent of their deeds ... And great Babylon was remembered before God, to give her the cup of the wine of the fierceness of His wrath." (Revelation 16:11, 19)

Following the destruction of the World Trade Center, Fitzgerald's thoughts turned to its implications for the nation as a whole. Was the 9/11 attack just an isolated fulfillment of prophecy, or did it portend an even greater future disaster that would affect the entire United States of America?

One objection to such a scenario is that the Lord will not destroy this Christian nation because He will be killing the righteous along with the unrighteous. However, in reflecting on the Civil War, which claimed the most American lives of any catastrophe in the nation's history and which Abraham Lincoln considered the execution of God's judgment on America, Fitzgerald observed that death had been no respecter of persons in that conflict, regardless of their faith or lack of it, or whether they were on the side of the North or the South. He also noted that for the Christian death is redemptive rather than punitive; it dooms the unrepentant sinner to Hell but frees the righteous in Christ from the bonds of this mortal life to be with Him in glory forever (cf. Philippians 1:21-23). Therefore, whether or not the Lord destroys a nation in judgment does not depend on the number of Christians in that nation but on the fidelity of the nation as a whole to the Lord's ways and the response of that nation to the Lord's warnings to repent and change its ways. Although, as prophesied in Revelation, the people of "great Babylon" will be severely chastised by disasters brought on by the judgments of the Lord, they will refuse to repent and will continue to blaspheme Him (Revelation 9:20-21; 16:21), and their nation or empire will finally be totally destroyed.

In *The 9/11 Prophecy*, published ten years after the destruction of the World Trade Center, Fitzgerald laments that America has exactly followed the course that Babylon the Great is prophesied to take. Immediately following the disaster, Americans flocked to churches where they were consoled, the attackers were demonized, patriotism was fueled, and retaliation was encouraged. There was very little soul-searching, mention of the Biblical reasons national catastrophes occur, or of the means of avoiding those disasters—repentance and obedience. Therefore, the incoming tide of church-goers in the U.S.A. soon abated and the nation was back to its ever-increasing godless ways—headed intractably for a date with her final destiny.

The Last Generation

"This generation will by no means pass away till all these things take place." (Matthew 24:34)

As recorded in Matthew 24, Jesus told His disciples that the Temple in Jerusalem would be totally destroyed. They asked Him not only when that would occur but, *"What will be the sign of Your coming, and of the end of the age?"* Brilliantly, He replied with a prophetic discourse that answered all their questions, not with dates but with *"signs of the times"* (Matthew 16:1).

Jesus warned his disciples of the coming destruction of the Temple, which occurred in 68 A.D.; of wars and rumors of wars, natural disasters, persecutions and deceptive false prophets and messiahs that would continue to proliferate through the centuries; and the preaching of the Gospel to all nations, which would be fulfilled just before *"the end."* He warned them of the coming *"abomination of desolation"* that would be set up in the rebuilt Temple, and the *"great tribulation"* that would claim the lives of everyone on Earth if it were not cut short. And finally, He told them how to recognize Him at His coming to gather His chosen ones from all over the earth.

Then, Jesus said, *"**This generation** will by no means pass away till all these things take place."* The question is: to which generation was Jesus referring? Although, because of different eschatological stances among denominations, churches and sects of Christianity, the answer to that question is a subject of great debate, it is obvious from a simple, common-sense reading of the text. *"This generation"* must be the last generation up to the *"end of the age,"* which includes the final events prophesied by Jesus in His discourse to His disciples and to the apostle John, as recorded in the book of Revelation.

James Fitzgerald agrees and, in fact, presents his case in *The 9/11 Prophecy* (Chapter 15) that, according to current events in the light of Bible prophecy, the final generation of 40 years began with the 9/11/2001 destruction of the World Trade Center.

The "Beginnings of Sorrows"

"For many will come in My name, saying, 'I am He,' and will deceive many. But when you hear of wars and rumors of wars, do not be troubled; for such things must happen, but the end is not yet. For nation will rise against nation, and kingdom against kingdom. And there will be earthquakes in various places, and there will be famines and troubles. **These are the beginnings of sorrows.**" (Mark 13:5-8)

According to Fitzgerald we are, at the present time, experiencing the events of the *"beginning of sorrows"* foretold by Jesus in Matthew 24:4-8 and Revelation 6:1-8. And those beginnings (in the Gospel of Mark, "beginnings" is plural) consist of the results of the "Four Horsemen of the Apocalypse" going forth on Earth.

The First Horseman, Riding a White Horse
"And I looked, and behold, a white horse. He who sat on it had a bow; and a crown was given to him, and he went out conquering and to conquer." (Revelation 6:2)

Some expositors teach that the first horseman will be the King of Kings when He returns to defeat His enemies and conquer the earth. Others think that he is Antichrist. Fitzgerald, consistent with his contention that the *"final generation"* and the *"beginning of sorrows"* began with 9/11, believes that the first horseman is a positive figure—President George W. Bush who declared the "War on Terror" after the attack on the World Trade Center, and who declared that the war would take a long time—perhaps 20 years—to win.

Please read this watchman's commentary on Revelation Chapter 6 for the correct identification of the first horseman, who represents the spirit of the anti-Christ controlling the rulers of the world during the *"beginnings of sorrows."*[6]

The Second Horseman, Riding a Red Horse

"Another horse, fiery red, went out. And it was granted to the one who sat on it to take peace from the earth, and that people should kill one another; and there was given to him a great sword." (Revelation 6:4)

Fitzgerald interprets the prophecy of the second horseman as foretelling "all-out global war"[7]—World War III. And, in his view, the basic conflict of that war will be between the combined forces of atheistic Communism and Islam and those of the western nations that have a Judeo-Christian heritage. More specifically, he believes World War III will be probably be instigated by an attack on western targets by Iran, who will be joined by Russia, and then other Communist and Islamic nations will be drawn into the conflict. And World War III will prepare the way for Antichrist, who Fitzgerald believes will be a Muslim. (Islamists anticipate their soon-coming messiah, the Mahdi, who they believe will arrive on the wings of all-out war between the Muslims and non-Muslims.)

The Third Horseman, Riding a Black Horse

"I looked, and behold, a black horse, and he who sat on it had a pair of scales in his hand. And I heard a voice in the midst of the four living creatures saying, 'A quart of wheat for a denarius, and three quarts of barley for a denarius; and do not harm the oil and the wine.'" (Revelation 6:5, 6)

Fitzgerald interprets this prophecy as referring to famine, which inevitably follows war. Most Bible expositions researched by this watchman agree.

The Fourth Horseman, Riding a Pale Green Horse

"I looked, and behold, a pale [greenish-yellow] *horse. And the name of him who sat on it was Death, and Hades followed with him. And power was given to them over a fourth of the earth, to kill with sword, with hunger, with death, and by the beasts of the earth."* (Revelation 6:8)

Death and Hades (the place of the dead) naturally follow war, famine and *"beasts of the earth"* (pestilence). Fitzgerald reasons that pestilence probably also refers to biological warfare, in which deadly microbes will take a terrible toll on populations during and after World War III.

The cumulative effect of the destruction brought on by the Four Horsemen of the Apocalypse will be the death of one-fourth of Earth's population.

The Rise of Antichrist

"[The day of the coming of our Lord Jesus Christ] *will not come unless the falling away comes first, and the man of sin is revealed, the son of perdition, who opposes and exalts himself above all that is called God or that is worshiped, so that he sits as God in the temple of God, showing himself that he is God ... And now you know what is restraining, that he may be revealed in his own time. For the mystery of lawlessness is already at work; only He who now restrains will do so until He is taken out of the way. And then the lawless one will be revealed ...* **Antichrist is coming.**" (2 Thessalonians 2:1-8; 1 John 2:18)

The One Who Restrains

Jesus' discourse with His disciples and His revelation to the apostle John concerning the events at the "end of the age" make it clear that the *"beginnings of sorrows"* will precede and set the stage for the global reign (Revelation 13:7) of the one called "the prince who is to come" (Daniel 9:26), *"the man of sin," "the son of perdition," "the lawless one,"* and *"Antichrist."* The Bible also states that someone is, at the present time, restraining Antichrist. But whoever is doing the restraining will be *"taken out of the way,"* then the satanic prince who is to come will be revealed.

As with his conviction that the *"final generation"* and the *"beginning of sorrows"* began with 9/11, Fitzgerald has a unique take on the identity of the one who restrains Antichrist. He believes that "he," the restrainer, is the United States of America personified. The reason he believes that is because America has led the world in the War on Terror and against the takeover of Islamists. So, in his view, it is the United States of America who will be *"taken out of the way"* before Antichrist is revealed.

Actually, in Fitzgerald's view, the whole Western world since the Roman Empire was Christianized has been restraining the arrival of the man of sin. But, because Europe has been greatly weakened by secularism and the influx of Islam, the U.S.A. has, to a large extent, taken on the sole role of the restrainer.

However, careful exegesis of the text reveals that *"he who re-strains"* is Michael the archangel. The identity of the U.S.A. in relation to Antichrist will be made clear later in this book.[8]

The Apostasy of the Church

There is also another precursor to the revealing of Antichrist that gives us a clue, if Fitzgerald is correct, as to just how close the U.S. is to being "taken out." And that is the "falling away" (apostasy) of the Church (2 Thessalonians 2:3). Fitzgerald observes that the American Church is just a rapidly fading shadow of what it once was in its impact on life in the nation. In fact, all vestiges of Christianity, including faith in God and prayer, are being removed from the public arena. And, most alarming in the light of Bible prophecy is the influx of and interest in Islamism in America, fully encouraged by the U.S. President and his administration. Islam, with its false god (Allah), false messiah (the Mahdi), and false "gospel" (conquering the world by force and violence rather than redeeming it by love), is **the** actualization of Antichristian religion, and the Mahdi is **the** Antichrist. America is rapidly approaching the spiritually emaciated and even anti-Christian state of Europe as she is coming closer and closer to being overrun by Islamists. And when that happens, the main antagonist, Antichrist, will enter the stage and steal the show . . . until the true Messiah comes to take back what is rightfully His.

When, not If

*"Now **when** these things begin to happen, look up and lift up your heads, because your redemption draws near."* (Luke 21:26)

Jonathan Cahn, because he, in concluding *The Harbinger,* did not make the connection between the Isaiah 9:10 prophecy, Jesus' *"end of the age"* prophecy, and the Revelation 18 prophecy concerning the fall of Babylon the Great, left the destiny of the United States of America contingent on whether or not the nation's people will repent and return to the Lord, as God's people Israel were exhorted to do (2 Chronicles 7:14).[9]

However, as he states in *The 9/11 Prophecy*, James Fitzgerald believes that the takeover and destruction of America by the Muslim horde led by Antichrist is "inevitable and imminent."[10] That is because, after the first attack by Muslim terrorists on New York City, Americans, as represented by their leaders, responded with a spirit of arrogance and defiance rather than repentance and turning to God, just as did ancient Israel after being attacked by ancestors of those same terrorists. Then, ten years later, the Northern Kingdom of Israel was conquered and totally destroyed by the Assyrians. Likewise, if Fitzgerald's conviction that the U.S.A. is the restrainer who will be "taken out of the way" before Antichrist takes global dominion is accurate, America must be conquered and destroyed during "this generation" (by about 2040).

Chapter 3

A Third Witness is Called

*"By the mouth of two or **three** witnesses every word shall be established."* (2 Corinthians 13:1)

"For to this you were called, because Christ also suffered for us, leaving us an example, that you should follow His steps." (1 Peter 2:21)

Through Jonathan Cahn's book *The Harbinger*, the Lord has opened America's eyes to the certainty that, if her people do not repent and turn to the Lord, the nation will be destroyed. Then, through James Fitzgerald's book *The 9/11 Prophecy*, published two years after *The Harbinger* was published, further revelation has been given which clarifies that, although individual Christians, by turning to the Lord in repentance, may be saved from the coming holocaust, the destruction of the U.S.A. as a sovereign nation is inevitable and imminent.

However, by overlooking a tenth harbinger that was revealed in the rubble of the collapsed World Trade Center, neither Cahn nor Fitzgerald have realized that the prophecies of Isaiah 9 and Revelation 18 are connected to hundreds of other Bible prophecies that confirm the **exact** identity of the United States of America in Bible prophecy and America's **three-fold** date with destruction at the end of the age.

What is the Tenth Harbinger and what does it reveal concerning the destiny of America? If you really want to know, keep reading.

But first, how the Lord brought this third witness, Watchman Bob, to the point of recognizing the Tenth Harbinger and its importance in foretelling the destiny of the U.S.A., plus the reason it was overlooked by Cahn and Fitzgerald, need to be explained.

[You are asked to be patient as you read through the autobiographical sketch of this chapter. Just be assured that knowing the spiritual, social and religious roots of Watchman Bob and how he was called to be a watchman will help you understand the importance and validity of the Tenth Harbinger in identifying the United States of America in Bible prophecy and foretelling her destiny.]

The Calling of a Watchman

Social, Religious, Spiritual and Moral Roots

Watchman Bob was raised in New Mexico and Texas—arguably one of the most religious, conservative, patriotic areas of America—in a staunch, Christian, church-going family. And, while growing up, he was (from all appearances) a model son, student, citizen, and church member. In high school, he was a member of the National Honor Society and he was selected as "Teenage Christian of the Month" one month by a national Christian publication for teens. Then, he attended and graduated from a college affiliated with the church in which he was raised. So, Bob was thoroughly instructed in church doctrine and Bible knowledge. Also, a strong conscience was instilled in him.

But, although he was quite adept at maintaining appearances of living a good, Christian life on the surface, in his mind and heart Bob was full of questions, self-doubt and turmoil. And during his first two college years, he found himself occupying much of his time with various amusements rather than focusing on his studies. Bob enjoyed sports, so he and his closest friend played golf during the day and tennis during the evenings. Then, virtually every night after playing tennis, they would go to their favorite restaurant and eat a big meal. On the weekends they would take their dates on outings to the lake, the amusement park or other places of entertainment or recreation, or would travel to another town and spend the day playing golf on the course there. So, with little effort or time invested in his schoolwork, Bob's grades were below average and he washed out of the pre-med program in which he was enrolled. But that was okay with him, because his main interest was sports, so he decided to become a coach. But when he went home after his sophomore year and told his mother that he was changing his major from pre-med to physical education, he could see the disappointment on her face and hear it in her voice.

So, filled with guilt because he had wasted so much time, effort, and his parents' money during his freshman and sophomore years of college, Bob changed his major to psychology, not because he had strong aspirations of becoming a psychologist, but he had taken a couple of psychology courses that were interesting. And he applied himself to his studies enough to make pretty good grades his junior and senior years, and was accepted into graduate school. He continued making good grades in his graduate courses and earned a master's degree in pre-clinical psychology. (Only those with PhDs are considered full-fledged clinical psychologists.)

During his entire time in college, although he maintained the façade of being a faithful, church-going Christian, Bob's moral and spiritual life continued to be in a state of turmoil, and he began to question the validity of his "Christianity."

Also, this was during the tumultuous 60s—the time period during which the entire American society, following the placid, post-war 50s, was in upheaval, shattering its image as a good, Christian nation. It was a decade of nationally demoralizing assassinations: In November 1963, during Bob's first year of college, popular President John F. Kennedy was assassinated; in April 1968, civil rights leader Dr. Martin Luther King was assassinated; in June 1968, John F. Kennedy's brother Robert F. Kennedy was assassinated. The 60s were the years during which the unpopular Vietnam War and the anti-war protests, especially on college campuses, started. It was also the decade of hippie "love-ins," the proliferation of the use of psychedelic drugs, the formation of counter-culture organizations like the National Organization for Women (NOW), and the popularity of anti-establishment singers like Joan Baez and Bob Dylan.

So, in addition to questions about the effectuality of the form of Christianity in which he was raised and the guilt and anxiety that plagued his personal spiritual and moral life, Bob was beset by strong doubts about the integrity of America, which he had always been taught was "God's redeemer nation" that would, as a banner of righteousness in the world and through its benevolence and missions to other nations, win the whole world to faith in Jesus Christ.

Personal and Religious Crises

In December 1968, the year America's involvement in the Vietnam War peaked, Bob was drafted into the U.S. military. He was completing the requirements for his master's degree, so he enlisted in the U.S. Navy's 90-day delay program, which gave him enough time to get his degree before starting active duty in the Navy on March 1, 1969. And, with his heavy baggage of personal and religious guilt and confusion, plus questions and doubts about the "goodness" of America and the righteousness of the nation's involvement in the Vietnam War, it was with strong mixed feelings that Bob entered the military.

Compounding his confusion and emotional turmoil, Bob was in a difficult marriage. He had married immediately following his senior year of college and, just before he entered the Navy, his wife gave birth to a girl. Bob loved his baby daughter dearly, but disagreed with his wife on how she should be raised, and on other issues. These conflicts combined with guilt over immoral behavior in which Bob had gotten involved prior to their marriage resulted in an unsatisfying emotional and physical relationship with his wife.

Finally, adding to the frustration and unhappiness of those years, Bob didn't like his Navy job. He had, because of his master's degree, been granted an officer's commission as a psychologist in the Navy's Medical Service Corps, which seemed, on the surface, like a pretty cushy job. But he did not enjoy doing psychological evaluations on military personnel who had returned from Vietnam with severe mental and emotional problems, and having to make recommendations (therapy, discipline, discharge, or return to active duty) based on those evaluations. Bob's recommendations were usually followed, and he was just not comfortable with those recommendations (that were based on 30-minute evaluations and theoretical psychology) being a key factor in making important, life-affecting decisions for those sometimes quite disturbed men.

From all appearances, as always, Bob lived a nice life. He was a Navy officer stationed in the states (didn't have to go overseas, especially to Vietnam), a family man with a beautiful wife and daughter, and a respected member of a local church congregation—teaching a junior high Sunday school class. But it was in teaching that class that his doubts and misgivings about the version of Christianity in which he was raised came to a crisis point. The young people in the class asked him some quite penetrating questions, for which he had weak answers . . . questions like: "Why are we taught pure, unselfish love, boundless joy, and 'peace that passes understanding,' but we see very little of those fruits of the Spirit in the Church?" "Why do we pray for sick people to be healed, but usually do not see them get healed?" and, "Why do we think that the members of our church are better than the members of other churches and the only ones going to Heaven?" Bob gave the standard, pat, church-contrived answers, but, more and more, the questions of those thirteen- and fourteen-year-olds hounded him.

Resolution of the Crises

Throughout his time in the U.S. Navy, Bob's doubts, guilt, confusion, and sense of futility continued. But near the end of his four years of active duty, something remarkable happened that started to turn things around. One day, he received a postcard in the mail. It was an advertisement for a subscription to a religious magazine. Bob had no clue as to how the magazine publisher had gotten his address, because he had just been transferred to his last duty station. Normally, he would have trashed "mail clutter" like that, but unexplainably, he subscribed to the magazine. Then, in about the second or third issue he received, there was an article by a man who had been a ministerial student at the college from which Bob graduated! And this man, who was now a pastor in a different denomination, explained how the church in which he and Bob had been raised had "the cart before the horse" because it emphasized correct doctrine (dogma) and practice (legalism) over a personal relationship with God the Father, His Son, and the indwelling, guiding, enabling Holy Spirit. And "the lights came on!" Bob suddenly understood what was missing (the active presence of the Holy Spirit) in his impotent, ineffectual profession of Christianity, which had proven to be incapable of delivering him from the mental, emotional, and moral morass that he was in. And when he asked the leaders, teachers and ministers of the congregation he and his wife were attending about the revelation he had received, they reacted in a way (defensively, with the same contrived, specious, pre-formulated answers that he had given to his junior high Sunday school students two years earlier) that confirmed his new understanding of the flaw in the form of Christianity in which he had been raised.

Then, when Bob was released from active duty, more shackles came off. He no longer felt trapped in the military of a government whose purposes in waging wars around the world were questionable at best. Next, he had more discussions with ministers and teachers in the Christian denomination in which he was raised, but when they gave him no more valid and satisfactory answers than he had already received, Bob finally decided to cut the umbilical cord and leave. That was frightening, because all his life, he had been taught that anyone who left "the only true church" was damned to Hell. But, the moment he made the decision to leave, it seemed that a thousand tons of dead weight lifted off his shoulders. . . . He was FREE to pursue a genuine relationship with the Lord and a fellowship of Believers who practiced True Christianity. Sadly, Bob's new-found understanding of Christianity came too late to save his marriage, which ended in divorce. Finally, he decided not to continue in a profession that was based on competing, confusing, and often contradictory, anti-Biblical theories of human behavior and that imposed therapies on disturbed people that, more often than not, worsened their mental and emotional maladies or, at best, temporarily relieved them, like prescribing aspirin for cancer. Besides, Bob was convinced from his own personal experience that most of the pathologies psychologists and psychiatrists attempted to treat were caused basically by unresolved sin, guilt, and the influence of evil spirits, which were beyond the domain of non-Christian and pseudo-Christian therapists, and even Christian therapists who attempted to mix psychotherapy with spiritual counseling and intercession.

Exploration, Discovery and Deliverance

However, it turned out that finding a doctrinally sound yet spiritually vibrant congregation with which to fellowship and a teaching/coaching situation in which he was free to share his Christian faith were elusive goals, even in "Christian America." Compounding his quest for "True Christianity" was that Bob had a lot of personal, spiritual, social and religious chaff from the first half of his life that needed to be threshed out. At times it was an arduous struggle. It was like learning to swim against a fast-flowing current. But the Lord graciously kept him moving forward toward his, as yet unknown, calling.

For the next 30 years after leaving the Navy, Bob moved from job to job and church to church. Each job and each church ended up being a dead end street.

An Insider's Experience with U.S. Education, the Mirror and Perpetuator of American Society

Bob's first teaching job was at a large junior high school. He taught ninth grade health and physical education. The school was located in an upper class part of the city. The parents were college professors, doctors, government officials, successful business owners and well-to-do others. It was a rude awakening for Bob. He expected to get to work with well-behaved, bright young people who were eager to learn and prepare for college so that they could become successful professionals and contributors to society, like their parents. But those "privileged" students were very difficult to teach. Bob mistakenly and naively started out the year giving his students the benefit of the doubt and a lot of freedom to regulate themselves. But, to his dismay, it immediately became almost impossible to maintain order in the classroom, much less teach. Most of the students couldn't care less about learning anything; all they wanted to do was to have fun and cause trouble—often at the teacher's expense and the expense of the few students in the class who did want to learn. So Bob spent most of the year struggling to regain the control in the classroom he had lost in the beginning.

Due to his poor performance that first year, Bob was transferred to an elementary school in a low income area of the same city, to teach physical education. It too was a large school, and he was the only physical education teacher. So, it was very hard work—an average of 45 wiggling, restless children per class (six classes), eager to get out and play, plus an after-school recreation program to run. But, although his classes were twice as large as those at the previous school, Bob found that the students were much easier to teach and control, and his job was much more enjoyable.

The next year, Bob got his first coaching job . . . in his home town, where he had graduated from high school. He taught ninth grade science and was the eighth grade assistant football coach and the tennis coach. It was nice being back where he had friends and family and memories of success as a high school student and athlete. But things had changed, or rather, Bob had changed. He wanted to develop close, personal relationships with his students so that he could share his Christian faith with them and minister to their spiritual needs. But his classes were too big and Bob was too busy preparing lessons and teaching and coaching to interact much on a personal level with his students. Also, few if any of them were interested in discussing spiritual or even personal issues.

So, the year after that, Bob got a job teaching science and coaching girls' basketball, helping coach football, and coaching tennis at a very small farming community school. That, it seemed, was a better situation, because he could interact with the students and other members of the community on a more personal level. However, there too, the students were much more interested in their games, sports, parties and other activities than they were in spiritual issues. And the bottom fell out of that job. Bob attempted to discipline some of the girls on the high school basketball team he coached because he caught them drinking on a game trip. But he quickly found himself in the superintendent's office in a meeting with two of the girls' fathers—Christian leaders in the community who also happened to be on the school board. They informed Bob that he was not going to discipline their daughters, because that would result in a blemish on their otherwise stellar high school records. So, having had the discipline rug jerked out from under his feet and his credibility destroyed in the eyes of his students and athletes, Bob started looking for another job.

And he found a similar teaching and coaching position, beginning the next school year, at a small Christian school affiliated with a Baptist church. Bob reasoned that his freedom to practice and share his faith and have a positive spiritual influence on his students and athletes would surely be less hindered in a church school than it was in the public schools. Again, he was mistaken. In fact, most of the students in that "Christian" school were just as worldly—interested in fun and games, partying, and glorifying themselves through their academic and extracurricular accomplishments—as those in the public schools. The only difference was that they were more pretentious and hypocritical—claiming to be good Christian kids while doing the same things as the public school students. And exactly the same thing happened to Bob's job in that school as had happened to it at the public school the year before: Bob caught a young woman on his high school girls' basketball team with a bottle of alcoholic beverage on the bus on a game trip. And the day after he suspended her from the team, the pastor of the church called together an assembly of all the school's students and staff, and told them that a mistake had been made—the player was not suspended from the team. Bob confronted the pastor on the spot, in front of the assembly, asking him why he had lied. And the pastor told him to pack his stuff and leave—that he was fired. So that was Bob's eye-opening first experience working in a so-called "Christian" school.

During the following years, Bob taught and coached in two larger, solidly established Christian schools. The Lord gave him success there: some of the basketball teams he coached won state championships and some individual track and field athletes he coached won state and even national private schools championships. Also, there were a few students who had real hearts for the Lord. And Bob, especially since he was respected for his coaching success, was freer to share his faith and to encourage his students and athletes to *"seek first the kingdom of God and His righteousness"* (Matthew 6:33). Nevertheless, the general spirit of those two schools was no different than that of the first Christian school where Bob worked—worldliness in Christian disguise. On the surface, wonderful Christian worship, ministry and service were practiced, but the main real emphases at those schools were on self-gratification and preparing for worldly success. Bob continually encouraged and even trained his athletes to express gratitude to the Lord and to glorify Him for their accomplishments, but in the end, when awards and recognition were handed out, it always seemed to come down to how proud they were of those accomplishments. And when Bob rocked those schools' worldly boats too much, his employment at both ended on a sour note. The first school had been accepting students because of their athletic ability rather than their Christian character. Some had been kicked out of public schools because of misbehavior and drug use. When Bob protested, he fell out of favor with the administration of the school, could see the handwriting on the wall, and resigned. At the second school, the pastor of the church affiliated with the school was trying to get the members of the church and the staff of the school involved in a get-rich-quick, pyramid marketing scheme. And when Bob wrote the pastor a letter explaining why he could not go along with that "enterprise" and would have to resign if it continued, although he had been a very successful and popular coach there, he was immediately fired.

The Last Straw

Bob could no longer get a job in a Christian school (bad references), so he took a job coaching and teaching in another small, farming community, public school. By that point in time (2002), Bob had studied enough prophetic Scripture and current events that his understanding of America's end-times role in the world and ultimate destiny (which, according to Bible prophecy, are as Jonathan Cahn and James Fitzgerald have described them) was pretty well crystallized. Unfortunately, patriotic fervor in the U.S.A., especially in the Texas farming community in which Bob worked at that time, one year after the 9/11/2001 attack on the World Trade Center, was at an all-time high. Also, President George W. Bush, who had declared the "War on Terror" following 9/11, was a Texan. Finally, two men who worked at the school where Bob taught and coached—a fellow coach and the head of school maintenance—were veterans of the Desert Storm War in Iraq and Kuwait. So Bob was in for a real test of his convictions.

But, he could not keep quiet. By this time, he had sensed God's call on his life (although he did not conceptualize it as being a watchman at the time), and there was no turning back. Bob wrote a series of newsletters in which he explained the meaning of "True Christianity" (see Chapter 4), explained the identification and destiny of the U.S.A. in Bible prophecy, and urged believers to *"come out of her, My people"* (Revelation 18:4), which he mailed to the entire community—about 300 addresses. Well, as can be imagined, the spiritual climate in the community quickly turned very cool toward Bob. There were a couple of positive responses to his newsletters and a few negative reactions, but mainly there was stone, cold silence.

By the grace of God, Bob managed to stick it out for three years there, probably because it was a very "Christian" community—most of the school staff and administration and other members of the community professed to be Christians and attended one of the three protestant churches in the town. Also, Bob's wife, who also taught at the school, unlike him, was very sweet, non-confrontational, and not outspoken concerning religious issues.

And everyone loved her. So, bless her heart, she provided a buffer between Bob and the rest of the community.

However, at the end of the school year 2005, the last straw was broken. At the annual awards banquet the week before the last day of school, Bob made a little speech in which he observed that not once during his three years at the school had he heard anyone in that "Christian" community—a teacher, administrator, student, faculty member, coach, minister, or other member of the community—give God the full credit and glory for the accomplishments being recognized at those awards ceremonies. All that he had heard were the words "pride" or "proud." The following evening, there was an emergency school board meeting. And the morning after that meeting, Bob was told to turn in his keys and leave the school campus immediately—he was finished there (and, by implication, his days as a teacher and coach were over).

That was the end, 30 years after his first teaching/coaching job, of Bob's career in education. And that was his experience with American education, as it reflects the society in general.

An Insider's Experience with American Christianity

Also for 30 years following Bob's release from active duty in the U.S. Navy, he went from church to church seeking true Christian fellowship. He visited and/or fellowshipped with Brethren Assemblies; Baptist, Methodist, Nazarene, Seventh Day Adventist churches; charismatic and Word of Faith churches; non-denominational, non-charismatic churches; a Catholic church; and Messianic/Hebraic Roots assemblies. He taught in some of their schools. And he studied their doctrines and teachings plus those of numerous other Christian sects and denominations. But Bob (and his wife, after he was remarried) never found a congregation, assembly, or church in which he sensed the Lord wanted him to place his membership.

There were numerous reasons that he did not fit in, including exclusive legalism (modern-day Pharisaism), anti-Semitism, quenching the Spirit, heresies, secular humanism, and cultism practiced or taught, to one extent or another, in many of the various denominations and congregations that Bob visited and/or studied.

But the main reason that he avoided seeking permanent membership in any denomination or sect was simply the worldliness, sometimes blatant and sometimes subtle, that pervades American Christianity. This worldliness is manifested in a spirit of pride, self-sufficiency, self-indulgence, and exclusivity (manifestations of American Exceptionalism[2]), rather than total dependence on the Lord and submission to His will. This worldliness has no real understanding of Jesus' radical call, *"If anyone desires to come after Me, let him deny himself, and take up his cross daily, and follow Me"* (Luke 9:23), or His command, *"Do not lay up for yourselves treasures on earth"* (Matthew 6:19). This worldliness seeks to set up its own "kingdom on earth" (cf. Daniel 7:23) through politics or, if necessary, by force rather than waiting on the King of Kings to return **in person** to establish His *"kingdom of Heaven"* on Earth (cf. Matthew 4:17; John 18:36; Revelation 19:11-20:4). This worldliness is apparent in the emphases in the churches on entertainment, fun and games, and good food, rather than in humbling ourselves, repenting, and seeking the knowledge of the Lord's Word and will in this rapidly deteriorating world.

And reciprocally, the congregations Bob visited invariably rejected his warning from the Lord, *"Come out of her, my people, lest you share in her sins, and lest you receive of her plagues"* (Revelation 18:4). At first, they received him (a new potential member) warmly. But, as soon as his views on America in Bible prophecy became known, the atmosphere chilled and they let him know that he was no longer welcome there.

The Lord Provides

After Bob was fired from his last teaching/coaching job in 2005, his wife Donna, who was a teacher at the same school, resigned from her job. So, they had to scramble to earn a living. They attempted to run a concession stand, but that didn't generate enough income. They managed a lodge at a mountain resort during the ski season, but that was temporary. They sold their home and moved into a travel trailer. Bob worked as the maintenance man at a motel and Donna worked as a cleaning attendant at an interstate highway rest area for a few months. But the rest area job—twelve hours per day—proved to be too stressful for Donna, so she resigned. Bob took over her job, which paid a little more than his maintenance job. Also he had been converting an old camping trailer into another concession stand—a mobile one (the first was stationary and in a bad location). After he completed the concession trailer, at 6:00 each morning he would move it to a location he had found on the main street of the little town in which they lived. Then Donna would run the concession trailer while Bob was working at the rest area. After work, he would return to help Donna for a couple of hours, clean up the concession trailer, then move it back to where they had parked the travel trailer in which they were living. That routine was exhausting, and Bob and Donna were still earning barely enough on which to subsist.

Finally, in clear answer to prayer, Donna was given another teaching job. She prayed, in September, "Lord, school has already started, so I'm not going to apply for another teaching position, but if You want me to have one, Your will be done." And, during her prayer, she visualized a friend, Pat—the secretary at the local school—asking her if she wanted to teach that year. That same day, Donna's friend came to the concession trailer when Donna was working there. Donna was excited because she thought Pat was going to buy some hamburgers to take to the school. But she asked Donna, "Do you want to teach this year?" Donna, of course, seeing that as an answer to her prayer, told Pat that she would like to teach, so Pat told her to come to the school office that afternoon. So Donna, thinking that the job was at the school where Pat worked and that she was just going to fill out an application, closed up the concession trailer that afternoon and went directly to the school office. But when she arrived at the school, Pat told her that the teaching position was at a school in a nearby town. The job had just opened up because the teacher who had been there had resigned, so it was an urgent situation. Pat called the other school to set up an interview for Donna, then turned to Donna and asked her, "How soon can you get up there?" So Donna, without changing from her concession stand work clothes or fixing herself up (the way professional women normally do for a job interview), drove to the other school for the interview. After the interview and she had left the interview room and closed the door, Donna heard the school administrators and teachers who had interviewed her laughing. So she said to the secretary sitting there,

"Well, I guess I didn't get that job." But the secretary told her to just fill out the application because she had the job. The interviewers were laughing because they were amazed and delighted that they were able to hire such a highly qualified teacher on such short notice after the school year had started. Later, a reporter from the town newspaper interviewed Donna, who told her how she had gotten the job. And the reporter said, "Wow! I'm just going write it up as an answer to prayer."

And so it went after that. Bob and Donna never had much, but the Lord always provided. In 2007, Bob was eligible for Social Security benefits, so those monthly payments helped relieve the financial pressure. He tried to get several enterprises started, but none of those worked out. And, at his age and with no job experience (except teaching and coaching), it was difficult to find employment. He worked temporarily at two manual labor jobs, but old back and joint pain problems flared up, and he had to discontinue those jobs. So Bob found himself spending a lot of time at home. But that was okay, because Donna's job was stressful, and it helped for Bob to do the housework and cooking. Also, it gave Bob time to focus on his real passion—what he wanted to do more than anything—study and write about current events in the light of Bible prophecy.

Accepting the Call

"Here am I! Send me." (Isaiah 6:6)

Like most Christians, Bob had always thought the end-times prophecies of the Bible, particularly the book of Revelation, were so enigmatic, allegorical, and difficult to understand that they had little literal application to the present times in which we are living. But then, he discovered a real key to understanding those prophecies. He learned that the book of Revelation is inundated with references to the Old Testament (the Hebrew Scriptures)—from over 200 to about 1,000, depending on how they are counted.[3] Then, he realized that the writer of Revelation, the apostle John, was a Jew and probably originally wrote the book in Hebrew, or at least from a Hebraic perspective, as did all the other writers of Bible prophecy, who were also Jews. So, Bob decided to study Revelation, the best he could, from that Hebraic perspective.

With a fine-toothed comb, using cross-references, he read through Revelation, looked up Old Testament Scriptures referenced there, and studied them. If he was not sure about some of the words or figures of speech used, he looked those up in reference books—concordances, Bible dictionaries, and commentaries—and online sources. He also studied the Feasts of the Lord and the Temple sacrifices, plus historical events, traditions, and practices of Israel alluded to in Revelation. And as Bob continued to scan mainstream and non-mainstream sources for news about current events, to read articles and commentaries, to listen to audio teachings, to watch teachings on the Internet and on DVDs, and to study the Bible from the Hebraic perspective of its writers, he was amazed at how clearly the implications of the prophetic Scriptures for the present times in which we are living started to come into focus.

Finally, Bob started writing what he had learned. And on July 1, 2010, he self-published, through CreateSpace (an Amazon-company), a 310-page commentary on the book of Revelation entitled *The Revelation of Yahushua the Messiah, a Clear, Common-Sense Commentary—and More—from the Hebraic Perspective of the Writer of the Last Book of the Bible.*[4] That is a rather cumbersome title and subtitle, but Bob felt that it was necessary to get the purpose of the book across to Christians who are not familiar with the Hebraic perspective. Also, to get the prophetic, last days message of the Revelation out to as many as possible, Bob simultaneously published the entire contents of *The Revelation of Yahushua the Messiah* online, at revelationunderstoodcommentary.com. The website also includes a blog on current events in the light of Bible prophecy and a "Contact Watchman Bob" page to encourage dialogue.

During the three years since *The Revelation of Yahushua the Messiah* commentary and the *Revelation Understood!* website were published, consistent with previous non-responses to Bob's newsletters and other warnings of the impending judgments of the Lord, responses to the book and the website have been very weak. Just as before they were published, a few have responded positively, a few have reacted negatively, but most shout, loud and clear through their silence, "Just leave us alone! We don't care about the warning you are giving us!"

Thank God for Jonathan Cahn and James Fitzgerald!

"A threefold cord is not quickly broken." (Ecclesiastes 4:22)

After shouting his warnings into the unresponsive silence and in a frequently hostile climate for over ten years, Watchman Bob was almost incredulous when he received, from one of his few supporters, a copy of *The Harbinger*, a New York Times Bestseller that very clearly and powerfully tends to confirm everything that Bob had been proclaiming about the destiny of the U.S.A. The only misgiving that Bob has about *The Harbinger* is that it does not definitely nail down the ultimate identity and destiny of America, as he believes the Bible does.

But then, just last year (2013), *The 9/11 Prophecy* was published by the same news website company, World Net Daily (wnd.com), that distributes *The Harbinger*. And Bob is even more encouraged to keep sounding the alarm, because *The 9/11 Prophecy* does concur with Scripture that the U.S.A. will definitely be taken over by evil Islamic forces in the near future.

However, there is more to the Bible's prophecies concerning the ultimate identity and destiny of the U.S.A. than either Jonathan Cahn or James Fitzgerald has perceived. There are hundreds of verses of prophetic Scripture that tell us **exactly** what the identity and the **three-fold** destiny of America are. And there was a tenth harbinger exposed in the rubble of the fallen towers of the World Trade Center on 9/11 that is the key to unlocking the door of our understanding of what is happening, from Heaven's point of view, in the United States of America at the present time, what will happen in the very near future, and what Father God tells His children, in no uncertain terms, to do about it, before it is too late. And the reason that Cahn and Fitzgerald have overlooked the Tenth Harbinger and its connection to those many other passages of Scripture is because they have not fully or correctly discerned the true spiritual foundation and character of the U.S.A. This book, *The Tenth Harbinger*, will correct that misperception.

And it is in praying that there are some who have the courage to face up to the reality of these terrible, awesome last days and who can, like Israel's smallest tribe Issachar, fully understand the times and know what to do (1 Chronicles 12:33), that *The Tenth Harbinger* has been published.

Caution and Encouragement

A word of warning, please: If *The 9/11 Prophecy* is more difficult to read than *The Harbinger*, *The Tenth Harbinger* is that much more daunting. This watchman anticipates (based on reactions to what he has written in the past) that many who read this book will be infuriated and some will be terrified. But if you really want to understand and are willing to face up to the Truth, you will be greatly enlightened through understanding the prophetic message of the Tenth Harbinger. And if you take what the Lord shows you to heart and act on it, you will be filled with great hope and joy as you, in seeing end-times prophecy rapidly being fulfilled before your eyes, anticipate the awesome, soon-coming Day of the Lord, sharing in His victory over the forces of evil, and reigning with Him over His redeemed and restored creation in the wonderful World to Come! (See Chapter 10—"In The End, there is GOOD NEWS!")

Chapter 4

Is the United States of America a True Christian Nation?

"Let no one deceive you by any means; for that Day will not come unless the falling away comes first." (2 Thessalonians 2:3)

W hat the Tenth Harbinger portends for The United States of America cannot be fully understood unless the spiritual condition of the nation is understood. Is The United States of America truly a Christian nation, as most American Christians believe? If it is—if America is truly the Lord's nation of people, in the same sense that Israel was called out of Egypt to be His nation of people (cf. Hosea 11:1)—then there is still hope that the U.S.A. will be saved from whatever economic, social, political, psychological, spiritual, or physical holocaust might be coming on the rest of the world. If America is truly the Lord's nation of people, God's promise, as recorded in 2 Chronicles 7:14, applies just as much to the U.S.A. as it did to Israel:

> *If My people who are called by My name will humble themselves, and pray and seek My face, and turn from their wicked ways, then I will hear from heaven, and will forgive their sin and heal their land.*

But if the United States of America is **not** truly the Lord's nation of people—if it is a nation of false Christians (apostate anti-Christians)—then it is doomed, because the Bible declares that **all** nations that are not His nation of people will be destroyed on the Day of the Lord (cf. Zechariah 14:1-3, 12-13).

So, please keep reading, because this chapter and the next will answer, irrefutably, whether or not the U.S.A. is God's nation of people—a true Christian nation. This chapter, by getting very personal, will examine the spiritual condition of the Christian Church in America at the level of its individual members, including you (if you consider yourself a Christian), to help you determine if the U.S.A., even in its churches, is made up of true Christians. The next chapter will answer the question: was the United States of America ever, from its beginning, a true Christian nation?

The Church's Deadliest Disease

Cancer—America's second deadliest disease (next to heart disease)—dreaded by everyone. AIDS—incurable loss of immunity to disease, deterioration of health, and finally death. But during the past few years, I, Watchman Bob (since this chapter is personal, I will write in the first person), have been made painfully aware of a far more insidious, pervasive, and devastating disease infecting the American Christian Church—an evil, spiritual malady capable of destroying both body and soul if not checked. Why so painful to me? Because I have had to admit that for most of my 68 years on Earth, I too have been infected by this disease, and I am presently striving, by God's grace, to eradicate it from my own soul. So please understand, dear friend, that I am not pointing an accusative finger at any individual, because I realize that when I do, there are always three fingers pointing back at me. Therefore, if you feel that what is written here is speaking to or about you personally, you'd better pay attention, because that conviction is not coming from me—it is probably the Lord speaking to you through your own conscience. And it is definitely not wise to ignore the voice ("Word") of God. If the shoe seems to fit, rather than getting offended at the shoe, no matter how much you do not like that shoe, I pray that you will wear it until you can replace it with a good shoe.

One other point: If you are not a Christian, some of this essay will not apply to you because it is directed primarily to Christians, or at least to those who claim to be Christians. But some parts may hit home with you too, and I pray that you will take those to heart. Your (eternal) life may be at stake. Also, reading this chapter will help you understand the difference between a True Christian and a false Christian, so that you can avoid the hypocritical fakes and, if you become a Christian, you can make sure that your faith and your life in Christ are genuine and will lead to eternal life rather than to Hell.

Three Spiritual Maladies

There are two terrible maladies closely related to and feeding the third, most insidious and pervasive evil—the Church's "deadliest disease."

The first is pride, which often manifests itself in a sense of self-sufficiency or a "we're better than you are" attitude, especially in competitive activities. Pride pervades our whole culture, doesn't it? America is the home of the rugged, independent, "self-made man." Pride is a primary motivation for most Americans' accomplishments. One Sunday, when my wife Donna and I visited a local church in the small farming community in which we lived, we heard the pastor preach an excellent sermon against the evils of pride. But later, we heard the same pastor, who was also the head science teacher at the high school in that community, going on and on about how "proud" he was of his students' accomplishments. Too bad his own sermon wasn't taken more to heart. Isn't pride what the "We're number one," "We're the best," and "We-are-proud-of-you" cheers are all about at sporting contests? And isn't building "self-esteem" (pride) in our children a basic goal of education? I use these examples because I was in education and coaching for 30 years. But doesn't this **un**godly spirit of pride pervade everything we do—our occupations, our accomplishments, and our accumulation of material possessions? Don't we take pride in our jobs, our achievements, our promotions, our homes, the vehicles we drive, our family members . . . *ad infinitum?*[1]

Some may object, "Well, hold on, Bob. That's not the kind of pride we're talking about when we say, 'We are proud of you' [as if there are two kinds of pride—one good and one evil]. We're simply showing our appreciation and support of the ones we love." Oh, really? Then why not say, "I appreciate what you are doing," or, even better, "I thank God for you," or simply, "Good job," or "I am very pleased with you" (what the Father told His Son, Jesus), rather than using a form of that horrible word "pride"? Or don't you know that pride is one of the three basic, fundamental sins (cf. 1 John 2:16) and that Jesus listed pride right along with other "evil things" that defile a person (Mark 7:20-23)? Perhaps you are not aware that it was pride that got Lucifer (later called Satan) kicked out of Heaven (Isaiah 14:11-14). It got Adam and Eve kicked out of Eden (Genesis 3:5). And pride will get those who are infected by it a hot reservation in Hell, excluded from Heaven (Proverbs 16:18).

What is the Christian alternative to pride? Obviously, it's humility. Scripture states, *"God resists the proud, but He gives grace to the humble"* (Proverbs 3:34). And how can we tell that someone is humble? Again, that's obvious: The truly humble person always gives credit, honor, and glory to whom credit, honor, and glory are due—and that is not to oneself or to any other human being. Jesus said, *"Apart from Me, you can do **nothing**"* (John 15:5). You see, my friend, unless Jesus (God the Son) gives us the will, the opportunity, and the power, we cannot inhale one breath, speak one word, take one step, or even think one thought, much less achieve other "accomplishments," whether we acknowledge God's omnipotence or arrogantly deny it (cf. Philippians 2:13). Later, the apostle Paul wrote, *"**Whatever** you do in word or deed, do **all** in the name of the Lord Jesus"* (Colossians 3:17), and again, *"In **whatever** you do, do it so as to bring glory to God"* (1 Corinthians 10:31). That's both specific and comprehensive, isn't it? Yet, we insist that pride is OK. In fact, in America, pride is considered a virtue, isn't it? That just goes to show how subtle and deceitful the Devil is, and what total control, apart from God's gracious intervention, he has over our hearts and thought processes.

At a high school activities awards banquet, just before I was fired from that school's staff, I mentioned that in my four years of teaching and coaching there, I had not once heard anyone—any student, any athlete, any teacher, any coach, any school administrator, any parent, any church leader or minister, or any other member of the community—give God the full credit and glory for the accomplishments being recognized at that banquet. In fact, the most frequent word heard there was "proud." Now, what's wrong with that picture? Didn't most of the people in the community, including the administrators, teachers, and coaches at the school, claim to be good, church-going Christians? And again, I'm not finger-pointing here, because much of my life, especially during my teaching and coaching career, I too was guilty of keeping credit and glory to myself, rather than praising God for what He had enabled my classroom kids, athletes, and me to do. All that I wanted to do at that awards ceremony and all that I want to do now is to light a little candle in the darkness of self-adulation (including my own). Acknowledging God in all that we do, rather than just patting ourselves on the back, is very, very important, with eternal implications, because Jesus said,

> *Whoever acknowledges Me before others I will acknowledge before my Father in Heaven. But whoever denies Me* [keeps the credit and glory for self] *before others I will deny* [disown] *before my Father in Heaven.* (Matthew 10:32)

Isn't stealing the credit and glory for what God has done, or even giving it to others to whom it doesn't belong, a form of denying Him?

The second spiritual malady pervasive in the American Christian Church is covetousness (greed). Jesus said,

> *Do not lay up treasures* [wealth] *on earth, where moths and rust destroy, and burglars break in and steal. Instead, store up for yourselves treasures in Heaven, where neither moths nor rust destroys, and burglars do not break in and steal. For where your treasures are, there your heart is also."* (Matthew 6:19-21)

"Now, wait a minute, Bob," you may again object. "I live in a community with very modest incomes. No one is extravagant. Everyone works together and shares. I certainly am not greedy—I give to the Church and I'm generous with others. I'm just trying to get by." Well, are you willing to test that assertion against God's Word (and again, I'm speaking primarily to "Christians")? Jesus said,

> *If anyone wants to follow Me, let him deny himself, take up his cross daily, and keep following Me. For whoever tries to save his own life will destroy it, but whoever destroys his life on My account will save it."* (Luke 9:23-24)

And He told a wealthy young community leader who asked what he needed to do to be saved, "Sell whatever you have, distribute the proceeds to the poor, and you will have treasures in Heaven. Then come, follow Me!" (Luke 18:22). So what does Jesus mean to "deny ourselves"? He means just what He said: Unless we are willing and in fact are in the process of giving up all of our prideful, self-indulgent, worldly pleasures and treasures to follow and serve Him (primarily in bringing others to Him - Matthew 28:19-20), we will have no place in His glorious, soon-coming kingdom with Him. And carrying that cross (the figurative instrument of death to self) is not a comfortable, painless thing to do. And what are "treasures in Heaven"? They are certainly not the things we accumulate on Earth, are they? We can't take anything (money, homes, vehicles, land, awards, fame, position, pleasure, unsaved family members, etc.) with us after this short "puff-of-smoke" life on Earth is over (Ecclesiastes 2:18). Let me submit to you that the only treasures we can lay up in Heaven are human souls (our own and those of others whom God saves through our influence). Proverbs 11:30 states, "He who saves souls is wise." And are you familiar with Jesus' Parable of the Pearl of Great Price? When a merchant found a very valuable pearl, he sold everything he had to purchase it. What is more valuable than a human soul? Get the picture? Saving souls is God's heavenly savings plan.

So, dear friend, let me ask you a few simple questions. Please answer them honestly, then decide for yourself if you are infected with the covetousness malady.

- Are your awards—your certificates of accomplishment, letter jackets, ribbons, medals, trophies, plaques, pictures in the newspaper and on the wall—treasures on Earth or treasures in Heaven?
- How is most of your time spent—trying to secure your own and/or others' success, comfort, and pleasure on this Earth, or helping those you love secure their place in Heaven?
- On what do you spend most of your money—on yourself and the worldly success, comfort, security, and pleasure of your family and others, or, either directly or indirectly, on the Gospel—getting your loved ones saved from this evil world?
- What do you talk about most of the time—temporal, worldly things, or, either directly or indirectly, the Lord and His great and wonderful plan of salvation?
- When someone compliments you, do you say, "Thank you," and keep the praise to yourself, or do you give the credit and glory to God?

64

- And here's a real soul-searcher: What do you think about most of the time—temporal, worldly success, things, pleasure, and relationships, or the Lord and His great and wonderful plan of salvation and how to get your loved ones saved?

Your honest answers to these questions should give you a pretty good idea of whether or not you are storing up treasures on Earth, which is covetousness, or in Heaven. And again, my friend, I have to admit that I have wasted most of my life working foolishly and futilely for worldly success and possessions. But, by the grace of God, I am changing that focus and direction in my life. I pray that you will join me.

But the third evil, spiritual "disease," which is the child of and is reinforced by pride and covetousness, is the most insidious and the deadliest of all, because most "Christians" are not even aware that it infects them, and when confronted with its existence in them, they tend to deny it. The good news is that, unlike many forms of cancer and AIDS, it is totally curable, **if** they will face up to and admit ("confess") it, reject ("repent of") it, and allow God to replace it with His alternatives—His Truth and pure, unselfish Love. Jesus spoke His strongest words of censure against the third evil—the Church's deadliest disease. What did Jesus call those who claimed to be good, "law-abiding" people, but who were really full of the first two spiritual maladies—pride and covetousness? That is correct; He called them "**hypocrites**—white-washed tombs [beautiful on the outside but full of dead people's bones and all kinds of rottenness on the inside]." (Matthew 23:27) Does that description fit you? Are you claiming to be a good Christian—perhaps even a church leader—but are really full of hateful bigotry—condemning and mistreating those who don't agree with your political, religious, or racial views? Do you claim to be a good Christian, but are really full of pride and covetousness—patting yourself on the back and denying the grace of God by refusing to give Him the credit for your accomplishments (and encouraging others to do the same), thereby laying up your treasures on Earth? Are you mainly preoccupied with maintaining your own materialistic, self-indulgent lifestyle, and just giving the "tithe" or the leftovers to the needy, the Church, or devote it to the Gospel?

And again, I'm not pointing my finger at any individual. I have been as guilty of all three of these deadly spiritual diseases as anyone, and it's only by God's wonderful mercy and amazing grace that He has saved me from them and their "eternal" consequences, although I pray daily for Him to continue to eradicate them from my own soul. (True Christianity is not a static state of goodness and holiness—it is a continual process of "putting off the old person and putting on the new person" or "growing in the grace and knowledge of our Lord and Savior, Jesus Christ"). I pray the same for each of you whom the shoe fits, before it is too late. Remember, the blatant sinners were not the ones who were primarily responsible for killing God's prophets and His Son; those were the hypocrites—the ones who claimed to be good religious people—especially the religious leaders. Are you considered a "good Christian" or even a church leader, but are really, deep in your heart, congratulating yourself and proudly accepting the praises of others? If so, that's pure hypocrisy. Please repent and start giving God **all** the credit, honor, and glory, and start devoting **all** that you have to the Gospel, before it is too late and you find yourself sharing a place in Hell with the Prince of Pride and Covetousness (Satan).

Are you an "*almost* Christian"?

God tells Believers to "Examine yourselves to see whether you are living the life of faith. Test yourselves. Don't you realize that Jesus Christ is in you?—unless you fail to pass the test" (2 Corinthians 13:5). In other words, search your heart, asking yourself and God if you are a True Christian or are really just a phony hypocrite—what the Puritan preacher, Matthew Mead, called an "*almost* Christian*." I've been doing a lot of that soul-searching lately, and I invite those of you who claim to be Christians to join me as we share a few points from Mead's book, *The Almost Christian Discovered.*[2] If you don't claim to be a Christian, this part may interest you anyway, because it will help you see who in your community is a True Christian and who to avoid because they are infected with the Church's deadliest disease.

A person may go through all the "steps" of becoming a Christian and even have a highly emotional and spiritual conversion experience in being "saved"—and still be but *almost* a Christian. The

Bible says that even the demons believe in God and know that Jesus is His Son—God in a human body—and tremble (Mark 1:34; James 2:19). There is a faith that is seated in the understanding but does not touch the spirit and permanently change the heart and the will. A person may believe in his mind every word of the Bible, be convicted of, confess, and repent of his sins (see the next section), believe in Jesus, be baptized, and become a member of a Christian Church, but still be as lost as one who hates Jesus and never sets foot in a church. His natural mind and conscience may be enlightened by God's Word, and he may be "saved" to avoid going to Hell or even out of gratitude to God for his saving grace in sacrificing His Son for us, but if his heart is not transformed by the Holy Spirit, his "conversion" is basically just a selfish device designed to get him the benefits of the Kingdom of Heaven without the totally new and unselfish life in Christ. And the new "Christian" is but *almost* a Christian.

A person may hate sin and go far in repenting of sin, overcoming sin in his own life, and opposing sin in others—indeed, be a great crusader against evil—and yet be but *almost* a Christian. Every human being, somewhere in his soul, although it may be seared over by much wrongdoing, has a conscience—a sense of right and wrong, good and evil. Most would agree that rape, murder, stealing, greed, abuse of others, arrogance, selfishness, and other attitudes and actions that the Bible calls "sin" are wrong. And they may hate that sin in themselves and others. And they may go far in eliminating sinful attitudes and behavior in themselves and helping others do the same. They may even make those changes in response to the enlightening of God's Word, the Bible. And so they consider themselves and others consider them "Christians." Yet those changes may be but natural and rational—not spiritual. Their natural and rational hearts, attitudes, and behavior are changed in hoping that they will receive the benefits of a sinless life (basically a selfish motive), but their spiritual hearts are untouched by the Holy Spirit of God. So they remain but *almost* Christians.

A person may be under great, visible changes—may become a "good," moral person and yet be but *almost* a Christian. There is a civil and moral change as well as a spiritual and supernatural change. Many are changed morally, even to the extent that it is said of them that they have become "new" people; but they are, in heart and nature, the same still. A person may be converted from a profane life to a form of godliness, from filthy to clean, wholesome conversation and behavior, and yet the heart is basically the same in one as in the other because it is not permanently renewed by the Holy Spirit. King Saul changed greatly when he met the Lord's prophets, even becoming a prophet himself. Indeed, it was written of him that God gave him "another" heart (1 Samuel 10:9). But in the end, Saul was not saved after all: an evil spirit entered him and the Spirit of God "departed from him" (1 Samuel 16:14). That's because there's a critically important difference between having "another" heart and having a "new" heart. God can give someone "another" heart to transform his outward attitudes and behavior temporarily, or he can give that person a "new" heart transforming him from the inside out eternally. A person whose outward attitudes and behavior are changed but who has not been given a new heart is but an *almost* Christian.

A person may be very religious—a zealous church leader and even a pastor and a pillar of the community—and yet be but *almost* a Christian. Jehu, a king of Israel, served God and did what He commanded, destroying all the worshipers and priests of the false god Ba'al, and was very zealous in His service, proclaiming, *"Come with me, and see my zeal for the Lord of Hosts!"* (2 Kings 10:16). And yet, in all this, Jehu was a hypocrite, making no effort to live wholeheartedly according to the Word of God and refusing to turn from the sins introduced into Israel by King Jeroboam. So a person may be a very religious, zealous, and devoted church member, and yet be but *almost* a True Christian.

A person may go farther yet. He may have a "love" for God, the People of God, his friends, and even his enemies, and yet be but *almost* a Christian. There is a natural affection for those who love us and bless us. Some will even go so far, Jesus said, as to give his life for his friends. But this is basically a selfish "love" which loves only those who return that love, even if it's just a "Thank you" from them. But when God gives a person a new heart and fills it with His totally unselfish love, which blesses and even lays down one's life for someone, including an enemy, expecting nothing in return, as Jesus did, then that person is a True Christian. But a person may even go so far as to give his life for his enemies— even to the point of being tortured or burned at the stake—and still be lost. How? Because when he does **anything** primarily for the purpose of getting something in return—perhaps only a reputation as a martyr or the salvation of his own soul—then his love is basically conditional and selfish. So, a person may have great "love" and make great sacrifices for others and still be but *almost* a true Christian.

A person may have great spiritual gifts and yet be but *almost* a Christian. God can use anyone or anything through whom or which to manifest His gifts. He spoke to the pagan prophet Balaam through a donkey (Numbers 22:28). That was a gifted donkey! He then spoke through Balaam to the pagan king Balak a true word of prophecy concerning Israel (Numbers 23:16). But neither the donkey nor Balaam were true believers, were they? So, a person may speak amazing prophecies that come true, do astonishing miracles, heal people, speak in other tongues supernaturally (Antichrist and the False Prophet will do all these things), and still be but *almost* a Christian.

Now you may ask, "If a person may hate, repent of, and go far in overcoming sin in his life, become a 'good,' moral person, be a zealous and devoted church member, love and make great sacrifices for others, and manifest powerful spiritual gifts from God in his life, and still be but *almost* a Christian, how in the world may I know that I am a True, saved Christian?" The answer is simple and takes us back to the beginning of this article: *"Whatever you do in word or deed, do all in the name of the Lord Jesus"* (Colossians 3:17), and again, "In whatever you do, do it so as to bring glory to God" (1 Corinthians 10:31). If there is the tiniest element of selfishness or pride in anything we think, say, or do as Christians, then that is not True Christianity—that is hypocrisy—the deadliest spiritual disease. Fear of going to Hell may drive us to God, or gratitude to God for what He has done for us may draw us to Him (self-interest is what motivates unsaved people), but fear of Hell or hope of Heaven, by themselves, will not keep us saved. When we are truly saved, He gives us a new heart and fills it with His pure, unselfish love, and we are no longer as concerned about the consequences or benefits to ourselves as we are in glorifying Him and blessing others. Yes, of course, in our humanity, we all want to be blessed in this life and saved from the horrible destruction soon to come on this world, but, as Christians ("new creations in Christ"), those basic human desires are no longer our focus and no longer provide the **primary** motivation for our lives. If any impulse other than the pure, unselfish love of God governs our attitudes or behavior, then we are but *almost* Christians and will perish with the rest of the unbelieving world.

The Bottom Line

So, what is the conclusion—the real difference between a True Christian and a phony, "almost" Christian? It is very simple: The True Christian is a person who has come to the full realization that he is not basically and naturally a good person—that, in fact, apart from the indwelling Spirit of God, there is absolutely no goodness or righteousness in us (Romans 3:10-12). And whatever goodness is in us or whatever good thing that we do is really Christ in us— that, as the apostle Paul affirmed, *"It is no longer I who live, but Christ lives in me"* (Galatians 2:20). The True Christian is one who has come "to the end of his rope" as far as attempting to live the Christian life in his own goodness or power, repented of his sin in arrogantly attempting to do that, surrendered his life totally to God in the name of Jesus Christ, and allowed Jesus the Holy Spirit, to totally take over his life. The phony Christian has never gotten to the point of absolute surrender to God. He still clings to the delusion of Satan that he is basically a good ("God-like") person (Genesis 3:5) and can live a good, Christian life in his own righteousness and strength, except, maybe, for needing God's help occasionally when the going gets tough. He lives by the old deluded, self-sufficient dictum: "God helps those who help themselves." He does not understand Jesus who said, *"Without Me, you can do **nothing**"* (John 15:5). And he does not understand nor has he ever experienced the wonderful *"mystery of godliness"* which is *"Christ in you"* (cf. 1 Timothy 3:16; Colossians 1:25).

The New Covenant

And the reason that most Christians do not understand and have never experienced the Spirit-filled life in the Christ is because they do not understand the New Covenant which was promised to God's ancient People Israel (Jeremiah 31:33) and ratified by Jesus' death on the cross (Matthew 26:28). They think that, when the New Covenant went into effect, the Old Covenant of God with His People Israel, which was His promise to bless them if they kept His commandments or Law (*Torah*), was replaced by the New Covenant. But what they do not understand is that the Hebrew *Torah* was not comprised of just the legal requirements of the Law of God, but was all the instructions for living righteous, good, happy, prosperous, successful lives as His People. That is why Jesus said,

> *Do not think that I came to destroy the Law* [Torah] *or the Prophets. I did not come to destroy but to fulfill. For assuredly, I say to you, till heaven and earth pass away, one jot or one tittle will by no means pass from the Law [Torah] till all is fulfilled. Whoever therefore breaks one of the least of these commandments, and teaches men so, shall be called least in the kingdom of heaven; but whoever does and teaches them, he shall be called great in the kingdom of heaven.* (Matthew 5:17-19)

And how did Jesus fulfill the *Torah*? In two ways: (1) He fulfilled the legal requirements of the *Torah* by keeping all of its commandments perfectly, so Christ is actually the living personification of the *Torah*, and (2) He fulfilled the prophetic implications of the ceremonial aspects of the *Torah*. For example, the *Torah* required that blood be shed in animal sacrifices for the sins of the people. The shedding of Jesus' blood on the cross to atone for the sins of the world fulfilled, once and for all, the prophetic significance of all those animal sacrifices throughout Israel's history. But, as Jesus stated, the *Torah* has not been done away with, because its commandments (especially the Ten Commandments) and instructions are still being fulfilled in the lives of Christ's Body of People on Earth.

So, if the Old Covenant, which is the promise of God to bless those who keep the commandments of His *Torah*, is still in effect, what is the New Covenant? The Bible tells us exactly what the New Covenant is:

> *But the Holy Spirit also witnesses to us; for after He had said before, "This is the covenant that I will make with them after those days, says the LORD: I will put My laws into their hearts, and in their minds I will write them," then He adds, "Their sins and their lawless deeds I will remember no more."*
> (Hebrews 10:15-17)

In other words, according to the New Covenant that God has made with His People the Followers of Jesus, we are not only no longer required to continually make bloody sacrifices for our own sins (the once-for-all sacrifice of His Son on the cross has taken care of that), but He has put his *Torah*—his instructions for living a happy and successful life in Christ—into our hearts and written them on our minds, so that, with the enabling of His indwelling Spirit, we can keep His commandments from our hearts in the Spirit of God's wonderful love rather than just going through the religious motions, keeping the commandments of the Lord out of duty or in a perfunctory, legalistic way. That is why Jesus said,

> *He who has My commandments and keeps them, it is he who loves Me. And he who loves Me will be loved by My Father, and I will love him and manifest Myself to him.* (John 14:21)

And that is why it is so important for Christians to embrace their Hebrew roots, which is basically keeping the *Torah* of the Lord God from our hearts and in His love. When we do that, we discover that, rather than being a burdensome exercise, keeping the Law of the Lord is a wonderful way to live our religious lives— joyfully keeping the commandments of our God out of pure love for Him and others, not because we are afraid of what will happen if we don't obey Him! Thank God for His wonderful New Covenant!

The Apostate American Church

Sadly, the vast majority of American Christians have neglected the Lord's eternal *Torah*, which is the foundation of life in Christ. And in attempting to establish their own righteousness through good works apart from the Lord's *Torah*, kept by His enabling Spirit, they have fallen out of love with their heavenly Father and forfeited His presence and blessings in their lives. It is as the apostle Paul predicted,

> *Now, brethren, concerning the coming of our Lord Jesus Christ and our gathering together to Him, we ask you, not to be soon shaken in mind or troubled, either by spirit or by word or by letter, as if from us, as though the day of Christ had come. Let no one deceive you by any means; for that Day will not come unless*

the **falling away** *comes first, and the man of sin is revealed, the son of perdition, who opposes and exalts himself above all that is called God or that is worshiped, so that he sits as God in the temple of God, showing himself that he is God.* (2 Thessalonians 2:1-4)

"That day" is the *"Day of the Christ"* (the Day of the Lord). And the *"falling away"* (Greek: *apostasia*), which must occur before the son of perdition (Antichrist) is revealed, is what is called the Apostasy of the Community of Believers in Jesus—falling away from true Christian faith and practice—just going through the religious motions.

So, is American "Christianity" True Christianity? If we take a realistic, honest look at the Church in America, it is blatantly obvious that it bears little resemblance to the first century apostolic "Church" of the Lord Jesus the Christ. In fact, American "Christianity" is thoroughly permeated with the sin—the pride, the covetousness, and the hypocrisy—described in this essay.

The Reason for it All

Now, you may be asking yourself, why is Bob writing all this stuff? Does he have an ax to grind—something against Americans or members of the Church? Or is he trying to cover up his own inadequacies as a Christian by judging us? Believe me, my friend, I have done a lot of praying and soul-searching regarding my own motives for putting together this essay and this book. But I believe that God does want me to publish it, and this is why: As a chief offender, I have tasted the sweet relief and joy of God's forgiveness and His grace in grafting me, a wild branch, into the cultivated olive tree (cf. Romans 11:24), and I want to share that with others! As I have mentioned throughout this essay, no one has been more arrogant, self-centered, and hypocritical than I have been. But God, through His wonderful grace and mercy, has shown me the way out of that bondage into the exhilarating freedom of His pure, unselfish love. And I believe that He wants me to share that way out of selfishness, pride, and hypocrisy with you, just in case you too want to be free—gloriously, joyfully FREE—to love others unconditionally and to serve and glorify your Lord in everything you do. And what He has shown me is that I first need to fall on my face daily and continually—every time I have a proud or selfish thought—confessing that to God, repenting of it, and begging Him to replace that sinful impulse with gratitude to Him and His special God-kind of love for Him and others. And as He enables me to do that more and more, I am finding that, more and more, I am being liberated to enjoy His wonderful presence in my life—His special, spiritual joy, peace, hope, and love. Have you ever done anything—competed in an athletic event, cleaned your house, done your job, helped another person, or anything else—out of pure love for others and the desire to glorify God, with no thought of what attention or profit (even just a "Thank you") that you were going to get out of it? If you have, then you've had a little taste of the unsurpassed joy that comes from being free from the bondage of selfishness and pride and free to love with the God-kind of love. And that, my friend, is why I'm writing this book—for, "*He who is free in the Son* (Jesus said) *is free indeed!*" (John 8:36) And I want that freedom and that joy for you. I don't want anyone to miss out on the joy of the Lord's salvation.

Meanwhile, I pray that you will take all the things you have read in this chapter and will read in the following chapters to heart, because The End is near, and Jesus said to His Disciples whom He sent out to share the good news of the Kingdom of Heaven,

> . . . *if the people of a town will not welcome you or listen to you, leave it and shake its dust from your feet! Yes, I tell you, it will be more tolerable on the Day of Judgment for the people of Sodom and Gomorrah than for that town!* (Matthew 10:1)

Chapter 5

The True Spiritual Roots of America

"Who is a liar but he who denies that Jesus is the Christ? He is antichrist who denies the Father and the Son. Whoever denies the Son does not have the Father either; he who acknowledges the Son has the Father also."
(1 John 2:22-23)

We American Christians have been taught all our lives that the United States of America is a Christian nation founded by Christians on Christian principles. But how many of us have really verified the historical validity of those claims? According to Wikipedia the "Founding Fathers" of the U.S.A. "were political leaders and statesmen who participated in the American Revolution by signing the United States Declaration of Independence, taking part in the American Revolutionary War, and establishing the United States Constitution." [1] Wikipedia lists John Adams, Benjamin Franklin, Alexander Hamilton, John Jay, Thomas Jefferson, James Madison, and George Washington as "the key Founding Fathers." Let us, in this chapter, take a close look at the "Christianity" of those seven notable and highly honored Founding Fathers of the U.S.A. plus other national leaders, and the principles and philosophies upon which they founded and have continued to lead the nation. But first, let us briefly summarize two of the basic tenets of "True Christianity."

What is True Christianity?

God Incarnate

True Christians believe that Jesus Christ is the only human being in history who could truthfully claim to be, in His basic nature, both human and divine—the only begotten (without a biological human father) Son of God.

Matthew, the writer of the first book of the New Testament, testified to that incredible fact from the witness of Old Testament prophetic Scripture and his own testimony of what an angel told

Jesus' human father Joseph, when Joseph was thinking about "putting away" Mary, to whom he was betrothed, because she was found to be pregnant before their marriage was consummated:

> *Now the birth of Jesus Christ was as follows: After His mother Mary was betrothed to Joseph, before they came together, she was found with child of the Holy Spirit. Then Joseph her husband, being a just man, and not wanting to make her a public example, was minded to put her away secretly. But while he thought about these things, behold, an angel of the Lord appeared to him in a dream, saying, "Joseph, son of David, do not be afraid to take to you Mary your wife, for that which is conceived in her is of the Holy Spirit. And she will bring forth a Son, and you shall call His name JESUS, for He will save His people from their sins." So all this was done that it might be fulfilled which was spoken by the Lord through the prophet, saying: "Behold, the virgin shall be with child, and bear a Son, and they shall call His name Immanuel," which is translated, "God with us."* (Matthew 1:18-23)

Then Jesus, although He never directly stated it, many times clearly implied that He was God in human flesh. For example, He told the religious leaders that whoever kept His Word would not die. Then, when those religious leaders asked Jesus, *"Whom do you make yourself out to be?"* He told them, *"Before Abraham was I AM."* Then they immediately picked up stones to kill Him, because I AM was the name the Lord had given to Moses when Moses asked Him what His name was, and claiming to be God was considered blasphemy, punishable by death, by the Jews. (cf. Exodus 3:14; John 8:51-59)

There are also hundreds of other passages of Scripture in both the Old and New Testaments that prophesy, state directly, or imply that Jesus Christ and God are identical.[2]

Jesus' many amazing miracles, some of which had never been performed before (e.g., healing a man born blind—John 9:32-33) were also evidences of His divine, supernatural powers.

Total Human Depravity Apart from Jesus Christ

As was explained in the last chapter, True Christians understand that, apart from the indwelling Spirit of God, *"no one is good but God"* (Luke 18:19).

When, in the beginning, Adam and Eve gave in to the temptation of the devil and rejected their Creator, sin entered them and broke the spiritual unity between them and the Lord. That was spiritual death, which eventually resulted in their physical death. And that sin that entered God's creation through Adam and Eve has infected the entire human race, resulting in the spiritual death (separation from God) and eventual physical death of every one of us (Romans 5:12).

Although, in our limited, self-centered human perception, some are "good people," not a single one of us is righteous or does any good thing apart from the indwelling Spirit of Jesus, who is God. (John 15:5; Romans 3:10-12). Apart from Jesus, our so-called "good" deeds and acts of unselfish "love" are really pretenses, and actually have a selfish motive, whether it is hope of reciprocal kindness, recognition, self-esteem, or some other benefit in this life or the next one.

Therefore, the true motive for everything we do, unless we do it in the Spirit of the pure unselfish love of God, is pride (which is directly opposed to faith in God), selfishness, or lust (cf. 1 John 2:16).

So now, with the spiritual criteria for True Christianity more clearly in mind, let us examine the actual religion of some leaders who have been guiding influences in the founding and development of United States of America during the past 240 or so years since the nation's founding.

The Pervasive Influences of Deism, Unitarianism and Freemasonry in the Founding, the Government, and the Spiritual Life of the U.S.A.

American "Christian" Deism (a contradiction in terms)

Deism is the belief that reason and observation of the natural world are sufficient to determine the existence of God, accompanied with the rejection of revelation and authority as a source of religious knowledge. Deism gained prominence in the 17th and 18th centuries during the "Age of Enlightenment"—especially in Britain, France, Germany, and in the United States—among intellectuals raised as Christians who believed in one god, but found fault with organized religion and did not believe in supernatural events such as miracles, the inerrancy of scriptures, or the Trinity. . . . Deistic ideas influenced several leaders of the American and French Revolutions.[1]

Did you get all that? Deism was a prominent religion during the 1700's—during the "Age of Enlightenment" when human reason was elevated above superstition and religious faith as the basis of human conduct and progress. The American Revolution occurred during this time. Deists are monotheistic—they believe in the existence of a god who may, in a general sense, maintain order in the world he created. But that god is not personally involved in the lives of people. In fact, the Deist god is a universal god—He does not have a particular group, church, or nation of people with whom He identifies. Nor does he reveal himself through visions, miracles, his inspired written word, or certainly not through his incarnation as a human being. So, Deism is basically humanistic—an attempt to elevate human beings to the level of God in managing their own affairs independent of Him. Yet, numerous Founding Fathers of the U.S.A., including four of the seven "key" founding fathers—Thomas Jefferson, Benjamin Franklin, Alexander Hamilton, and James Madison—who claimed to be "Christians," were actually Deists.

Thomas Jefferson[4], the principal author of the Declaration of Independence and the third President of the United States, claimed to be a Christian because he was a "disciple of the doctrines of Jesus"[5] who he considered a great moral person and teacher. But Jefferson did not believe the parts of the Bible that tell us that Jesus was the Messiah and the Son of God. He believed in neither the deity nor the miracles of Jesus, nor in the divine inspiration of the Bible. Jefferson even wrote a book entitled *The Life and Teachings of Jesus of Nazareth* in which he omitted any mention of Jesus' miracles or the supernatural aspects of Jesus' life (e.g., His virgin birth and His resurrection). In fact, Jefferson stated that he was a "materialist" rather than a "spiritualist" like Jesus. On the other hand and somewhat paradoxically, Jefferson believed in a Supreme Being and did not question the faith in God of others, which makes him a Deist rather than strictly a materialist (one who does not believe in the supernatural). He was also a regular church attender and a supporter of various churches, which makes one wonder about the soundness of the "Christian" doctrines being taught in those churches.[6]

Thomas Jefferson was also a racist. He was strongly opposed to the enslavement of anyone, black or white, but he considered blacks an inferior race who, like wild animals who could not really be tamed, should be freed only so they could be removed from the United States and deported to Africa or the West Indies.[7]

Benjamin Franklin[8] is called "The First American" because of his tireless efforts to unify the colonies and lobby on their behalf in England, in helping draft the Declaration of Independence and the U.S. Constitution, and in negotiating the Treaty of Paris, which ended the Revolutionary War. Franklin was self-educated, multi-talented, and highly accomplished in many pursuits, including: author, editor and printer of newspapers and books; civic activist, statesman and diplomat; political theorist, politician, Governor of Pennsylvania and Ambassador to France and to Sweden; United States Postmaster General; musician, scientist and inventor. Biographer Walter Isaacson wrote that Benjamin Franklin, because of his many accomplishments, writings, and involvement in the formation and founding of the U.S.A., "was the most accomplished American of his age and the most influential in inventing the type of society America would become."[9]

Ben Franklin was born into a Puritan family in Boston, Massachusetts, and received infant baptism at the old South Church in Boston, the congregation his family attended. He embraced the moral precepts of his family's faith, but, like the Unitarians, who split off from the Puritan church, he rejected the doctrine of the Trinity (the doctrine that God is three beings—God the Father, God the Son, and God the Holy Spirit—in one, supreme being). He also embraced the doctrines of Deism, including the belief that God is revealed only through nature and reason, rather than through direct, inspired revelation. He even wrote a treatise (*a Dissertation on Liberty and Necessity, Pleasure and Pain*) advocating determinism (the belief that "what will be, will be"—a denial that God is involved in human affairs).[10] And, in his 1771 autobiography, Franklin admitted that he was a Deist, although he still considered himself a "Christian."

Alexander Hamilton[11] was a lieutenant colonel in the Continental Army and General George Washington's chief of staff during the Revolutionary War. He was later a representative from New York in the Continental Congress, a delegate to the Constitutional Convention, and the primary author of the *Federalist Papers*, the primary document on which interpretation of the U.S. Constitution is based. Then, he served as the first Secretary of the Treasury of the U.S. in the cabinet of President George Washington.

Alexander Hamilton was raised in the Presbyterian Church and was quite devout—even wrote two Christian hymns. But, like numerous other Founding Fathers of the U.S., he later (during the Revolutionary War) rejected belief in a god involved in the personal affairs of humans and embraced Deism, including faith in reason rather than revelation. After the Revolutionary War, he joined the Episcopal Church and remained a nominal Christian until he died, even having received communion on his death bed. But his "Christianity," rather than being practiced in sincere devotion to the God of the Bible, was used by him to achieve political ends. Further evidence that the form of Christianity that Hamilton practiced was just a spiritually impotent façade was his insistence that Christianity and democracy were incompatible.[12]

James Madison[13], due to his leading role in drafting the United States Bill of rights and the U.S. Constitution, was known as the "Father of the Constitution." He then served as a leader in the U.S. House of Representatives, Secretary of State in President Thomas Jefferson's cabinet, and as the fourth President of the United States.

Although James Madison was educated by Presbyterian clergymen, nothing of the Christian religion stuck with him. He was an avid reader of English Deist writings, and although he wrote and spoke little of religion, some scholars state that he was a Deist.

Unitarianism: the Theological Basis of Deistic Churches

Unitarianism[14] is a church-establishing theological movement that came out of Europe and the "Age of Enlightenment" during the 1700s. Although there are many variations of specific beliefs among Unitarians, their theology is derived from Deism and, in general, rejects the doctrines of the Trinity and the deity of Jesus Christ. They also reject the doctrine of human depravity ("original sin"), believing that people are capable, in their basic nature, of both good and evil. Unitarians also elevate human reason and science as sources of truth to a level equal to Scripture. "Christian" Unitarians are so-called because they consider themselves followers of Jesus Christ who, they believe, was a great man or a prophet, although he was not God incarnate.

John Adams[15], a prominent Boston attorney and a delegate from Massachusetts to the Continental Congress, had written extensively concerning his theories about a strong, central, republican form of government. Then, he assisted Thomas Jefferson in drafting the Declaration of Independence and was the Declaration's leading proponent in Congress until it was ratified in 1776. He then served as Vice President of the U.S. during George Washington's presidency, then, following Washington's two terms, was himself elected the second President of the United States of America.

John Adams' ancestors were Puritans who split off from the Church of England (Anglican) and came to the colonies in the early 1600s to establish their own congregations free of the domination of the Church of England. They settled mainly in the Massachusetts Bay area and established independent Christian assemblies under the umbrella term Congregationalist. So, Adams was raised a Congregationalist in Boston. But, this was during the "Age of Enlightenment" when Christian faith in the personal, triune God was being eroded by Deism and its "Christian" counterpart Unitarianism. And Harvard University in Boston, where John Adams received his higher education, was a hotbed of Deistic philosophy and Unitarian religion. Also, during the mid-1700s, Congregationalist and other Christian churches, especially in Boston, were being heavily influenced by Unitarian theology. His whole life John Adams was a member of the First Parish Church of Braintree (a suburb of Boston) which, although nominally a Congregationalist assembly, beginning in 1750 (the same year Adams matriculated at Harvard) had a Unitarian minister.[16]

Although Adams, for the rest of his life, continued to be a church-going, devout "Christian," never openly denying the miracles and the redemptive role of Jesus, his writings and actions revealed his true humanistic, Deistic, and Unitarian convictions. For example, in an 1813 letter to Thomas Jefferson, he wrote, "The human Understanding is a revelation from its Maker which can never be disputed or doubted ... No Prophecies, no Miracles are necessary to prove this celestial communication."[17] And, as President, in 1791, he supported and signed the Treaty of Peace and Friendship with Tripoli, which states in Article XI:

> As **the government of the United States of America is not in any sense founded on the Christian Religion**—as it has in itself no character of enmity against the laws, religion or tranquility of Musselmen [Muslims]—and as the said States never have entered into any war or act of hostility against any Mehomitan nation, it is declared by the parties that no pretext arising from religious opinions shall ever produce an interruption of the harmony existing between the two countries.[18]

Satanic Roots of America

Freemasonry[19] was started as a formal organization (with the founding of lodges in England) also during the 1700's "Age of Enlightenment" and also has its roots in Deism. Freemasonry falsely presents itself as a beneficent civic organization, but, in reality it is a covert, secretive, insidious religion that undermines true Christianity and is actually, like Unitarianism, an **anti**-Christian religion in disguise. One of Freemasonry's primary exponents, Albert Pike, wrote,

> The doctrine of Satanism is a heresy; and the true and pure philosophic religion is the belief in Lucifer, the equal of Adonay (Jesus); but Lucifer, God of Light and God of Good, is struggling for humanity against Adonay, the God of darkness and evil.

This seemingly paradoxical statement is typical Masonic double-talk. Freemasons keep their initiates deceived into thinking they are seeking the "light" (intellectual enlightenment) of the one, true "God," without identifying who that god is until they reach the 19th Degree. Then, their understanding is illuminated by the deeper, esoteric secret that there are two, equal gods—Lucifer and Adonay (Jesus). And Lucifer (who the Masons falsely teach is not Satan) is the god of light and good, but Adonay is the god of darkness and evil.

Hopefully, you can see that this is just the opposite of what Jesus, who was not an angel, taught. He said, "I am **the** way **the** truth and **the** light. No one comes to **the** Father [God] except through me" (John 14:6). And the apostle Paul taught, *"Satan himself transforms himself into an angel of light"* (2 Corinthians 11:14). The prophet Isaiah identifies this angel of light (Satan) as Lucifer, who aspires to ascend into Heaven and exalt his throne above the stars of God (Isaiah 14:12-14). Antichrist, the incarnation of Satan, will, at the "end of the age" (Matthew 24:3), not appear as a sinister, evil character, but indeed as an angel of light masquerading as the true Messiah, and the whole world will follow after him in wonder and awe and worship him (cf. Revelation 13:3, 8).

Numerous Founding Fathers of the U.S.A., including "George Washington, Thomas Jefferson, Benjamin Franklin, Ethan Allen, John Hancock, John Paul Jones, Paul Revere, Robert Livingston, and 35 other lesser known men who were signers of the Declaration of Independence and/or the Constitution" were Freemasons.[20]

George Washington[21], the commander-in-chief of the Continental Army and Revolutionary War hero, presided over the Constitutional Convention that established the office of President of the United States of America. Then, by unanimous choice of the electors, in 1788, he became the first President of the U.S.A. What were the religious beliefs of "the father of his country"?

Washington, a member of the Episcopal (Anglican) Church, was perceived as a devout "Christian." He was frequently seen with his Bible, praying, when he was commanding general of the Continental Army. A few of his typical statements were,

- It is impossible to rightly govern the world without God and Bible.
- Make sure you are doing what God wants you to do—then do it with all your strength.
- What students would learn in American schools above all is the religion of Jesus Christ.[22]

But, was George Washington a **true** Christian? Did He acknowledge belief in the basic tenets of the Christian faith (the depravity of human beings apart from the indwelling Holy Spirit and the deity of Jesus Christ)? A survey of his writings reveals that he did not. Jesus told His disciples, *"If you ask anything in **My name** [implying that He is God], I will do it"* (John 14:14). But there is no evidence that Washington ever prayed any of his prayers in the name of Jesus. There is one of his alleged prayers displayed in St. Paul's Chapel in New York City, where Washington worshiped the first two years of his Presidency, in which he prayed in the name of Jesus Christ. But, research has revealed, that prayer was derived (and modified) from a letter Washington wrote to the states' governors in which he did not mention the name of Jesus Christ:

> I now make it my earnest prayer, that God would have you, and the state over which you preside, in His holy protection; that He would incline the hearts of the citizens to cultivate a spirit of subordination and obedience to government; to entertain a brotherly affection and love for one another, for their fellow-citizens of the United States at large, and particularly for their brethren who have served in the field; and finally, that He would most graciously be pleased to dispose us all to justice, to love mercy, and to demean ourselves with that charity, humility and pacific temper of mind which were the characteristics of the Divine Author of our blessed religion, and without an humble imitation of whose examples in these things, we can never hope to be a happy nation.

In fact, Washington very seldom mentioned the name of Jesus (the above quote about "the religion of Jesus Christ" is an exception), much less that He was the Son of God, the Savior, or the Messiah.[22]

So, what was George Washington's true religion? The fact that he was a high ranking, highly dedicated, and highly honored Freemason might give us a clue. In fact, we might say that he was the prototypical Mason. He joined the Fredericksburg, Virginia, Masonic lodge in 1752, at the age of 20. After just nine months he was given the title Master Mason. During the War for Independence, he was very active in Freemasonry, attending Masonic celebrations and "**religious**"[24] observances in several states, and supporting the formation of Masonic lodges in army regiments. During the war, Washington was recommended to be Grand Master of the Grand Lodge of Virginia, but he declined because he had not yet served as Master of a local lodge. At his inauguration as President of the United States, he took the oath of office with his hand on a Bible from the St. John's Lodge in New York. During his two terms as President, Washington remained a very active Mason and visited lodges in several states. After he retired from public service, he became Charter Master of Alexandria (Virginia) Lodge Number 22. And when he died in 1799, Washington was buried with Masonic rites conducted by the Alexandria lodge. And on Shuter's Hill, on property owned by the Alexandria-Washington lodge, the multimillion-dollar George Washington Masonic National Memorial, a "lighthouse to Washington," was constructed. It was located there because ancient religious temples were located on hilltops or mountaintops. On the Memorial's website, George Washington is referred to as "the cornerstone of American civilization" and "Freemasonry's 'perfect ashlar' [building stone] upon which countless Master Masons gauge their labors in their own lodges and in their own communities."[25]

The Exception

John Jay, a New York City attorney, was elected to the Continental Congress and served as its president. He was a key figure in getting the new U.S. Constitution ratified and wrote five of the *Federalist Papers* on which its interpretation was based. Both during and after the Revolutionary War, Jay was an ambassador to Spain and France, and he served as Secretary of Foreign Affairs. Together with Benjamin Franklin and John Adams, he was a signer of the Treaty of Paris, which ended the Revolutionary War. He then served as the first Chief Justice of the United States from 1789-95. Following that, he was Governor of New York for six years.[26]

Of the seven "key" Founding Fathers of the United States of America, John Jay came the closest to espousing a true understanding and practice of Christianity that was uncompromised by Deism, humanism, Unitarianism, or Masonic Luciferianism.

Jay's paternal grandfather Augustus was a French Huguenot. The Huguenots were a sect of Protestant Christians who were severely persecuted by the Roman Catholic Church. So, Augustus fled France and settled in New York City in the early 1700's. And, as Huguenots who migrated to the British colonies frequently did, Augustus joined the Church of England (Anglican Church).

John Jay was profoundly influenced by the faith of his grandfather and stories of the persecution of the Jay family in France. And while he was growing up on a farm owned by his father Peter, also a devout Anglican, he was educated at what is now called a "Christian school"—the school run by the pastor of the Anglican congregation in nearby New Rochelle, New York. And Jay shared the orthodox, Protestant faith of his father and grandfather his whole life and was a devout member of the Episcopal Church (called the Anglican Church in Britain) until the day he died.

John Jay's religious convictions, which shaped his philosophies of government and justice, included an unshakable belief in the deity of Jesus Christ, belief that true religion consists basically of a personal relationship with God rather than church liturgy, rejection of Roman Catholicism as Biblical religion, belief that slavery was morally wrong, and strong opposition to Deism as a valid philosophy or religion. His views frequently resulted in conflicts with other Founding Fathers, especially Benjamin Franklin with whom he had some heated exchanges over the differences between Deism and true Christianity. But Jay was so strong in his convictions and influence that he was able, almost single-handedly, to get some strongly opposed enactments passed. For example, because of the persecution of his French ancestors, Jay was keenly aware of the dangers of mixing religion and politics. And when he served as a member of the New York Constitutional Convention, he was concerned about the separation of church and state—especially that the Catholic Church would not interfere with government functions. And he got the Convention to pass a requirement ...

> barring Catholics from State citizenship and government service unless they pledged to "abjure and renounce all allegiance and subjection to all and every foreign king, prince, potentate, and state in all matters, ecclesiastical as well as civil."[27]

Was The United States of America Founded on Christian Principles?

A frequent claim by American Christians is that the U.S. was founded on Christian principles. But was it? To examine the truth of that assertion, let us see, in the light of Scripture, how it stacks up against reality.

Jesus was not a pacifist. When the merchants and money-changers were making the Temple a place of doing business rather than the center of worship, He furiously overturned their tables and drove them out with a whip (John 2:14-16). Nor was He against self-defense or defending others against aggressors. He never told his disciple Peter not to carry his sword (cf. John 18:10). And He told His disciples that if any of them did not have a sword, he should sell his garment and purchase one (Luke 22:36). To Jesus, it was that important in a hostile world to have a weapon.

What He taught against was retaliation, revenge, and rebellion against authority. In Israel, it was the role of the government to try criminals and exact justice, not individuals. In fact, Jesus, in keeping with the God-ordained principles of tolerance, mercy, and love, counseled his disciples to show far more restraint in retaliating against those who damaged their persons, their property, or their liberty than was normally humanly possible (e.g., Matthew 5:39-44). And He was strictly against rebelling against those in authority. When Peter chopped off the ear of one of the troops sent to arrest Jesus, He rebuked Peter, not because he had used his sword to defend his Master, but because he was rebelling against the Jewish authorities and, consequently, against God (John 18:10-11). And it was a transformed Peter who later clarified what he had learned from Jesus about not rebelling against either government or non-government authorities (even slave masters), even if those authorities were abusive (1 Peter 2:13-20).

But how did the United States of America gain its independence? Was it through, in the Spirit of Christ, patient endurance of the oppression of Great Britain, peaceful negotiations, and praying for the Lord's deliverance? Or was it through **un**godly, violent rebellion? What does the National Anthem glorify? Is it the wonderful providence of God, or is it the bloody fruits of violence and rebellion (the "bombs bursting in air" ... what a glorious sight!).

And were the concepts and principles on which the new nation was based, as expressed in its foundational documents, truly Scriptural? Consider the most quoted statement of those principles, from the Declaration of Independence:

> We hold these truths to be self-evident, that all men are created equal, that they are endowed by their Creator with certain unalienable Rights, that among these are Life, Liberty and the pursuit of Happiness.

This foundational statement is totally contrary to Scripture. Where does the Bible tell us that "all men" are created equal, with certain "unalienable Rights"? The Bible states that we belong to our Creator, were created to serve and to glorify Him, and to love others unselfishly—not to insist on our own rights (Romans 14:7-8; 1 Corinthians 10:31, 33; 13:4-5). And where does Scripture tell us that these "Rights" (which are really God-given *privileges* which he gives or removes according to His perfect will) include "Life, Liberty and [especially] the pursuit of Happiness"? Jesus said, *"Whoever desires to save his life will lose it, but whoever loses his life for My sake will find it"* (Matthew 16:25). Then, regarding personal liberty, He stated, "Whoever compels you to go one mile, go with him two" (Matthew 5:41). Finally, the Bible has nothing positive to say about the "pursuit of Happiness." Does it not make exactly antithetical statements like, *"He who loves pleasure will be a poor man"* (Proverbs 21:17) and, *"She who lives in pleasure is dead while she lives"* (1 Timothy 5:6). Jesus was the perfect example of sacrificing His "Rights" for the good of others. And He tells those of us who want to be His disciples (true Christians) to follow His example (Luke 9:23), trusting the Lord to meet all our needs if we are more concerned about pleasing Him and meeting the needs of others than we are about insisting on our own rights.

Therefore, it is clear that the founders of the United States of America had no real understanding of the fundamental principles of true Christianity, which include trusting our Heavenly Father to take perfect care of us, in this life and in the World to Come, if we will submit to His commandments and seek His kingdom and His righteousness, rather than seeking, in arrogance and self-centeredness, to establish our own kingdom on Earth. The old saying that "God helps those who help themselves" is not found in the Bible. What Jesus says is, *"Apart from Me, you can do **nothing**"* (John 15:5). Yet, how many of the founders of the U.S.A. even acknowledged our Savior's involvement in human affairs, much less submitted to His ways of doing things, the faith in Him and His Heavenly Father that He told His followers to have, and applied those principles to the founding of the nation?

The Declension of Christianity in America

Have whatever traces of true Christianity that existed in the formation and founding of the United States of America developed into a more substantial national religion? Hardly. Of the forty-four U.S. Presidents, most have been nominal Christians when they took office, but very few have been active in their churches after taking office, other than attending Sunday services. Five have been Deists, as indicated by their stated religious beliefs if not their church affiliations. Four have been Unitarians and three others explicitly have not believed in the Trinity (the deity of Jesus Christ). Seven have indicated no religious affiliation.[28] Fourteen have been Freemasons. Many Members of Congress have been Freemasons. Seven of those have been 33rd Degree (the highest level) Freemasons.[29]

Also, the past 200 years have seen the rise of many quasi-Christian and even explicitly anti-Christian religious cults in America, some with significant cultural and political impact, including the Church of Jesus Christ of Latter Day Saints (Mormonism), Christian Science, Islam, Jehovah's Witnesses, Theosophy, Unity, The Way International, the First Church of Satan, and the Neo-Luciferian Church. All of these religious organizations and numerous others deny the key doctrine upon which true Christianity is based: Jesus Christ is the only begotten Son of God (1 John 4:9). In fact, He *is* the one, true God—God manifested in human flesh (John 1:1-3, 14; 8:58; et al.)—the only human being in history who could truthfully make that claim. According to the Bible, any person who denies this fundamental Truth is not only a liar but is manifesting the **anti**-Christian spirit (1 John 4:1-3).

Third, numerous non-religious and explicitly anti-religious organizations and movements, which deny or minimize spiritual reality, have proliferated in America, including the American Humanist Association which has as its subtitle "Good Without a God," the Secular Coalition of America, the Naturalism Philosophy Forum, Rationalist International, and American Atheist.

The Results

So, what are the net effects of the seeds of apostasy that were sown in the "Christianity" of The United States of America when it was founded plus all the quasi-Christian, pseudo-Christian and anti-Christian influences that have been injected into the spiritual bloodstream of the nation's religion during the past 200+ years?

The results are tragic.   Even   the superficial façade that was "Christian" America in the beginning is but a perverse caricature of itself.

Look again at American religion. We claim to be a "Christian" nation, but are we not awfully tolerant of all the other religions and cults of the world, just like ancient Babylon? Just as America is the melting pot of the races of the world, she is also the melting pot of all the world's religions. And the distinctions between the religions in the USA are getting very blurry. Many groups are being formed for dialogue, action, and even common worship among various religions—Protestants and Catholics Together, Promise Keepers, Buddhism and Christianity, Islam and Christianity, New Age ideas and practices in the Church, Yoga in the Church, Eastern mysticism in the Church, Masonic Luciferianism in the Church ... *ad infinitum*. True Christians believe that there is only one way to God, and that is through Jesus Christ, who is the only human being in history who could truthfully claim to be God.   But more and more nominal "Christians" believe that there are many paths to "God" and that all the different religions worship, ultimately, the same god. (That is what George Bush said about other religions and Christianity when he was President and what Barack Obama says about other religions and Christianity now that he is President.) True Christians believe that there are basically two "gods" impacting this world. One is the false god, Satan or Lucifer, and the other is the one, true God, the God of the (true) followers of Jesus Christ, and that all the other religions of the world are, whether they realize it or not, following Satan. So, to the extent that the American "Christian" Church is uniting with other religions, philosophies, and practices of the world, she is not truly Christian, is she? She is really a false (anti-) Christian church, following the false god of this world.

In the next chapter, the true, Biblical identity and destiny of the religious and secular United States of America will be explained. Then, the implications of the Tenth Harbinger that was found in the rubble of the collapsed World Trade Center towers will be clearly and fully understood.

Chapter 6

The Identity and Destiny of America in Bible Prophecy

"The merchants of these things, who became rich by her, will stand at a distance for fear of her torment, weeping and wailing, and saying, 'Alas, alas, that great city that was clothed in fine linen, purple, and scarlet, and adorned with gold and precious stones and pearls! For in one hour such great riches came to nothing.' Every shipmaster, all who travel by ship, sailors, and as many as trade on the sea, stood at a distance and cried out when they saw the smoke of her burning, saying, 'What is like this great city?' They threw dust on their heads and cried out, weeping and wailing, and saying, 'Alas, alas, that great city, in which all who had ships on the sea became rich by her wealth! For in one hour she is made desolate.'" (Revelation 18:15-19)

Most expositors see very little if any mention of the United States of America in Bible prophecy. But this chapter will prove, beyond a shadow of doubt, based on historical and Biblical evidence plus current events, that New York City is the "great city" of Revelation 18. And America (especially after she is taken over by Islamists) and the many countries she controls economically and politically comprise the city-state/empire called "Babylon the Great" that, until she is destroyed, will dominate all the nations of the earth, setting the world stage for the takeover of Antichrist.

Two Babylons

The Bible goes to great lengths to clearly tell us about two different (but similar), literal Babylons: ancient, historical Babylon and modern, prophetic Babylon. There are more verses of Scripture (over 250) that speak of the two Babylons than of any other city or nation on Earth, except for Jerusalem and Israel. Entire chapters of the *Bible* devoted to Babylon include: Isaiah 13, 14, 47, 48; Jeremiah 50, 51 and Revelation 17, 18. Each Babylon is not only identified by a "*great city,*" but by the land, nation or empire in

91

which its great city is located (cf. Jeremiah 50:8, 12, 38); by other nations or territories it dominates politically, economically, militarily, and religiously; and by its treachery against Israel. Two entire chapters plus other passages of the book of Revelation are devoted to modern Babylon. The great exultation of the Redeemed of the Lord before He returns to establish His kingdom on Earth is because of the final (third) destruction of modern Babylon (Revelation 18:21-19:2). If you are interested in really understanding the events, players, and plot of the book of Revelation, realize that a main key to unlocking that understanding is knowing the identity, activities, and destiny of modern, prophetic, "mystery" Babylon. So, brace yourself, put on your face-up-to-reality hat and let us first take a look at ancient, historical Babylon to see what clues about modern Babylon we can gather.

Ancient Babylon[1]

Actually, there were three ancient Babylons: Babylon the religious center of the Akkadian Empire, Babylon the capitol of the first Babylonian Empire, and Babylon the capitol of the neo-Babylonian Empire. Aspects of all three ancient Babylons are reflected in Bible prophecies concerning modern Babylon.

The Bible tells us that, after the Great Flood, Noah's great-grandson Nimrod founded the world's first multi-national, multi-ethnic and multi-cultural empire (cf. Genesis 10:10-12). Coincidentally, thousands of cuneiform (clay) tablets from that same time period (about 2300 BC) tell us that, in the same location (the *"land of Shinar"*—Mesopotamia) the Akkadian Empire, which most secular historians acknowledge as the world's first empire, was founded by Sargon. Close examination of Biblical, Akkadian and Summerian records reveal that Nimrod and Sargon are the same person. Nimrod was his given name and Sargon (which means "True King" or "Legitimate King") in Akkadian was his royal title. According to both the Biblical (Genesis 10:10) and secular records, the Kingdom of Akkadia included the religious center that was later named Babylon and the cities of Erich (Uruk) and Accad (Akkad). Also, according to both records, this king invaded and conquered what was then the relatively small, insignificant kingdom of Assyria, built several cities there including Nineveh and Calah, and incorporated it into his growing empire. Thirdly, both the Bible and Akkadian records call this king a *"mighty hunter"* (Genesis 10:9). All Akkadian kings were celebrated as mighty hunters and warriors and were worshiped as deified humans.

To establish himself as a god in the public's perception, Sargon ceremonially married the principal deity of the Summerians and Akkadians, the "Queen of Heaven" Innana (later named Ishtar in Babylon). Scripture states that Nimrod *"began to be a mighty one on the earth"* (Genesis 10:8), which may indicate that he was not only the first empire-building ruler or king, but that he had supernatural satanic powers. His powers certainly were not from the one true God God, because he practiced a totally idolatrous religious system and attempted to build a tower to heaven—the infamous "Tower of Babel"—reminding us of Satan's enticing statement to Adam and Eve, *"You will be like God"* (Genesis 3:5), and the boast of Lucifer, the (spiritual) king of Babylon (Isaiah 14:4), *"I will ascend into heaven, I will exalt my throne above the stars of God"* (Isaiah 14:13). The title "mighty hunter," spiritually speaking, may mean one who hunts for and destroys the souls of men.

So, virtually all translations (from Hebrew) of the Genesis 10 and 11 account of the history of Nimrod's Babylon are incorrect, and all expositions and teachings based on those translations are incorrect. Nimrod/Sargon was the founder of the Akkadian Empire, not the Babylonian Empire. And the city of Akkad was the capitol of the empire, not Babylon. Nimrod/Sargon conquered the Sumerians, who ruled southern Mesopotamia before he arrived, and, to include the Sumerians seamlessly into his empire, although he was a direct descendant of Noah who believed unwavering in the one, true God, he adopted the Sumerian religion which included the worship of their gods, especially Innana, the "Queen of Heaven." He then built a city which later came to be called Babylon because the ziggurats (towers) built there to honor and worship the Sumerian/Akkadian deities were called, in Akkadian, *babylons*. (Actually, *babylon* is a Greek variation of the Akkadian word *babilum*).

Another error based on mistranslations of the original Hebrew Scriptures, which greatly distorts and diminishes our understanding of how Nimrod's Babylon is reflected in prophecies regarding modern Babylon, is the notion that, at the time of the building of the "Tower of Babel," the whole world spoke one language. Archaeological discoveries of the thousands of Sumerian and Akkadian cuneiform tablets and linguistic studies have proven that, by the time Nimrod arrived on the scene, about 500 years after the Flood, many languages were spoken in the world. In Mesopotamia several languages were spoken, including Sumerian, and, after Nimrod arrived, Akkadian was spoken there. Then, Babylonian and Assyrian (dialects that developed from Akkadian) were spoken. The error that the whole world spoke a single language arose from a mistranslation of Genesis 11:1 which states in virtually all versions of the Bible, *"Now the whole earth had one language and one speech."* There are three words in that statement that have been mistranslated down through the centuries. The Hebrew text literally states, *"And the whole **earth** was of one **lip** and of one **word**."* The Hebrew term for "earth" *(erets)* may also mean "land," as in the "land of Israel." And in the context of Genesis 10 and 11, that is apparently how *erets* should be translated, because it is all about the Mesopotamian empire of Nimrod, which certainly did not cover the whole earth. Also, in the ancient Akkadian and Sumerian cultures "one lip" was an idiom that meant "one government," and "one word" was an idiom that meant "one command" as in, "Just say the word and it will be done." So, Genesis 11:1 should be correctly translated, *"And the whole land* [of Mesopotamia/the Akkadian Empire] *was of one government and one commander* [ruler]." In other words, what Nimrod did, in total rebellion against the Lord God, Whose original intention for human beings was that they would *"have dominion over ... all the earth"* and Who told Adam and Eve, *"Be fruitful and multiply; fill the earth and subdue it"* (Genesis 1:26, 28), was to attempt to bring all languages, cultures and nations together under his rule as the deified sargon ("true king") of the world. Notice that the Lord nowhere told humans to rule over one another. His later concession to Israel, allowing them to have a human king, was because of their hardness of heart in refusing to submit to Him alone.

Another grievous error in translation that has reinforced the error that the *"whole earth"* spoke one language is naming the ziggurat that the Akkadians were attempting to build to Heaven (probably for worship of their principal deity Innana/Ishtar) the "Tower of Babel." There are only two places in Scripture (Genesis 10:10 and 11:9—the text we are clarifying) where, in translations from the Hebrew, *"Babel"* is identified as a city the Akkadians, under Nimrod, were building. However, there is no such term "Babel" in Hebrew. In every other place in Scripture (280 times) where the He-brew term translated "Babel" in Genesis 10:10 and 11:9 is used, it is translated *"Babylon."* The original translators of the Hebrew might have thought the Hebrew term was *balal* which means "confusion," and that mistaken translation supported their belief that the Lord stopped the building of the tower and scattered the people of "Babylon" by confusing their language.

Until recently, the sudden collapse of the Akkadian empire in 2154 BC, within 180 years of its founding, was a mystery to histori-ans. Many Akkadian writings told of the gods raining disasters from the heavens, but historians could not put two and two together. However, archaeological and geological discoveries, especially, in 2001, of the two-mile wide Umm al Binni lake crater in the Amarah region of southern Iraq, only about 125 miles from ancient Akkad and nearby Babylon, plus Akkadian writings like "The Curse of Akkad," have proven that the Akkadian civilization was destroyed suddenly by a comet impacting the earth and exploding with the force of thousands of Hiroshima-size atomic bombs (190 to 750 megatons of TNT). That impact must have totally destroyed "by fire" everything within over 100 miles from the impact. It also rendered the land of much of the empire uninhabitable for a num-ber of years and scattered survivors far and wide.

This scientifically, historically correct explanation of what hap-pened to Nimrod's empire and the city of Babylon throws brilliant light on the Revelation's prophecy of what will happen to modern Babylon. In the same way that Nimrod set himself up as the deified ruler of the world's first empire, the ultimate anti-Christ will declare himself to be *"god"* (2 Thessalonians 2:4) and will establish a (true) global kingdom (cf. Revelation 13:8; 17:17). Nimrod was the first type and foreshadow of the *"beast"* of Revelation (13:4; 17:12). Al-so, Nimrod/Sargon's Akkadian Empire was the original type of Antichrist's global empire which will be destroyed in the same way but on a much larger scale than the Akkadian Empire was de-stroyed.

Also, the annihilation of Babylon will not be an isolated event. There are strong scientific, historical and Biblical indications that **every one** of the trumpet and bowl judgments of the Wrath of God will involve the impact of comets, God's *"weapons of indigna-tion"* from the *"storehouse"* of those weapons (the Oort Cloud of billions of comets) located at the *"farthest border"* (surrounding our solar system) (cf. Jeremiah 50:25, 26).

Incidentally, it was about 200 years after the fall of the Akkadian Empire, about 1900 BCE, that Abram (renamed Abraham) left Ur, the ancient capital of Sumer, located in southern Mesopotamia, and moved to Haran, a city in the north. Later, Abraham left Haran and migrated into the land of Canaan (modern-day Israel) under God's promise that he would become the father of a great nation (cf. Genesis 12).

The second phase of Babylon, when it became a great city-state/kingdom, was ruled by the Amorite dynasty. The most famous Amorite King over Babylonia was Hammurapi (sometimes spelled Hammurabi), who ruled from approximately 1792-1750 BCE. Hammurapi is most famous for his legal judgments, which evolved into the "Code of Hammurapi," from which many of our modern, western laws are derived. The Babylonians had numerous gods which were assimilated from the earlier Sumerian/Akkadian culture which the Babylonians and Assyrians displaced. In fact, basically the same Sumerian religious system with the same gods was in place in Hammurapi's Babylon as during Nimrod's rule hundreds of years earlier. Their chief male god was Marduk the sun god or the god of life and death (whose earlier name was Tammuz). But in Babylon, males and females were seen as equals, and, in fact, the main Babylonian deity, and the god most pertinent to our study, was still the "Queen of Heaven," Ishtar (the Sumerian goddess Inanna, the daughter of the moon god and goddess), the goddess of temple prostitutes (the "Mother of Whores"), also called the "Goddess of Liberty." (Make a note of Ishtar's names; they will be important when we discuss the religion of modern, "mystery" Babylon.) In fact, Sumerian/Babylonian religion may be traced through all the false religions of the world, especially those that impacted Israel. The gods (particularly the goddess Inanna/Ishtar) of Canaan, Egypt, Assyria, Greece, Rome, and, yes, modern Babylon are the same as those of ancient Babylon, just with different names. About 1270 BCE, the brutal, merciless Assyrians (the world's first terrorists) overpowered Babylonia. The Assyrian takeover of the Babylonian Empire also has clear prophetic implications for modern Babylon, as will be explained below. For the next 700 years, the Assyrians dominated the ancient world.

In 626 BCE, a leader named Nabopolassar led Babylonia to regain its independence from Assyria. Under him and his son, Nebuchanezzar, who took over as King in 604 BCE, the neo-Babylonian empire became one of the greatest city-state-empires in world history. And it is this **third phase of Babylon** with which Scripture is most concerned, because it was the Babylon of Nebuchadnezzar, starting even before he officially became king, that took the Israelites (the descendants of Abraham), primarily of the tribes of Judah and Benjamin, into 70 years of captivity, beginning in 605 BCE when Daniel, Hananiah, Mishael, Azariah and other members of the royal family of Judah and other children of Israel's southern kingdom (the other ten tribes having been dispersed and many taken captive by the Assyrians about 120 years earlier) were taken to Babylon.

So, to help us understand the many Biblical prophecies concerning both ancient and modern Babylon, let us take a closer look at some of the features of ancient Babylon.

Government and Religion

The Babylon of Nebuchadnezzar and its few other kings who reigned from 626-539 BCE, when it fell to Cyrus, King of Persia, was an absolute monarchy. Although Babylon worshiped the same gods as always (Marduk, Ishtar, and others), its religion became very eclectic as it added Sumerian gods and gods from other parts of the world to its pantheon. Various forms of the occult—witchcraft, divination, sorcery, necromancy, and so forth—as well as eastern mysticism were practiced. And Nebuchadnezzar was a ruthless tyrant who demanded that he also be worshiped. Remember the story of Daniel's three friends, Shadrach, Meshach and Abednego, who refused to worship Babylon's gods or bow down to an image of Nebuchadnezzar (Daniel 3)? Although they were three of Nebuchadnezzar's favorite administrators, he was infuriated and had them thrown into the royal incinerator. So, we might say that Babylon's government was a religious dictatorship in which religion was inextricably intertwined with government. One could be executed either for not submitting to the laws of the land or for not practicing the national religion. We will see that in modern, prophetic, "mystery" Babylon, religion is also in bed with the government.

Economy, Culture, and Citizenry

Babylon was the trade and cultural center of the world. It was called the "Golden City." It had the highest standard of living of any nation on the earth. By the standards of the rest of the world, Babylon's citizens lived in great wealth and luxury. It was the world center for education, the arts, and religion. It was the location of the famous "Hanging Gardens," which, from a distance looked like a lush, green, tropical paradise. It was dotted by temples and ziggurats (religious towers) built for the worship of Babylon's many gods, especially for its main gods, Marduk and Ishtar. Babylon was located on the mighty Euphrates River in southern Mesopotamia, which was not an arid, desert area like it is today. In fact, Babylon was located on the alluvial plain drained by the Tigris and Euphrates rivers, watered by an amazing system of canals built by the Babylonians—boasting probably the most fertile soil in the world, covered by rich crops and other vegetation. It was called the "beautiful land." Babylon was the crossroads of trade for that part of the world. Trade routes passed through Babylon from all points north, east, south and west. Boats sailed up and down the Euphrates, which passed right through the middle of the city of Babylon, from the Persian Gulf in the south into Assyria (modern-day Syria and Turkey) in the north. Because Babylon had been occupied by so many peoples down through the centuries, and because people from so many places passed through Babylon, the citizenry of Babylon was very diverse; it was a real "melting pot." Just like ancient Babylon, modern, prophetic Babylon is the economic, trade, and cultural center of the modern world and also the "melting pot" of the world. Sound familiar?

Morality

Babylon was an extremely licentious, immoral city. As was mentioned above, sex outside of marriage was not only acceptable, but was considered the highest form of religious and spiritual practice. All forms of sexual perversion—homosexuality, bestiality, incest, pedophilia, etc.—were widely practiced. Drunken orgies were common entertainment. Modern Babylon is also very libertarian in its morality.

Defense

Babylon was considered the "invincible city." Built in a square pattern, approximately 15 miles on each side, with wide boulevards running at right angles to each other, north to south and east to west, she was a very large city, but carefully designed for rapid access to all parts of the city. As was mentioned above, the Euphrates River flowed right through the middle of Babylon. And a system of canals from the river provided plenty of water to the whole city for gardens, drinking water, cleaning, and other purposes. So, if under siege, the city could be sustained with water and food indefinitely. Along the river banks on both sides of the city and surrounding the city were two huge walls, 100 feet high and 50 to 60 feet wide (wide enough on top for a chariot pulled by a team of four horses to make a U-turn), with intermittent watch towers and huge, copper-plated gates. Then, other parts of the city, like the King's palace, were also partitioned off by similar walls. So, with soldiers constantly manning the watch towers and patrolling the tops of the walls, Babylon was the most impregnable city in history. Unfortunately, the Babylonians got complacent in their "invincibility" and liked to party. So, one night in 539 BCE, when the Babylonians were in drunken revelry, the army of Cyrus, King of Persia, having dammed up the Euphrates River, stealthily entered the city from the river bed, sneaked into the palace, killed the King, and took over the city without a struggle. The next morning, the citizens of Babylon awoke to find themselves conquered! The Bible says that in the same way, modern Babylon, who thinks she is invincible, will be destroyed by a sudden, sneak attack in just one hour. Actually, as we continue, we will see how this prophecy has two fulfillments: the fall of political, economic and military Babylon (like the fall of Hammurapi's Babylon to the Assyrians and the fall of Nebuchadnezzar's Babylon to the Persians) and the total annihilation of Babylon *"by fire"* (like the burning of the Babylon of Nimrod).

Imperialism

Babylon, under the reign of Nebuchadnezzar, was the most economically, politically, and militarily dominant city-state (nation/empire) in the world. She controlled every nation from Egypt to the Persian Gulf in the South to the Black and Caspian Seas in the north. In the same way, modern Babylon will, and to a large extent already does, rule the world.

Modern, Prophetic, "Mystery" Babylon

Of course, modern, prophetic Babylon is not named in the Bible because she was not in existence when the Bible was written. But you probably already know who she is, if you read the commentary on Revelation Chapters 17 and 18, don't you? And, if you have read through this page, you are probably starting to get a gnawing feeling that it is obvious, aren't you? When confronted with plain evidence from history, current events, and the Bible, the identity of modern Babylon is crystal clear, undeniable, and irrefutable. Then, why do very few Americans acknowledge that Babylon is the United States of America? This commentator has often asked himself that question. Citizens of other nations do not seem so blinded to that reality. I think it is because it is just very, very difficult for us to be objective about something in which we have a very high personal stake, especially if our whole lives we have been taught something different. What do you think?

So please, let me beg you, if you love the Truth and are one of those rare few who are really willing to face up to reality, especially if your eternal destiny and the eternal destiny of your loved ones depends on it (and in this case, it certainly might), please suspend any automatic negative reaction that you might have to the idea that the U.S.A. is indeed Babylon long enough to read the rest of this essay. Then, if you want to crucify this watchman for his horrible, unpatriotic lies, that is okay, because he has done his best to share with you what he believes the Lord has shown him, before it is too late and, if he is right, you perish with the rest of the Babylonians.

Historical Evidence

Remember, Bible history repeats itself. Modern Babylon must be very similar to ancient Babylon. Think about all the characteristics of ancient Babylon listed above: totalitarian, dictatorial government led by a self-deified ruler; eclectic, idolatrous religion blended with the government; strong sense of national pride and patriotism; luxury and wealth—dominates world economy and trade; by far the most powerful military in the world; powerful defense—seemingly "invincible"; world cultural center; center for world government; the "melting pot" of the world; a very immoral nation, tolerating all kinds of sexual immorality and perversion; a "party" nation, centered on entertainment and revelry; imperialistic—dominating the governments of other nations of the world.

Some may take issue with a few of these characteristics. For example, is the USA a totalitarian government ruled by a self-deified ruler? Please allow me to suggest that the U.S.A. is quickly moving in that direction. President George W. Bush garnered more powers for the top executive than any other President in history. While he was in college, President Bush (as did his father, George H.W. Bush) became a member of Skull and Bones—an organization based on the belief that its members have been "born again" into a state of superhuman spirituality (their own spirit, not the Spirit of the Lord God). And President Barack Obama, with widespread and intrusive enforcement of the Patriot Act, has continued that trend. In the event of another "national emergency" of the magnitude of 9/11 or greater—a terrorist attack, an economic crisis, or World War III—the President could declare national martial law overnight, just as Adolf Hitler did in Germany on November 9, 1938, the date he started having Jews and others who opposed his government killed and millions of them shipped off to concentration camps. President Obama also practices self-worship, believing that the way one rises above the common and mundane is to develop the god-person within.[2] Plus, in her final form, just before her total destruction "by fire," modern Babylon will be ruled by a totalitarian government with a mandated religion, exactly like ancient Babylon, as will be explained below.

Or, you might object to the suggestion that America is imperialistic. It would probably boggle your mind to know how many nations of the world, including Honduras, Uruguay, Afghanistan, Iraq, several African nations, and many others around the world are just client states of the USA; their economies would immediately collapse if America's multi-national corporations pulled out or stopped importing their goods. Therefore, the USA calls the shots in how those countries are run: Their "elected" leaders are virtual puppet governors controlled by the USA.[3]

The Evidence of American Religion

But, the greatest similarity of all between ancient and modern Babylon is religion. Now many, especially American Christians, will flatly deny that assertion. But, please consider the evidence of current events in the light of the history of American religion as to how American "Christianity" compares with Babylonian religion.

As was thoroughly explained and documented in chapters 4 and 5, American religion is based primarily on the humanism and Deism of the "Age of Enlightenment" of the 1700s. And, according to the Deists, human beings still have the Creator's (the universal, impersonal "God") nature; all humans are still basically good and have the knowledge, wisdom and power, somewhere in their beings, to regain dominion of the world. We just needed a god-man, a perfect, sinless man, a "messiah" and savior, to show us the way back to our natural godliness. And, according to the Bible, that Messiah and Savior is Jesus Christ. So, all that "Christians" need to do is to believe in Jesus as a great god-man, teacher and prophet (albeit not the incarnation of the one, true God), follow his teachings, and by the wisdom and power of "God's" (whoever that is) spirit, which He put in them in The Beginning, bringing them back in touch with their basic, natural goodness, bring the rest of the citizens of the world into actualization of their godliness, and reestablish Paradise on Earth and their dominion over it.

Sounds (to the undiscerning) true to Scripture, right? So, what is wrong with American "Christianity" according to the above analysis? Do you see the subtle deceit—the Lie of the devil—in it (cf. Genesis 3:5; 2 Thessalonians 2:4, 11)? If you do not, then you are probably a part of America-Babylon's false religious system. But please, do not stop reading yet. In the next section, many evidences from the Bible for exactly which city-state (nation/empire) is modern, prophetic, "mystery" Babylon will be given. If you can honestly face reality, please keep asking yourself which nation, other than the USA, in the present-day world can come anywhere close to manifesting the characteristics of historical ancient Babylon and the biblical identification of modern Babylon.

Scriptural Evidence

Revelation 17 and 18 are devoted to describing modern Babylon and her destiny. Revelation 17 presents religious Babylon and

Revelation 18 presents secular Babylon.   (See Appendix A for commentaries on Revelation 17 and 18.)

Many insist that modern *"mystery"* Babylon is the Vatican or Rome.   And yes, the Roman Empire and the Roman Catholic Church were the original political and religious prototypes of modern Babylon. The "harlot who rides the beast" (religious, "mystery" Babylon) of Revelation 17, with her robes of purple and scarlet, does bear a remarkable resemblance to the Roman Catholic Church, whose colors are purple and scarlet, and she sits on "seven mountains" (Rome is called the "City of Seven Hills"). But a close examination of the text shows that the conclusion that modern religious Babylon is limited to or consists of the RCC or to Rome is fallacious—she is much, much more than that. The Greek word that is translated *"mountains"* or, in some translations, *"hills"* in Revelation 17:9 is *oros,* which means "mountains" or "large land masses" (like continents or large areas of imperialistic rule), rather than "hills." The Greek word (basically a Latin word borrowed from the Romans that commonly referred to Rome) that is translated "hills" or "mounds" (as in Luke 23:30) is *buonos,* which is **not** used in Revelation 17:9. And when we look at the context of Revelation 17:9, we see that it is talking about world-dominating kingdoms or empires, which hardly describes the city of Rome. The Roman Catholic Church does have worldwide influence, but it can hardly be said to rule the kingdoms of the world. Also, the religion of ancient Babylon was very eclectic—a mixture of all religions and cults. The Roman Catholic Church has made overtures to other religions, but only to bring them under the influence, and ultimately the control, of the RCC. The RCC is not about to give up its autonomy and belief that it is the one, true Church, and that ultimately all the world's religions will be part of the Catholic Church.

Others believe that modern Babylon will be a revived ancient Babylon, located where Iraq is today. Common sense, looking at the sad state of affairs in Iraq at the present time, should immediately dispel that absurd notion. Besides, which nation is in control, behind the scenes, of Iraq at the present time? Is the USA really interested in helping Iraq rebuild Babylon and regain the world dominance Babylon once had?[4]

Since Iraq, the site of ancient Babylon, does not fit the Scriptural description of modern Babylon, some attempt to shift the location of modern Babylon to Saudi Arabia, stating that Mecca, Islam's main holy city, is the modern city of Babylon, the nobility of Saudi Arabia live in lavish luxury, immorality in Saudi Arabia is rife, the anti-messiah will arise out of Middle Eastern Islam, the oil wealth of Saudi Arabia controls the nations of the world including the USA, and so forth. Indeed, there are many characteristics Saudi Arabia has in common with modern Babylon and may be a precursor to Babylon the Great. But the argument that Saudi Arabia is, in fact, the final modern Babylon the Great is specious, because many of the over 60 identifying characteristics in the *Bible* of modern Babylon cannot possibly pertain to Saudi Arabia. But, far more than with any other nation on Earth, those characteristics fit the USA perfectly. For example, Babylon is called the "hammer [oppressor] of the world" (Jeremiah 50:23). That description does not remotely fit Saudi Arabia, but, with its military, political and economic dominance of the other nations of the world, America fulfills the prophecy perfectly. Also, just as ancient Babylon was a very idolatrous nation, adopting the gods of the nations over which it held sway, and modern Babylon is prophesied to be very idolatrous (Jeremiah 50:2, 38), the U.S.A., with its "freedom of religion" mantra, is the melting pot of the religions of the world, just as it is the melting pot of the ethnic groups of the world. However, Saudi Arabia is fanatically monotheistic, tolerating no other gods but Allah. And as to oil wealth, at the present time, Russia is the world's number one oil exporter and Saudi Arabia is second. But, with shale oil deposits that are being developed in North Dakota, Texas and other locations, the USA is projected to be the world's number one oil exporter by 2015.

Others insist that modern Babylon, the kingdom of Satan (cf. Isaiah 14:4), will be a "revived Roman empire"—probably a confederation of European nations—that will rule the religious and secular world as ancient Rome did. Well, that is somewhat confused and limited thinking; ancient Babylon fell long before the Roman Empire was in existence. Also, modern Babylon will be the world-dominating nation/empire at the End of the Age only **until** she is destroyed, then replaced by the global kingdom of Antichrist—the ultimate revived Roman Empire which will probably have its headquarters in Turkey—the location of the capital of the

Roman Empire under Constantine, a type of the false messiah (see the commentary on Revelation Chapters 17 and 18 for details).

So, let us see if we can discern who the latter days Babylon the Great is by correctly interpreting Scripture. And as you will see, that is not difficult once we realize and accept the possibility that the USA is indeed modern, prophetic Babylon.

Recall the Chapter 5 description of the present status of American religion: We claim to be a 'Christian' nation, but are really a melting pot of the races of the world, and are also the melting pot of all the world's religions.

And that brings us back to the above analysis of American "Christianity." Under which "god" and under in what spirit was America really founded? The Deistic founders of the USA believed that Americans are basically good people, ordained by "God" to establish His kingdom on Earth—by violence if necessary. And that is why we rebelled against Britain and fought the Revolutionary War—not because of some little disagreement over "taxation without representation." And that is why our National Anthem glorifies violent revolution. The real reason we fought the Revolutionary War was for freedom, is that not correct? But freedom from what?—freedom from anyone else telling us what to do or how to spend our money. In other words, we wanted to set up our own little "Christian" kingdom where we could do whatever we please without having to be subservient to anyone else. And there is a lot of evidence that the ultimate goal of the real movers and shakers behind the American Revolution was (and still is) to bring the rest of the world into the American-led New World Order. (Remember President George H.W. Bush talking about the New World Order" in a famous speech to Congress in 1991?)[5]

So, what is wrong with that? What is wrong with fighting for our freedom from unjust treatment by those who rule over us? It is totally UNBIBLICAL and UNCHRISTIAN, that is what. Where did Jesus tell us to rise up in rebellion to violently fight against those who rule over us, even if they mistreat us? Did He not tell us that if someone forces us to go with him one mile, to go two (Matthew 5:41)? Did not the apostle Peter tell us to do just the opposite of resisting or rebelling against those in authority over us, even if they mistreat us (cf. 1 Peter 2:13-19)? Yet, America was founded on violent rebellion, was it not? And the basic assumption was that we are good, Christian people who do not deserve that kind of treatment and who deserve to be free to take our place as "God's" chosen people in dominion over the earth. The next step in that kind of logic is to "preemptively" invade a small, weak nation like Iraq, who had done nothing to us (except for her president, Saddam Hussein, bad-mouthing America), virtually destroying the whole nation and killing and maiming hundreds of thousands of its citizens—old men, women, and children, besides military personnel. And this was all done, according to President Bush, in the name of Christianity, in the war of good against evil. Again, what is wrong with that kind of atrocious thinking and behavior? It is totally UNBIBLICAL and UNCHRISTIAN, that is what. Where did Jesus tell us that we Christians are good people who deserve to rebel against those in authority over us and to impose our will on the rest of the world, killing them if they, or even just their leaders, threaten us (but show no signs of attacking us)? No, He did not, because that, my friend, is the Lie of the devil. Did Jesus not say just the opposite? Did He not say, "No one is good but God alone" (Luke 18:19). Where did He tell us, because we are Christians (or a Christian nation), to attack and destroy and conquer and lord it over others, even if they threaten us? Did He not say that is what the nonbelievers do (cf. Matthew 20:25)? (Again, as was explained in Chapter 5, Jesus was not a pacifist—against defending oneself and others against attackers—but He was against retaliation, rebellion against authority, and especially attacking others for personal gain.)

Did Jesus not tell us that if we wish to be true Christians, to be everyone's servant (cf. Mark 9:35)? I submit to you that the whole idea that Americans (including Christians who are involved in America's agenda) are basically good (god-like) people who deserve to have dominion over the earth before the Lord returns in person to establish His kingdom (a religious manifestation of the doctrines of American Exceptionalism and Manifest Destiny) is a nationalistic version of the great Lie of the devil (cf. 2 Thessalonians 2:11). And it is that kind of satanically-deluded thinking that resulted in ancient Babylon's downfall, that resulted in Adolf Hitler's and Nazi Germany's downfall, and will result in the total annihilation of modern Babylon in "one hour" (Revelation 18:10, 19).

106

The Lie of the devil has always been the same from the beginning, when he told Adam and Eve, *"You shall be as gods"* (Genesis 3:5). Did Jesus not tell us just the opposite: *"Apart from me, you can do nothing"* (John 15:5)? Apart from Jesus, we fallible human beings are totally powerless against the spiritual forces that control this world. If Jesus dwells in us, we have some, limited power over those forces, but the book of Revelation tells us very clearly that the Kingdom of God—total peace and order—will not be established on Earth until the true Messiah—the Lord Jesus, King of Kings and Lord of Lords—returns **in person** to do that (cf. Revelation 19:11-20:4). So, if anyone tells you that the USA—"God's" Redeemer Nation—or the Manifested Sons of "God" or anyone else is going take dominion and establish the Kingdom of Heaven on Earth **before** the return, **in person**, of the Messiah, do not be a fool and believe it! That is the Lie of the devil! Or, if anyone tells you, "That's the Messiah, follow him," do not believe it! That is the anti-Christ (false messiah), and that is the Lie of the devil. When the true Messiah returns, no one will have to point Him out; it will be obvious (cf. Matthew 24:27). And then, it will be too late to become His disciple.

So, here is a quick, self-test question to help you see if you are a false "Christian" or a True Christian—a spiritual citizen of Babylon the Great or of the Kingdom of Heaven: Do you think that you are basically a good person? If you believe in your heart that you or anyone else is, by nature, basically good, then you have believed the Lie and are not a True Christian.

So, American religion is much more like Babylonian religion than it is True Christianity. It was founded and still operates more on a spirit of pride and self-sufficiency than true dependence on and faith in God. And, rather than being just one religion, i.e., True Christianity, modern American-Babylonian religion is an amalgamation of religions serving, often unwittingly, the false god, Satan. That is why Lucifer is called the (true, spiritual) King of Babylon (Isaiah 14:4). Like Babylon was, the USA is the most religious nation on Earth—the headquarters, as it were, of Satan's false, global, religious system. No other nation has as much worldwide religious influence—sending out missionaries, "apostles," and "prophets" all over the world. No other nation is as hospitable to or tolerant of all forms of religion. Like in Babylon,

American religion is extremely nationalistic—to be Christian is to be patriotic. Christians in America, contrary to the teachings of Scripture (cf. 2 Peter 2:20) are very involved in politics. Consider the Religious Right's symbiotic relationship with the Republican Party, for example. Like in Babylon, American religion is very materialistic, sensual, and self-indulgent—the churches are centers for social interaction, good food, fun and games, and entertainment rather than self-sacrificial service to others and God. They have it backwards: Most church members give a very small part of their income to the ministry and keep the rest for themselves. But did Jesus not say, *"If anyone wants to follow Me, let him deny himself, and take up his cross daily, and follow Me"* (Luke 9:23)? Then He said, *"Sell what you have, and give to the poor, and you shall have treasures in heaven: and come and follow Me"* (Matthew 19:21). To me that sounds like, "Keep only what is absolutely necessary for yourself and give the rest for ministry of the Gospel and meeting the needs of others"—just the opposite of what is happening in American "Christianity." In 2011, the United Nations reported that over 17,000 children (not counting adults) were dying from starvation daily around the world—over 6 million per year! Another report states that 99% of the people of the east African nation of Somalia are Muslims, and those of all other religions, especially Christianity, are being aggressively sought out and killed. Yet, what are most "Christians" most concerned about here in America—what we are going to have for dinner, what TV shows we are going to watch, what we are going to do for recreation on the weekend? How utterly disgusted God must be with American (Laodicean) "Christianity" (Revelation 3:17-19).

Hopefully, you are beginning to see the truth about American religion. Let me mention another item to drive the point home. What is the main symbol of American Freedom? What do the passengers on all ships that sail into New York Harbor see? What welcomes all the peoples of the world to America? What makes Americans' hearts swell with pride when they see it? That is correct; it is the Statue of Liberty.

Do you know who designed and built the Statue of Liberty?—the French, specifically a French Freemason, sculptor Frederic Auguste Bartholdi, who wanted to honor a Masonic doctrine that dates back to the time of Nimrod, the builder of Babylon! Bartholdi intentionally clothed Liberty as a classical Roman deity, the goddess Libertas. She wears a palla, a cloak that is fastened on her left shoulder by a clasp. Underneath is a stola, which falls in many folds to her feet. Around her feet is a broken chain, symbolizing freedom from all restraint—religious, political, moral, or otherwise. Libertas, also called the "Queen of Heaven," is a Roman version of Ishtar. By the way, there is a city just up the coast of Long Island from New York City named Babylon. People on ships sailing into New York Harbor from the northeast can see its sign: "Welcome to Babylon." Ironic, is it not? Babylon, New York, was founded and named by poor Jewish immigrants who, because of their circumstances, identified with the Jews of ancient Babylon.

Speaking of Freemasonry, as was explained in Chapter 5, several of the founders, fourteen presidents and many other high government officials throughout the history of the United States of America have been Freemasons—many of them Masons of the highest order (33rd degree). Do you know what the spiritual roots of Freemasonry are? They are basically derived from Babylonian religion and involve the worship of Lucifer. One of the Masonic deities is Isis, the Egyptian name of Ishtar.

More Scriptural Evidence

Still not convinced that America is Babylon the Great? Well, that is OK, because we have just scratched the surface of Biblical evidences for the identification of modern, prophetic Babylon. Please keep reading.

Revelation 18 tells us about modern, prophetic, secular Babylon. But the Babylon of Revelation 18 is the same Babylon as the religious Babylon of Revelation 17 because she has exactly the same name, "Babylon the Great," in both chapters (cf. Revelation 17:5 and 18:2) and she suffers the same fate, destruction by fire, in both chapters (cf. Revelation 17:16 and 18:8).

Actually, there are over 250 verses of Scripture that identify modern, prophetic Babylon the Great and the "great city" that is her head. When all of those Scriptures are studied, it is astonishingly clear who modern, prophetic Babylon is. The following quiz is borrowed and slightly modified from the 2-volume, 613-page work, *America the Babylon—America's Destiny Foretold in Biblical Prophe-*

cy, by R. A. Coombes, who did many years of research and study on the identification and destiny of modern, prophetic Babylon.[6]

The Babylon Quiz—Name that City-State/Nation/Empire

The following is a fun quiz to test your knowledge concerning the identifying characteristics of modern, prophetic Babylon. Each question refers to an identification characteristic of "mystery Babylon," with Scripture references given for each. The answers may surprise you.

What City-State/Nation/Empire . . .

Q: Is the location where all the world's leaders come to meet - the headquarters of world government (Revelation 17:18; Jeremiah 51:44)?
A: New York City, USA, is the location for the only world-governing body, i.e., the United Nations, which is dominated (behind the scenes) by the USA.

Q: Is called the "Queen of Kingdoms" - controls the other kingdoms/nations of the world (Revelation 17:2; Isaiah 47:5)?
A: The USA rules the nations of the world through her trade with them in sensual and material goods and services. It is projected that by 2015, America will be the number one oil exporter in the world, making the nations of the world "drunk with the wine of her fornication."

Q: Is the leading center of world commerce - the "engine of wealth" of the world's economy (Revelation 18:11, 15, 16, 19, 22, 23; Isaiah 47:15)?
A: NYC, the home of the World Trade Center, the NY Stock Exchange, the American Stock Exchange, NASDAQ, the New York Commodities and Mercantile Exchanges, the Federal Reserve Bank - the largest bank in the world—as well as the most powerful concentration of American banks. Also correct with this answer is the United States of America, with its numerous great cities of international commerce - Seattle, San Francisco, Los Angeles, Houston,

Chicago, Dallas, New York, et al. If the economy of the U.S. collapses, virtually all the economies of the world will collapse.

Q: Is the leading center of imports and exports (Revelation 18:11-13?
A: The ports of New York/Jersey make NYC the leading deep water port city in the Western Hemisphere, especially as the marketplace center and gateway to America, where world prices are most often correlated to NYC/USA prices. The NYC port, together with all the other deep water ports surrounding the nation, make the USA by far the leading import/export nation of the world.

Q: Is a leading center of manufacturing (Revelation 18:22)?
A: NYC has been the leading center of corporate headquarters for manufacturing in the world. Certainly, the USA is the world's industrial giant.

Q: Is the center for world trade in gold, silver, copper, oil, precious gems, cloth/clothing/fashions, lumber, containers, household items, furniture, iron, marble, ivory, spices, cosmetics, health products, wine, grains/foods, livestock, transportation, and services (Revelation 18:11-13)?
A: NYC is the world's foremost city of commodities trading, with these commodities exchanges trading daily: Coffee, Sugar, Tea & Cocoa Exchange; New York Cotton Exchange (also trades orange juice); New York Mercantile Exchange: crude oil, gasoline, natural gas, heating oil, platinum, palladium; New York Mercantile Comex Division: gold, silver, copper. Chicago is also a world leader in commodities trading with the following exchanges: Chicago Board of Trade: wheat, corn, oats, soybeans, soybean oil, soybean meal, also U. S. Treasury notes, and stock indexes; Chicago Mercantile Exchange: cattle, hogs, bacon, wood-lumber, and all major world currencies. World prices for the following "cash" commodities are also set or keyed from the USA. (Source: Wall Street Journal): barley, bran, burlap, butter, broiler chickens, eggs, coconut oil, cottonseed oil, palm oil, lard, tallow, wool, aluminum, lead, mercury, steel, tin, zinc, rubber. Also, Chicago is where the world's currencies are traded and is the location for trading all U. S. Federal Treasury Securities on a 'futures' basis, though initial offerings are derived

from the NYC Fed Reserve. Also, Chicago holds futures trading on the Standard & Poor's 500 Index and the Major Market Index, plus stock options trading as well as commodity options trading. New York City is also a leader in the marketing of: diamonds, precious gems, iron, ivory, marble, spices, cosmetics, legal pharmaceutical drugs, professional services especially related to media and the arts. NYC is also the main import city for fine foreign wines from around the world.

Q: Is the center for expertise in marketing, merchandising, public relations, advertising & sales (Revelation 17:2; 18:3, 23; 19:2)?
A: New York's Madison Avenue is the 'nerve center' and informal world headquarters for the world's best and most prestigious advertising, marketing & merchandising companies. Madison Ave. is home to the world's best salesmen those from advertising and the public relations fields, where the whole world learns and follows the latest techniques of how to 'move' or sell goods and services. It is the largest marketing center in the U. S. and the world.

Q: Is noted for its culture and aesthetics (music, art, dance, theater, etc.) (Revelation 18:22)?
A: New York is the key cultural city of the world: Carnegie Hall, Madison Square Garden, Radio City Music Hall, Lincoln Center, Broadway theaters, Greenwich Village, Manhattan's world class restaurants, TV networks, newspapers (NY Times, etc.), magazine and book publishers, Rockefeller Center, world-famous museums & art galleries, Times Square, Manhattan, and the whole City of New York, immortalized in songs and movies. It is also the location of more book publishers, plays, and movies than any other city in the world.

Q: Is noted for its intoxicating High Society, elegant, and sumptuous lifestyle (Revelation 17:2; 18:3, 14; Isaiah 47:1, 8; Jeremiah 51:13)?
A: Park Avenue, penthouse lifestyles of the rich and famous, Trump Towers, the noted lifestyle of New York is glamorous, glitzy, and sumptuous.

Q: Is noted for its bright, gaudy, colored lights and nightlife (Revelation 18:14)?

A: NYC is called the "city that never sleeps" as Sinatra's song says about New York, … "I wanna wake up in the city that never sleeps … to find I'm king of the hill, top of the heap … these little town blues keep melting away …" New York offers the glitter of Manhattan, Broadway's lights, and the lights of Times Square, plus the entire nighttime skyline of NYC. Another U. S. city world-famous for its lights and nightlife is Las Vegas, Nevada.

Q: Is noted for its drug consumption and importation (especially illegal) (Revelation 18:23 - Note that the primary meaning of the Greek word pharmakeia, translated "sorceries" in Revelation 18:23, is "the use or administering of drugs.")?

A: NYC is the largest center of legal and illicit drug consumption in the world, especially hard-core drugs, like heroin and cocaine. The USA's lengthy sea coast borders and borders with Canada and Mexico make it especially vulnerable to illicit drug traffic.

Q: Is noted for its architecture, buildings and skyline (Isaiah 13:22)?

A: New York's architecture - its super-tall or mega-story skyscrapers like the World Trade Center (the world's tallest building before it was destroyed), the Empire State Building, Rockefeller Center, the UN building, reach into the sky, similar to the Tower of Babel and the ziggurats of ancient Babylon.

Q: Is noted for being a city/nation of immigrants from all over the world - an international city (Jeremiah 50:37; 51:44)?

A: NYC is a city of immigrants, and always has been. It has been the historic point-of-entry for immigrants and is epitomized by the quote on the Statue of Liberty: "Give me your … huddled masses yearning to be free." NYC is host to the UN. It has "China Town", "Little Italy", "Little Moscow", "Little Bombay", "Little Tokyo", "Little Mexico", "Little Havana", etc. Unlike any other city in the world, every single ethnic group has its own little community in NYC. The USA in general is known as the "melting pot of the world."

Q: Is a cosmopolitan and urban nation (Jeremiah 50:32)?
A: America started as a rural, agricultural nation, but the life of the nation revolves around the cities now.

Q: Is noted for being both hated and envied by the world (Revelation 17:16; 18:9, 11,15, 17, 19)?
A: The city that seems to inspire the most animosity, disgust, and even hatred is New York City. The most denounced country in the world is the United States. "Yankee go Home" has been a popular slogan in many countries around the world for the last generation. Yet, at the same time, the U. S. is the most admired nation for its accomplishments and affluent lifestyle.

Q: Is noted for its waste and wasteful extravagance - overconsumption (Revelation 18:3, 7, 9, 16)?
A: NYC is like no other in consumption - noted for its extravagance. The waste by-product volume is so enormous as to be mind-boggling, practically bringing the city to a stand-still at times. One of the first impressions a visitor gets is the dirtiness of the streets and the city as a whole.

Q: Is noted for spiritual and moral 'dirtiness' and impurity (by implication: wantonness, reveling, involvement in the occult, etc.) (Revelation 17:1-6; 18:2, 4-9, 23; Isaiah 47:8, 9, 12)?
A: NYC is morally and spiritually impure in its sensual, hedonistic lifestyle, pandering to sexual interests - prostitution, pornography, and so forth - drug use, wild "partying," and its occult connections. NYC is the largest occult merchandising center in the world. Besides the immense number of fortune tellers, psychics, and occult shops, there are mail order houses for occult items. There is also an aspect of the occult exemplified by the "Amityville Horror" (Amityville is a town in the NYC metropolitan area, next to Babylon, NY), where there are reportedly "doorways to Hell."

Q: Could be said to worship materialism or things (Revelation 18:6-7)?
A: NYC, like no other city on the earth, epitomizes the worship of materialism. NYC newspapers abound with gossip and news about the wealthy, like the Trumps, the Leona Helmsleys, the Rockefel-

114

lers, the Kennedy family, the magnates of Wall Street, Madison Avenue, and Broadway, along with movie stars and other famous celebrities and artists. Wall Street is where some of the temples of materialism (called "capitalism") abound. Manhattan is crammed with temples to capitalism of every kind.

Q: Reflects the image of hyper-selfishness and pride (Revelation 18:7)?
A: NYC carries an image of hyper-selfishness and rudeness, not only the rich with their extravagant lifestyles, but the common people convey it through everyday rudeness, as exemplified by cab drivers and subway passengers. Also, scenes from sporting events of sports fans pushing and shoving, and arguing, and insulting each other, along with their fickleness toward even the hometown teams and stars.

Q: Promotes itself - is extremely proud and arrogant—to the point of "self-deification" (Revelation 18:7; Isaiah 47:8, 10; Jeremiah 50:31, 32)?
A: NYC - "the Big Apple" . . . again, through songs like Sinatra's "New York, New York", but also through its media, through its publications, through Wall Street, and its show biz. Its leaders worship their own accomplishments in the city, and the city itself, especially the Statue of Liberty, giving a religious-like homage to the statue, to capitalism, and to liberty that the city "gave birth to."

Q: Promulgates and exports Idolatries - is "insanely idolatrous" (Revelation 18:3-7; Isaiah 21:9; Jeremiah 50:38)?
A: The leaders of NYC and the U.S.A., through the media - the networks, newspapers, and magazines - and through Madison Avenue and Wall Street, promulgate the religion of capitalism-materialism (i.e., worship of material riches) more blatantly than does any other city/nation on the earth. Worship of sports heroes and celebrities is also pure idolatry. (Why do you think one of the most popular TV shows is called "American Idol"?)

Q: Is treacherous and deceit-filled in its political and business dealings (Revelation 18:23; Isaiah 21:2)?
A: Wall Street and American business in general is cut-throat. The

U.S. government has a long history of deceiving its own people, including but certainly not limited to the effects of scientific experiments involving nuclear radiation upon innocent civilians, the reasons for invading Vietnam, Bosnia, Iraq, etc., scandals like Watergate, sexual affairs in the White House, hiding information about UFOs, detention (torture) facilities for political prisoners, tax loopholes for the wealthy elite, dealing treacherously with other nations (like Israel) ... ad nauseum.

Q: Shares a similar distinction with ancient Babylon as being the host country for the majority of the world's Jewish population (from about 600 BCE, when Israel was taken into captivity, until 400 CE, Babylon had the world's largest Jewish population) (Revelation 18:4; also Jeremiah 50:8, 28; 51: 6, 45; Isaiah 48:20)?
A: NYC has the largest population of Jews in America, and the U. S. is home to more Jewish people than anywhere in the world, except perhaps Israel, most of whose ancestors came to America during the Russian pogroms against the Jews between 1821 and 1905.

Q: Has been a persecutor of Jews and is treacherous in her dealings with the Jews (Jeremiah 50:11)?
A: When Hitler offered to let the Jews leave Germany just before World War II, the USA refused to accept them, in fact, sent a shipload back, where they probably died in the Nazi death camps. There is strong evidence that the American government is dealing treacherously with Israel today - claiming to be her ally, but really using her as a pawn to keep us involved in the Mideast, while setting her up to be destroyed by the surrounding, hostile Muslim nations.

Q: Is the "daughter" of another great superpower nation (Jeremiah 50:12)?
A: The USA was founded by citizens of England, the world's greatest superpower nation at the time - until the 1920s. America is the only superpower nation in history that has been produced by another superpower nation.

Q: What city/state/nation is the lone and last ("hindermost") "superpower" in the world (Revelation 17:18; 18:7; Isaiah 47:5, 8, 10;

Jeremiah 50:12)?

A: Since the demise of the Soviet Union in 1989, the USA has been the only, and probably the last, "superpower" nation in the world.

Q: Is considered to be the "world's policeman" - the "hammer of the world" (Jeremiah 50:23)?

A: The USA has over 7,000 military installations and/or bases all over the world, in 63 nations, especially in the world's "hotspots." For example, Iran is completely surrounded by ten U. S. air bases, located in countries bordering Iran. Just stop and consider all the incidents in which the U. S. has used military power to intervene and stop conflict: Bosnia, Somalia, Haiti, Kuwait, Panama, Grenada, Vietnam, Korea, Afghanistan, and Iraq come to mind.

Q: Has no fear and little reason to fear invasion of its home soil by foreign armies (Isaiah 18:1-2; 47:7-8)?

A: The USA has, including its Star Wars technology and massive air defense, its "stealth technology" and "black ops" project, by far the most powerful, seemingly impenetrable national defense in the world. Protected by two oceans and a gulf, America is isolated geographically from the turmoil of Europe, Asia, and Africa. It would be seemingly impossible to launch a naval/amphibious invasion against America by any or all nations combined. The world's combined naval strength could not transport enough armed units to successfully invade America. With the demise of the Soviet Union, the main concern at the present time is the possibility of terrorist action (by which Scripture indicates America will be destroyed).

Q: Has carried over and incorporated many aspects of the old Babylonian religion, particularly in regard to art symbols and figures (Jeremiah 50:2, 38)?

A: NYC is the world's only city whose image is so closely linked to Babylonian religion. The Statue of Liberty and NYC are inseparably linked, and such a union is unprecedented in world history. Not even in Rome or Greece could a city boast of such an identification with such a profound or dominant figure as that of "Liberty." No other city has had such an imposing statue of a woman with an ideal or philosophy to uphold or to offer to the world. Meanwhile, Revelation 17:5 refers to the woman as "The Mother of Harlots" (practitioners of false religion). The Statue of Liberty may very well be said to be the main American idol. Other examples of Babyloni-an-type symbols used in America include the statue of freedom on the Capitol Dome in Washington D. C., the symbols on the currency, such as the pyramid with the 'eye' at its top, the 'Apollo' (the Greek name of an ancient Babylonian god) space program, many of the Masonic symbols spread throughout the land, including those at the Denver Airport.

Q: Is noted for the natural created beauty of its land (Isaiah 13:19)?
A: "America the Beautiful" ... for spacious skies, for amber waves of grain, for purple mountains majesty, from sea to shining sea ...The Shenandoah Valley, The Mississippi River, the Rocky Mountains, the Grand Canyon, Old Faithful, Redwood Forests, the Great Lakes, etc.

Q: Is noted for being highly and overly optimistic, confident of its success, with a "can-do" attitude, especially about its future (Isaiah 47:7-10)?
A: America has always been the nation of optimism - a John Wayne type of "can-do" attitude.

Q: Is considered by the world to have had a unique and remarkable beginning, different from all the other nations before it, has been awe-inspiring since its birth with regards to its ingenuity, resourcefulness, and power, and is still awe-inspiring - considered powerful and oppressive - to the world today (Isaiah 18:2)?
A: No nation other than America has had such a unique beginning, overcoming, against all odds, her own parent nation (Great Britain), the most powerful nation on the earth at the time; then quickly establishing herself as a mighty nation with a unique, representative form of government.

Q: Is noted as a land of rebels, not only in its birth, but now in its judgment for rebellion against Yahuah (Jeremiah 50:24; 51:1)?
A: The U. S. started out as a land of rebels. There was the rebellion for independence, and the rebellion of the South against the North, causing the Civil War, the student rebellion against the Vietnam

118

War, etc. Indeed, stubbornness and rebellion are practically considered virtues in America.

Q: Is noted for its cultural insanity (Jeremiah 50:38)?
A: The U. S. and NYC, Hollywood, Los Angeles, San Francisco, and much more. You pick the topic: abortion, movies, TV, music, pornography, child abuse, cloning, drugs, murders, gangs, divorce, celebrity and hero worship . . . ad infinitum - a culture gone crazy.

Q: Is noted for its being a land of many fresh waters, with a broad river in its middle and divided by many rivers (i.e., abundant, clean, fresh water for drinking, which is unique in that most nations have poor water supplies) (Jeremiah 51:13, 36)?
A: The USA is blessed with the far more fresh water sources than any other nation on the earth - tremendous numbers of rivers, including the Mississippi, which divides the country as did the Euphrates in Babylon, and other large rivers, which divide the rest of the country; hundreds of fresh water lakes, including the Great Lakes, plus abundant underground aquifers for most of the nation.

The above quiz is not exhaustive—there are other identification characteristics of modern Babylon listed in Scripture (over 60 in all). But hopefully you can tell that when the time arrives for modern, prophetic, *"mystery"* Babylon to play her part on the world stage, God does not want anyone who studies and believes His Word to have any doubt about who she is; Scripture is crystal clear about that. Don't you agree? Babylon, claiming to be a good, Christian nation, is actually the ultimate false (anti-) Christian nation—the most evil, "beast" nation in the history of the world, whose true ruler is Satan himself. And can there be any doubt at all in anyone's mind who has even a tenuous grip on reality that modern Babylonia is indeed the United States of America, with her "great city," New York City? If you cannot accept that clear, Biblical Truth by now, then you might as well stop reading this book and go on about your business, because it is doing you no good. The only question is not whether Bob is right or wrong; the question is whether or not you believe the Bible. Right?

But, if you can now see that America is Babylon, and you want to know the destiny (in the very near future) of America-Babylon, please keep reading.

What is Modern Babylon's Destiny?

The Assyrian Connection

Besides direct comparisons with Ancient Babylon, the identification of the USA as modern Babylon the Great can be proven another way.

It can be argued that pride (blind patriotism) has been the root cause of the fall of every nation and empire throughout history (*"Pride goes before destruction, and a haughty spirit before a fall."*—Proverbs 16:18). Even God's own nation of people Israel fell to the Assyrians in 722 BCE because of her disobedience of the Lord's command to repent of her idolatry, especially self-idolatry (pride). As Jonathan Cahn has vividly explained in *The Harbinger* (reviewed in Chapter 1), after an initial "warning" attack on Israel by the Assyrians, the Lord gave His People a series of nine signs (harbingers) that, if not heeded, would result in total destruction of the northern kingdom of Israel. And, ten years later, because those warning signs not only were not heeded but were arrogantly defied, Israel was attacked, demolished and replaced by those same cruel, merciless Assyrians (the original terrorists).

In *The Harbinger*, in a gripping, eye-opening way, Cahn explains how that same prophecy (Isaiah 9:10) applies in exactly the same way to the USA! Exactly the same nine signs of Israel's coming destruction apply to the soon-coming destruction of America. In the same way that in Assyria's first attack on Israel the wall around Samaria, the capital, was breached, the USA's seemingly impenetrable "wall" of air defense was breached by terrorists from the same part of the world (the Near East) and the World Trade Center towers were destroyed on 9-11-2001. And in the same way the leaders of Israel, rather than repenting and turning to the Lord for help, responded to the attack by defiantly proclaiming, "We will rebuild, and we will rebuild stronger!" America's leaders replied to the 9-11 attack by arrogantly proclaiming, with exactly the same words, "We will rebuild, and we will rebuild stronger!" And, if the Isaiah 9:10 prophecy is followed to its conclusion, in the same way that the government, the economy and the military of the northern kingdom of Israel were totally destroyed and replaced by the harsh control of the Assyrians, the USA will be taken over and replaced by a confederation of terrorists and nations from the same part of the world—the location of the ancient Assyrian Empire.

Cahn also points out that the USA's first capital was its *"great city,"* New York City. And immediately after his inauguration as the first President of the United States of America, George Washington went with some leaders of Congress to pray to their Deistic god (not in the name of Jesus) for the newly-formed nation at St. Paul's Chapel in New York City. St. Paul's Chapel, the oldest active church facility in New York City, is, ironically, across the street from the fallen and currently being rebuilt World Trade Center towers—America's greatest monument to her **un**godly spirit of pride and arrogance.

Then, James Fitzgerald, in his book *The 9/11 Prophecy*, takes Jonathan Cahn's application of the Isaiah 9:10 prophecy to the destiny of the U.S.A. a step further in identifying the U.S.A. as a "type" of the Babylon the Great of Revelation and in stating that America will definitely be taken over by the same descendants of the Assyrians who destroyed the World Trade Center.

So, are you connecting the dots? You do see that the Assyrian terrorists who attacked, destroyed and replaced Israel were predecessors of exactly the same terrorists who attacked the USA on 9/11/2001, do you not? But now, to correctly comprehend the whole picture, make this connection: Exactly the same terrorists from exactly the same part of the world (modern Turkey and Iran) are prophesied to attack, utterly destroy, and replace modern Babylon, as will be documented in detail in the next chapter and is augured by the Tenth Harbinger.

Chapter 7

The Tenth Harbinger

"Now the whole land had one [government] and one [commander].... And they said, 'Come, let us build a city, and a tower whose top is in the heavens; let us make a name for ourselves, lest we be scattered abroad over the face of the whole [land].' But the Lord came down to see the city and the tower which the sons of men had built. And the Lord said, 'Indeed, the people are one and they all have one [government], and this is what they begin to do; and nothing that they propose to do will be withheld from them. 'Come, let Us go down and there [confound] their [government], that they may not understand [their commander].' So the LORD scattered them abroad from there over the face of all the [land], and they ceased building the city. Therefore its name is called [Babylon], because there the LORD [confounded] the [government] of all the [land]; and from there the LORD scattered them abroad over the face of all the [land]." (Genesis 11:1, 4-9 Extrapolated Version)

On January 31, 2002, four months after the 9/11 attack on the World Trade Center, a remarkable discovery was made. The official 9/11 photographer for the New York Fire Department, Gary Marlon Suson—the only photographer allowed unlimited access to Ground Zero by the FDNY—spotted some wet, charred pages in the rubble of the collapsed North Tower. Not really paying close attention to the contents of the pages, Suson nevertheless photographed them. But when he received the developed photos from the lab, he was astonished by one of them. It was the photo of a page from a Bible that contained the verses from Genesis 11 quoted above concerning the destruction of the Tower of "Babel" (Babylon) and the scattering of the residents of Babylon.[1] And verse 7, *"Come, let Us go down and there disrupt their [government], that they may not understand [their commander],"* was highlighted in yellow. Suson states that the Genesis 11 photo is the "most memorable for me" of the thousands of photos he took at Ground Zero.

As was explained in the last chapter, the translators of Genesis 11 from Hebrew into other languages did not clearly understand what those verses stated. They thought that the Lord destroyed the empire by confusing its single language, so they translated the terms of the passage accordingly. But, as Dr. Jeffrey Goodman has thoroughly clarified and documented in his book *The Comets of God* [2], the original Hebrew term that should be translated "one government" was mistakenly translated *"one language"*; the term that should have been translated "one word (cause or command)" was mistakenly translated *"one speech"*; and the term "Babylon" was mistakenly translated *"Babel."* "Babylon" is a translation of an Akkadian word (*babilum*) that means "gate of god," not *"confusion"* (cf. Genesis 11:1). And, as was also explained in the last chapter, "babylons" were what the pagan ziggurats (towers) or temples where they met with and worshiped their deities were called. And the city—the religious center—that was built at the location of the *"tower"* of Genesis 11 (probably a ziggurat for the worship of Ishtar), and ziggurats/temples built for the worship of other Summerian/Akkadian gods, came to be called Babylon—the city of "the gate of god."[3]

So, it was the government of the world's first empire (the Akkadian Empire), ruled over by one "commander" (Sargon/Nimrod), practicing, in defiance of the Lord, a false religion (primarily the worship of Ishtar) that God determined to destroy, not merely the *"language"* of the people (actually, several languages were spoken there). And He did that by sending a heavenly "messenger" of His wrath—a comet—that impacted the earth (at the site of the recently discovered Amarah crater) about 100 miles from the capital city Akkad and nearby Babylon. The shock waves, the heat, and the fallout from that exploding comet no doubt destroyed everything within over 100 miles from its point of impact—including, probably, the *"tower"* of Genesis 11—and scattered the surviving citizens of the empire far and wide.[4]

The Exact Identity and Destiny of the United States of America Foretold

The Harbinger opened America's eyes to the astonishingly precise accuracy of the Isaiah 9:10 prophecy in predicting the 9/11 attack on the World Trade Center, the Pentagon, and the failed attempt to strike apparently some building in the nation's capitol city.

And it suggested the *possible* future fall of the U.S.A. to brethren of the same descendants of the Assyrians who carried out the 9/11 attack. Then, *The 9/11 Prophecy* correctly made the connection between the Isaiah 9:10 prophecy and the Revelation 18 prophecy to the extent that it identified America as a "type" of Babylon the Great who *will definitely be* taken over by the Antichrist—a Middle Eastern Muslim—and his forces. However, neither Jonathan Cahn nor James Fitzgerald have recognized the importance of the Tenth Harbinger (the page from Genesis 11) in confirming the **exact** identity and **triple** destruction of the U.S.A., as foretold in Bible prophecy. That oversight by Cahn and Fitzgerald is probably neither intentional nor subconscious; they both seem to be very honest and diligent watchmen and expositors of Scripture. Their failure to recognize the significance of the Tenth Harbinger is probably because of two factors: (1) like the vast majority of Americans, they do not fully understand the true spiritual roots of the United States of America (which were anti-Christian rather than truly Christian) and the present spiritual bankruptcy of "Christianity" in America; and (2) like virtually all Bible translators and expositors, they do not understand how ancient Babylon was destroyed, perfectly foreshadowing the destruction of modern Babylon the Great.

This book, *The Tenth Harbinger*, is an attempt to correct those two misconceptions, for anyone who has "eyes that see" and "ears that hear" the truth of God's prophetic Word.

How will the destruction of America-Babylon occur?

Now that we understand what really happened to Nimrod's empire and the Akkadian city of Babylon, as well as how the first Babylonian empire of Hammurapi and the neo-Babylonian empire of Nebuchadnezzar fell, and if we believe that the fall of those three empires were precursors to the fall of modern Babylon the Great, the answer is obvious, is it not? According to Bible prophecy the destruction of Babylon the Great will occur in three phases.

In the same way that the first Babylonian Empire, ruled by Hammurapi, was conquered by the Assyrians and the neo-Babylonian Empire, ruled by Nebuchadnezzar, was conquered very quickly without resistance by the Medo-Persians, Scripture indicates that modern Babylon will first fall to her enemies—terrorists and a confederation of nations led by Turkey and Iran (descendants of the ancient Assyrians, Medes and Persians) (cf. Jeremiah 50:29-30; 51:2-5; 27-31). The attack will come from within and without the borders of the U.S.A. Since Muslims have, for many years, been allowed relatively free entry into the U.S., especially during the administration of the current President (who is a supporter of the largest anti-American, terrorist-supporting Islamic group—the Muslim Brotherhood), it is easy to see that hundreds of terrorist cells might be festering within America's borders. And if hundreds—or thousands—of bombs, including suitcase-size nuclear devices, are simultaneously detonated in major population centers of the U.S.A., including New York City and Washington D.C., and organized, fanatical Muslims also attack police stations, National Guard facilities, and military bases all over the nation, the resulting chaos and carnage will be unimaginable. U.S. police departments are not prepared to cope with that kind of chaos and organized attacks, National Guard units will not have time to muster and respond, and virtually all of America's national defense is focused on preventing attacks from **outside** the nation. So, Americans who resist the terrorists will be sitting ducks for armed, trained and coordinated terrorists to mow them down. Millions of Americans, especially college students, who have been indoctrinated to favor the Islamists, will offer no resistance to the terrorists when given the choice to join them or die. Also, since there will be no clear direction from a paralyzed and chaotic Washington in the case of such an attack (which may even be facilitated by the President), America's foreign military installations will be vulnerable to simultaneously executed missile attacks. And America might very well be overthrown by descendants of the same people who conquered both ancient Babylonian Empires! If that happens, the USA will truly become in every way (politically and religiously, as well as spiritually) modern Babylon the Great. Also, this may be the event that begins the Final Seven Years (the "tribulation" period), because the whole world, which is dependent on America's economy, will also be thrown into chaos, giving rise to Antichrist going forth to conquer the world.[5]

But also, as is noted in the description of the destruction of Nimrod's empire, Scripture indicates that all life in Babylon-

America will suddenly, in *"one hour"* of *"one day"* be *"utterly burned with fire"* (Revelation 18:8, 10). R. A. Coombes, noted in Chapter 6 as the author of *America the Babylon*, believed the destruction of Babylon in one hour by fire may come directly from God, in the same way He destroyed Sodom and Gomorrah. In fact, both the prophets Isaiah and Jeremiah compare the destruction of Babylon to the destruction of Sodom and Gomorrah (Isaiah 13:19; Jeremiah 49:18; 50:40). Coombes notes numerous Scriptures (Isaiah 13:3, 5; Jeremiah 51:48, 53; et al.) that may refer to the attack against Babylon as being carried out by "angels" from "heaven."[6] However, the same Greek word *(aggelos)* that is translated *"angels"* is also translated *"messengers"* in Scripture. And Jeffrey Goodman, in his eye-opening book *The Comets of God* notes that the ancient Akkadians considered comets, comet fragments, meteorites and asteroids that impacted the earth "messengers" from "heaven" (far outer space).[7] And, extrapolating from the damage caused by the comet fragment that exploded over Siberia in 1908, a comet less than a mile in diameter exploding in the atmosphere above an area the size of the U.S.A. will immediately annihilate *"by fire"* all living plants, animals and humans in America.[8] But, regardless of how it happens, according to both the Old and New Testaments, Babylon-America will be annihilated suddenly and quickly by fire. Incidentally, Psalm 78:47 in the Amplified version of the Bible states, *"He destroyed their vines with hail and their **sycamore trees** [recall the sixth harbinger] with … great chunks of ice"* (comets are great chunks of ice with a rocky crust).[9]

When will this happen? Again, there are differing opinions. As stated above, this commentator believes that the political, economic and military fall of America will be the event that precipitates global chaos at the beginning of the Final Seven Years when the anti-Christ goes forth to conquer the world (see the explanation of the probable identification of the anti-Christ in Appendix 1, Footnote 9 of the commentary on Revelation 17). Then, the total annihilation of all life in Babylon-America by fire will occur at the midpoint of the seven years, just before the "beast" (Antichrist) declares himself to be god and is given his global *"kingdom"* (singular), the Revived Roman Empire (cf. the commentary on Revelation 17:16-17).

Then, finally, Babylon the Great, the headquarters of Satan's horde of evil spirit-beings, will, at the end of the Final Seven Years, be totally physically annihilated by a giant object from space (probably also a comet), never to rise again (Revelation 18:21).

What choice are you making?

But, regardless of exactly when the **three** destructions of America-Babylon occur, the events of world history and current global events, in the light of Bible prophecy, seem to be pointing to the reality that they are very near—right at the door. Are you ready? The most appropriate question for Americans (as well as the rest of the world) is not, "How can I survive the coming holocaust?" or "How can America be saved?" but, "Am I prepared leave this present life and enter the World to Come?" Yes, that is reality. We are all going to die, very soon. Therefore, realistically, we have only two choices: (1) deny ourselves, take up our crosses daily, seek the Kingdom of God and His righteousness with all our hearts, help every person who will listen to us to do the same ... and follow Jesus to Paradise, or (2) continue to lay up our treasures on Earth, seek worldly pleasures, comfort and security ... and perish in Hell with those who do the same. What is your choice?

What's next?

When will all this occur, and how does the Muslim takeover of the U.S.A., the annihilation of all life in America "by fire," and the final, physical destruction of Babylon the Great—the headquarters of Satan's global empire (Isaiah 14:4)—fit into the Lord's plan for this world at the "end of the age" (Matthew 24:3)? In the next chapter we will explore what the Bible states about that apocalyptic scenario.

Chapter 8

The Final Seven Years

"For then [at *'the end of the age'] there will be great tribulation, such as has not been since the beginning of the world until this time, no, nor ever shall be.* (Matthew 24:3, 21)

The "Tribulation"

Since the beginning of Creation, when Adam and Eve were deceived into forfeiting their dominion over the earth (Genesis 1:28) to Satan (the devil), he has held sway over the people of this world, except for the ones chosen by the Lord to be redeemed from the devil's power (Psalm 107:2). But, the Bible prophesies that, at the *"end of the age,"* there will be a seven-year period of time (cf. Daniel 9:27)[1]—what many call the "tribulation"—when Satan will be given the power to, first, conquer the whole world, including the parts of it presently controlled by the people of God[2], then, at the midpoint of the seven years, establish his global kingdom, ruled by Satan's incarnation the *"prince who is to come,"* the *"one who makes desolate,"* the *"man of sin,"* the *"son of perdition,"* the *"lawless one,"* the *"beast,"* or *"Antichrist"* (Daniel 9:26, 27; 2 Thessalonians 2:3, 8; 1 John 4:3; Revelation 13:4-5).

The first half of the seven years, during which time Satan will be gaining complete control of the world, is called the *"beginning of sorrows"* by Jesus (Matthew 24:8)[3]. Then, at the midpoint of the seven years, Antichrist will set up what both Daniel and Jesus called *"the abomination of desolation"* in the Temple in Jerusalem (Daniel 9:27; Matthew 24:15). This abomination was foreshadowed when, in ca. 167 B.C., the evil Seleucid ruler Antiochus Epiphanes defiled the Temple by sacrificing a pig and setting up a statue of the Greek god Zeus in it.[4] The ultimate abomination will occur when Antichrist *"sits as God in the temple of God, showing himself that he is God"* (2 Thessalonians 2:3-4).

Then, "all hell" will break forth on Earth. This will be the time when the *"great wrath"* of the devil is poured out on the earth. During the last half (42 months) of the seven years, Antichrist will be given unlimited power over the people of the world, except for a remnant of Israel who will receive special provision and protection from the Lord during that time. It will be a time of unprecedented persecution and martyrdom of true Christians and others who refuse to take the *"mark"* of the beast. The last 42 months of the Final Seven Years will be the period of time that both Jesus and the elder in Heaven speaking to John called the *"great tribulation"* which, if not *"shortened,"* will be so terrible that even the global kingdom of Antichrist will be destroyed and *"no flesh will be saved"* (cf. Matthew 24:21-22; Revelation 7:14; 12:12).

But, that time *will* be cut short—by the coming of the King of Kings and Lord of Lords and the armies of Heaven to destroy the forces of the world that oppose the Lord, cast the beast and his false religious leader into the lake of fire, cast the would-be ruler of this world (the devil) out and lock him away in the *"bottomless pit,"* and restore the earth to its original, wonderful, Edenic beauty (John 12:31; Revelation 19:11-20:4).[5]

Babylon the Great During the Final Seven Years

How does Babylon the Great, formerly known as the United States of America, fit into the end-times scenario of the Final Seven Years? This watchman will not be dogmatic, but, as a result of his years of prayerful study of current events in the light of Bible prophecy, he believes that the Lord has led him to the following understanding:

The U.S.A. is, at the present time, the latent Babylon the Great. But, once America is taken over by Islamists, she will become (with her "great city" New York City—the perfect antitype of ancient Babylon) Babylon the Great de facto. So, the takeover of the U.S.A. by Islamists may be the event that sets the stage for Antichrist (who will initially be a Muslim; see Appendix 3—"Who is Antichrist?") to go forth and conquer the world (Revelation 6:2). And Babylon the Great will dominate the Islamic global empire (Revelation 17:15).

However, Scripture (Revelation 17:16-17) clearly prophesies that all human life in Babylon the Great will be annihilated very quickly *"by fire"* (to end her domination of the nations of the world), so that the ten *"kings"* of the world (spiritual entities?) can give their *"kingdom"* (singular) to the beast, which the Lord has instilled in their hearts to do, to fulfill prophecy. As R.A. Coombes, in his monumental work *America the Babylon*, has explained, all the translations of Revelation 17:16 from the original Greek are mistaken and misleading.[6] The subject of the statement is *"fire,"* not *"kings."* Yes, the kings hate Babylon, but it is the fire that destroys her, not the kings. In other words, Babylon the Great will be destroyed by the Lord with fire (an exploding comet?)—an appropriate judgment on the "command center" of Satan—just as the destruction of Nimrod's empire by fire (an exploding comet) was an appropriate judgment. And, as the nations of the world look with horror at the destruction of Babylon—the sustainer of their economies (Revelation 18:3, 9-19)—the world stage is set for the entrance of Antichrist, offering himself as the solution to the chaos. So, the annihilation of Babylon the Great, formerly the United States of America, must occur just prior to the midpoint of the Final Seven Years, at which time Antichrist declares himself to be "god," the messiah, the savior of the world, and the solver of all the world's problems. And, at that time, he will establish his global *"kingdom"* and global religion, which will synthesize all the religions of the world.[7]

But, even after the destruction of all natural life in Babylon by fire, she will still be the spiritual command center of Satan—the habitation of his hordes of evil spirit beings (cf. Jeremiah 50:39; 51:37; Revelation 18:2). So, her final, total, physical destruction will be the event that prompts the celebration in Heaven just before the Marriage Supper of the Lamb and His return to Earth as King of Kings and Lord of Lords (Revelation 18:21; 19:1-16).

For more details and Scriptural support for the above explanation of the role and destiny of Babylon the Great during the Final Seven Years, read the commentary on Revelation 17 and 18 in Appendix 1 or visit the commentary website at www.revelationunderstoodcommentary.com.

A Narrative of the Final Seven Years

This watchman has come to realize that many have trouble digesting detailed study, but prefer parables and narratives. And that is fine, because that is the way Jesus taught. So he prays that the following "story" will heighten your interest so that you will really want to get into the Word to see for yourself if these things are true. This narrative is based on a common-sense, face-value, literal interpretation of Scripture, which I believe is the way our Heavenly Father wants His Word to be understood. I, Watchman Bob, do not claim to be a prophet or that all the events are in exactly the correct sequence or that their timing is precisely accurate. Although I have been studying current events in the light of Bible prophecy many years, I am simply a teacher who presents my understanding of what Scripture says is happening at the present time and will happen in the near future the best I can. And the identification of future characters, dates and circumstances in the following scenario should be evaluated by Scripture references given to determine if they are reasonably possible. If any of those future characters, dates and events turn out to be inaccurate, they will be changed in revisions to this narrative as the Lord gives further insight. On the other hand, the following narrative is not just a figment of my imagination. It is based on over 20 years of study of current events in the light of Bible prophecy. And I do believe that the interpretations on which it is based are as solidly based on Scripture as any out there. The current events portrayed (as of 2013) are actual. And please note especially that every future character, place and event that is included in the following narrative does occur in Scripture and could happen very much as portrayed. Again, the reader is encouraged to verify the feasibility of the following narrative by studying the Scriptures referenced and especially the commentary on the Scriptures in the book of the Revelation referenced. Also, three recently published, eye-opening books referred to frequently throughout this book—*The Comets of God* by scientist Jeffrey Goodman, the New York Times Bestseller *The Harbinger* by Jonathan Cahn, and *The 9/11 Prophecy* by James Fitzgerald—have provided additional, powerful support for "The Final Seven Years." For more details and documentation, the reader is encouraged to read those three books.

The Final Seven Years

A Quasi-Fictional End-of-the-Age Scenario

The Kingdom of Heaven

Jesus is, at the present time, establishing the Kingdom of God in Heaven *("I go to prepare a place for you ..."*—John 14:2), in the hearts of His regenerated People, His Disciples (Luke 17:21), and in its various spiritual manifestations on Earth (Matthew 12:28). But His People (His "Bride") will not physically dwell there until He comes to change them into glorified, heavenly beings, gather them to Himself, and take them there *("that where I am, there you may be also"*—John 14:3). Then, later, after the wedding ceremony and feast in Heaven (Revelation 19:7-9), He will return with His heavenly armies (glorified Saints and angels—Revelation 17:14; 19:8, 14; Matthew 16:27; 2 Thessalonians 1:7) to defeat his enemies on Earth and set up His millennial kingdom here (Revelation 19:11-20:4; Luke 13:29).

Meanwhile, while the Bride (the Church) is in her new home in Heaven (specifically, New Jerusalem), what is happening on Earth? Well, all Heaven is breaking forth, that is what. The final execution of the Wrath of the Lord is being poured out on Earth, big time (Revelation 16:16-21). But, to get the whole picture, let us back up a few years.

The Setup—The First Three and One-Half Years

For years, the United States of America—the world's only remaining "superpower" nation after the fall of the Soviet Union in 1989—had been gaining more and more global hegemony through subverting one government after another and converting them into "client states" with puppet leaders. In 2009 her only serious rival for dominance of the world's economy was the European Union. But then, in 2010, several of the EU's member nations—Portugal, Italy, Ireland, Greece, and Spain—having greatly overextended their credit and having accrued tremendous deficits that they could not service, got into serious financial trouble. Greece was on the verge of collapse; riots were breaking out. So, other EU member states bit the bullet and bailed her out, further weakening the stability of the whole Union. But then, by October 2011,

Greece's bailout had failed, causing massive protests and rioting, threatening bankruptcy of the nation and a calamitous domino effect in other European nations. And the United States, having accrued more that sixteen trillion dollars in debt, which was owed at home and abroad and was growing rapidly because of having to fund natural disaster recovery efforts in the homeland and constant involvement in foreign wars, was in no position to help the ailing nations although they were dependent on her as by far the largest consumer of their commodities and services. If the economy of the USA collapsed, the economies of the whole world would collapse. In fact, in spite of assurances of the government through the mainline media to the contrary, the stability of the US economy was quite precarious. One major national catastrophe could cause it to collapse. Then, in 2014, reality overtook America's worst fears. First, because of the economic stress caused by full implementation of the national health care plan ("Obamacare") and increased taxation resulting from the unsustainable national debt ceiling, nations around the world, beginning with China, France and Russia, began to abandon the U.S. dollar as their medium of exchange and it was devalued and replaced as the global reserve currency. This caused widespread panic, riots and looting in the U.S. Martial law was declared and a police state was established, making the President a virtual dictator.

Then, the following year, 2015, exactly as prophesied (Isaiah 9:10; Jeremiah 51:8, 27-28), there was a massive terrorist attack on America from within and outside her borders. For many years, Muslims had been freely allowed into the USA, and thousands of them had been clandestinely developing hundreds of Jihad terrorist cells around the country. A confederation of Muslim nations led by Iran and Turkey had been funding, training and coordinating the terrorist cells and was also planning to attack US military installations and ships abroad. The attack was meticulously planned and coordinated because the aggressors knew that if the US military, with its awesome fighting capabilities, was allowed to respond in a cohesive way they would not succeed. And the attack went exactly as planned! Simultaneously, all over the nation, thousands of bombs, including suitcase nuclear devices, were detonated—mainly in large population centers including Washington D.C. and New York City. And, because there was no plan to counter such a devastating and widespread attack from within the nation (the US Defense establishment was almost totally set up to respond to attacks from outside the borders of the US), the whole nation was thrown into total chaos. National Guard units could not be called up and activated instantly and police departments were not logistically prepared to counter the multi-faceted, massive attack. There were some joint police-military anti-terrorist units and plans in place, but strangely, no orders came from the President to activate them. So, Americans, in their panic, were sitting ducks for the armed, trained and coordinated terrorists, and all who resisted were mowed down in the streets and in their homes. The terrorists also took over all National Guard and police units around the country and bombed and forced the surrender of military installions, which were totally unprepared for such an attack, especially with no directions coming from Washington. Meanwhile, simultaneously, air, ground and missile attacks were being carried out on U.S. military installations, troops and ships all over the world—especially in the Near East. And also, having no directions from Washington, which was totally occupied with the attack at home, those installations, troops and ships could mount no coordinated response, were either destroyed or immobilized, and were taken over by the Muslim forces. In fact, the attacks at home and abroad were so effective that, within just a few hours, the government of the United States of America was in the hands of radical Islamists.

Then, the confederation of anti-Israel, anti-America nations from the Near East and North Africa (Jeremiah 51:27-28; Psalm 83:2-8; Ezekiel 38:2-6) that had caused the downfall of America, with the USA out of the way, immediately turned their attention to Israel—to invade and annihilate that tiny nation. Mobilizing rapidly, they set up support facilities all around Israel and came like a vast, menacing pack of wolves through the mountains of northern Israel. Surrounded by the anti-aircraft and anti-missile weaponry of her enemies and without the support of the USA, there was virtually nothing the Israelis could do to retaliate. But then, an amazing thing happened: All kinds of natural calamities began to occur in and around Israel, focused, incredibly, on the invading armies of her enemies: Comet fragments rained from the sky on them. The impact of a large fragment caused a tremendous earthquake, like the world had never seen, and collapsed the cliffs of the mountains on those armies; torrential rains flooded their camps; ten-pound comet fragments destroyed their equipment and killed large numbers of personnel; and even volcanic eruptions caused by comet fragments penetrating the earth's crust burned camps and covered them with lava. Then, in total panic and confusion, what was left of Israel's enemy forces attacked and destroyed one another (Ezekiel 38:20-22)!

Of course, in the aftermath of the attacks on the US and Israel, the economies of all nations had immediately collapsed and the whole world was in chaos.

But there was a man, Kurtarici Mesih, the new head of the Turkish branch of PNB Paribas, the largest global banking organization in the world, who had been rapidly garnering a reputation as being an incredibly persuasive, charismatic leader, and many said that he was a financial genius. In his first few months as head of PNB Paribas Turkey, Mesih had been able to develop powerful financial ties with some of the wealthiest investors from all points east and west of Turkey—from China to Paris (the location of the main bank and headquarters of PNB Paribas). The leaders of the EuroMed Partnership (a consortium of 44 European, North African, Middle Eastern, and Balkan nations formed in 1995 to promote mutual economic support and development) had started to tout Mesih as the potential leader of the EMP because Turkey was a key, centrally-located member with strong political and economic ties to both Europe and the Mediterranean Basin nations as well as being the leading nation, financially and militarily, of the trans-EuroMed area. Also, Turkey (together with Iran) had led the Islamist nations in their attacks on the US and Israel, and Mesih emerged as the primary leader of those who were already executing plans to re-establish the (former) USA (but now under Islamist control) as the anchor and stabilizer of the global economy. So when, in an emergency meeting in Barcelona, the leaders of the EMP frantically stormed their brains for a solution to their dilemma (economic chaos), one name dominated their thoughts—Kurtarici Mesih. They called him and asked him to meet with them. Much to their relief, he agreed. And the next day, in Barcelona, Kurtarici Mesih, by consensus acclamation, was named President of the EuroMed Partnership.

Then, the EMP, with Mesih as its President, working closely with other Muslim leaders who had been involved in the attack on the USA, took over all the USA's domestic and foreign political, industrial, commercial and economic institutions and her military installations, quickly (re-) establishing that nation as the "super-power" of the world. Also, in recognition of her new, Near Eastern rulers and of the many characteristics she uncannily had in common with ancient Babylon, the former United States of America was re-named New Babylon. And with New Babylon now established as the main sustainer of the economies of virtually all of the world's nations, and either by persuasion, political intrigue, violent force or economic coercion—to even greater an extent than the USA had accomplished before her fall—all the nations of the world were made "client states" of New Babylon.

Meanwhile, although most of her own people had survived the destruction of the armies of her enemies, the land of Israel was devastated. She was left without the wherewithal to sustain or to protect herself if her enemies should regroup and attack her again or if another enemy (e.g., Russia or China) should attack her. So, Israel's leaders were very happy when the EuroMed Partnership (of which Israel was also a member), although many of their forces had been destroyed in "the War of Gog and Magog" (cf. Ezekiel 38), offered to come to her aid. Representing the EMP as its leader, Kurtarici Mesih signed a military peace treaty with Israel, agreeing to protect her from further invasion or attack (cf. Isaiah 28:18; Daniel 9:27a). Mesih and the EMP also agreed to restore total sovereignty over her land to Israel, to help her clean up the mess left by the destruction of her enemies, and to allow her to re-establish all the religious practices of ancient Israel. And after Mesih's peace treaty with the leaders of Israel was signed, making Israel an (apparent) safe harbor for Jews, millions of other Jews from around the world (the vast majority of the world's Jews), with the assistance of the EMP, immediately migrated to the land of Israel. So, although the fall of the USA and the economies of all the other nations caused global desperation, chaos and violence, there was "peace" in Israel, allowing the Jews to start rebuilding their nation and their Temple.

Nevertheless, wars, bloodshed, food shortages, unsanitary conditions, disease, and death continued all over the world, resulting in about a quarter of the world's population dying during the next few years (Revelation 6:3-8).

But, with his charismatic personality, dynamic persuasive powers, and amazing organizational skills, Mesih was being more and more recognized as the de facto leader of the world and the solver of the world's problems. Conformity in government, commerce, and religion were mandated. All the world's religions were brought under the banner of Islam. Dissidents were persecuted, even martyred. (Strangely, the Israelis, who were allowed to practice their own religion, were the exception.) And some semblance of world order was maintained.

But then, approximately three years after the peace treaty with Israel had been signed, the greatest catastrophe in history, since the Great Flood, occurred. A large comet exploded in the atmosphere above North America totally annihilating all life in New Babylon and in much of the neighboring nations Canada and Mexico, in exactly the same way ancient Sodom and Gomorrah had been destroyed (cf. Isaiah 13:19, 20; Jeremiah 49:18; 50:40; Revelation 17:16; 18:8). And again, the whole world was thrown into chaos as the nations looked on in horror as the smoke of New Babylon and it's "great city," New York City, that had sustained their economies, rose into the sky (Revelation 18:9-19).

But Kurturaci Mesih rose to the occasion. He immediately mobilized the EMP's worldwide military forces and economic institutions and, over the next six months, again restored order to a devastated world. And he expanded and established his headquarters in Istanbul as the headquarters of the New World Order. Having so quickly restored order to the world after the annihilation of all life in New Babylon, and now as leader of, by far, the most powerful global empire in world history, Mesih garnered the wonder of the whole world. Many were even suggesting that he was the true Messiah—the god-man anticipated by all the world's religions.

The Takeover and the Great Tribulation

And Mesih seized the moment. He stood in the Most Holy Place of the Temple and, filled with the spirit of His spiritual father, Satan, declared himself to be the messiah—"god" incarnate (Daniel 7:25; 8:23-25; 11:36-37; 2 Thessalonians 2:4; Revelation

13:6-8). And virtually all the people of the world pledged their allegiance to him and worshiped him (Revelation 13:3-4). Then Mesih immediately brought in his top aides, military commanders and 100,000 elite military forces from Turkey and, with the full cooperation of the Israelis, who also accepted him as the long-anticipated messiah who would establish his throne in Jerusalem from where he would rule all the nations of the world (cf. Isaiah 9:6, 7), he took over the Knesset building and other Israeli government facilities as well as all of Israel's military installations, making Jerusalem his new global headquarters. And all the leaders of the world, as though they were mesmerized, rallied around him and quickly formed a ten-region global government and economic system under martial law (Revelation 17:12, 17).

The man who had been the head of religion of the EMP now took center stage as Mesih's Chief of Religion and World Order. He was also empowered by Satan, working all kinds of supernatural signs and wonders to deceive the world into worshiping Mesih. He even somehow developed a lifelike image of Mesih that could be made to appear all over the earth. And he set up a system in which every person, in order to participate in the global economy, had to take an oath of allegiance to worship the "Messiah Mesih" as "Lord of the World" and receive an identification chip under the skin of their hand or forehead. Immediate execution was the consequence of failure to take Mesih's mark or to worship his image. (Revelation 13:15-16)

But prior to the fall of the USA to the Muslims, 144,000 Jewish men, including 12,000 orthodox Jews (Revelation 7:4), and their families had left the USA and migrated to Israel, being convinced that somehow the Lord's command, "Come out of her, my people" (Jeremiah 51:45), applied to them. And when they saw Mesih standing in the Temple proclaiming himself to be "god," the 144,000 remembered the words of Daniel and what he had spoken about the diabolical "prince who is to come," the abominations and desolation the evil prince would cause (Daniel 9:26, 27), plus the prophecies about the coming time of "Jacob's trouble" (Jeremiah 30:7; Daniel 12:1), and they refused to take the mark or to worship Mesih. And the 144,000 and the Messianic Believers in Jerusalem and throughout Israel who remembered the words of Jesus (Matthew 24:15-21) immediately fled to hiding places in the mountains of Israel and the wilderness area east of the Dead Sea, where they were led by the Lord to places of safe refuge and sustenance (cf. Isaiah 16:3-4; Revelation 12:6). Also, about one-third of the Jews in Jerusalem and Israel who did not flee refused to take Mesih's mark and to worship him. But, rather than have them executed, Mesih stripped all Jews who refused to take his mark of ownership of their property, gave them bare, subsistence provisions, and subjected them to the harshest of slave labor conditions. Many of them died daily under those conditions.

Then, as if to add more aggravation to the escape of the Jews and Messianic Believers, an angel was seen streaking through the sky proclaiming,

Fear God and give glory to Him, for the hour of His judgment has come; and worship Him who made heaven and earth, the sea and springs of water. (Revelation 14:7)

And another angel followed, saying,

Babylon is fallen, is fallen, that great city, because she has made all nations drink of the wine of the wrath of her fornication. (Revelation 14:8)

Then, a third angel followed, saying with a loud voice,

If anyone worships the beast and his image, and receives his mark on his forehead or on his hand, he himself shall also drink of the wine of the wrath of God, which is poured out full strength into the cup of His indignation. He shall be tormented with fire and brimstone in the presence of the holy angels and in the presence of the Lamb. And the smoke of their torment ascends "forever" and ever; and they have no rest day or night, who worship the beast and his image, and whoever receives the mark of his name. (Revelation 14:9-11)

Finally, something else was happening that was a continual annoyance and distraction to Mesih. There were two men with appearances like ancient prophets, dressed in sackcloth (the Jews said they were Moses and Elijah), who appeared and were warning everyone in Jerusalem and the surrounding area not to accept Mesih as "Lord of the World" and were proclaiming that they needed to repent and accept Jesus, whom they crucified, as their true Messiah. Mesih sent some of his commandos to kill them, but the two "witnesses" (Revelation 11:3) seemed to have supernatural powers that created all kinds of disasters and havoc, and they were not able to succeed.

Mesih, being enraged by all these events, made a terrible and treacherous proclamation that no Jew would be allowed to take the mark and participate in the global economy. Just as in Hitler's Third Reich, all Jews in Israel were required to wear special identification badges. Those who resisted were to be executed. The Israeli Jews were then given a bare subsistence allotment of food, clothing and shelter and were subjected to excruciatingly hard labor in maintenance, support and production work in the land and government facilities of Israel. The elderly Jews and others in failing health or who were disabled, unable to serve some useful purpose in Israel, were executed. Mesih also ordered his followers worldwide to report any they spotted who had not taken the mark and bowed to his image, especially Jews and Followers of Jesus, and that they be killed on the spot (Revelation 12:17; 13:15-17).

This was a time of great tribulation (Matthew 24:21; Revelation 7:14) and carnage for Jews who had not migrated to Israel and Believers in the true Messiah Jesus. During the next 42 months, almost all of them, except the ones who had escaped into the wilderness, were killed. And the millions of Jews in Jerusalem and Israel who had been subjected to virtual slavery by Mesih were also under great tribulation and hardship, thousands of them dying daily from the terrible conditions to which they were subjected.

As he tightened his grip on the global control that his father Satan had given him (Revelation 13:4, 7), Mesih was totally convinced that he was indeed Lord of the World. Because of advanced surveillance technology, his "eyes" all over the world, and supernatural reconnaissance, it seemed obvious that his enemies, those despicable Jews and Disciples of Jesus, would not be able for long to escape their inevitable end.

The Day of the Lord Begins

But then, about a year into the "Great Tribulation," all Heaven broke forth—what the prophets had frequently referred to as the "Day of *the Lord*" (cf. Joel 2:1, et al.). Exactly as foretold (Joel 2:10, 11; 3:4; Matthew 24:29; Revelation 6:12-13), fragments of comets showered the earth with the force of thousands of nuclear bombs, the sun and moon were darkened because of clouds of smoke and debri produced by the commentary impacts; the stars disappeared; the sky looked like it was being rolled up like a scroll as the atmosphere was largely evaporated by heat from the explosions; and there was a violent, world-wide earthquake, moving every mountain and island out of its place. It was like the whole cosmos was being shaken. People everywhere were crying out in terror to be hidden from or even to be killed to escape the Wrath of the One who was doing this, because it was obvious that an awesome supernatural power was in control. Then, as suddenly as it had begun, it ended. The sun, moon, and stars once again gave their light, though dimly through the dense haze. The whole earth was in disarray and traumatized; millions had lost their lives. But compared to the awesome events that had just transpired, it was eerily quiet, like a spooky calm in the midst of a great storm. The wind was not even blowing (Revelation 7:1).

Mesih was trying to gather his wits and his lieutenants to deal with the situation. Then, the 144,000 who had fled into the wilderness a year earlier were seen marching into Jerusalem from the direction of Petra! They all had a peculiar seal on their foreheads. And they were being led by the true Messiah— Jesus! They marched right up to the top of Mount Zion, the highest peak in Jerusalem, and they were standing there with Jesus, singing a serenely beautiful song that apparently only they could understand (Revelation 14:1-3). Mesih was told about the 144,000, but just as he was attempting to marshal his forces against them, terrifying, surreal noises, like those who had been murdered crying out for vengeance (Revelation 6:10), were heard; deafening claps of thunder and blinding flashes of lightning came out of the darkened sky! Then, another great earthquake shook the whole earth, causing many buildings to tumble (Revelation 8:5). Mesih forgot about the 144,000 as reports of great damage poured in from all over the world. He blamed the disasters on the two witnesses who were still walking the streets of Jerusalem boldly proclaiming gloom and doom on those who took the mark of the false messiah and destroying, with amazing personal powers and control of the forces of nature, all those who opposed them.

For the next two and one-half years, the same cycle of events continued, but with increasing intensity. Mesih continued to seek out and kill any he could find who had not taken his mark or who failed to worship his image, and to attempt to kill Moses and Elijah. But, as time went on, he was more and more preoccupied with disaster management. And the two witnesses continued to prophesy while God sent a series of plagues of increasing intensity on the world in the following order: giant, burning "hailstones" (comet fragments) exploded in the atmosphere causing a third of the trees and all green grass to be burned and released toxic substances which caused great, foul-smelling, pus-filled, oozing sores to appear on the humans (although, amazingly, those who had not accepted the "mark of the beast" were not affected) (cf. Revelation 8:7; 16:2); a great, burning "mountain" (a large comet) "thrown" into the sea causing a third of the ships to be destroyed and a third of the world's salt water to turn blood red from the reactions of the comet's toxic chemical radicals with the sea water, which in turn caused a third of all living creatures in the sea to die (cf. Revelation 8:8-9; 16:3); fragments from a large, disintegrated, toxic comet contaminated a band of rivers and lakes around the earth's northern hemisphere, including the Great Lakes of North America and Lake Baikal in Siberian Russian—sources of over one-third of the earth's fresh water—causing close to a third of the world's remaining human population to die (cf. Revelation 8:10-11; 16:4); then, the light and heat from the sun, moon and stars were affected by all the cometary explosions so that one-third less light reached the earth and temperatures plummeted around the globe an average of 40 degrees Farenheit, but also much of the ozone layer protecting the earth from ultraviolet radiation was destroyed, so at the same time people were chilled by the cold, their skin was being scorched by the ultraviolet radiation (cf. Revelation 8:12; 16:8-9).

But, as terrible as the first four plagues of the Wrath of God were, the last three ("woes") were much more dreadful. First, another giant "star" (comet) fell from "heaven" (outer space—the Oort Cloud of billions of comets that surround the earth's solar system), causing a "bottomless" crater (one that penetrates the earth's crust) and releasing a huge plume of deadly bacteria-filled smoke that darkened the sky. (When magnified, these bacteria exactly resembled bizarre-looking locusts with horse-like heads and tails like those of scorpions.) This plague, with these bacteria which caused horrible, unbearable sores and skin diseases, lasted an agonizing five months. (cf. Revelation 9:1-10; 16:10-11). Next, four large comet fragments impacted the Euphrates River, drying it up, while simultaneously spraying millions of small comet fragments high into the atmosphere from where they were scattered all over the earth, killing all people (about one-third of the remaining world's human population) with whom the intense heat of the burning sulfur in the fragments came in contact (cf. Revelation 9:14-19; 16:6-12).

From the time the Day of the Wrath of the Lord began until the end of the seven years, all of Earth's inhabitants (except for about one-third of the Jews in Israel [cf. Zechariah 13:8] and several million Gentiles who had helped the Jews and who had not taken the "mark of the beast" during the "Great Tribulation" of the previous 42 months) suffered tremendously from the first six sets of plagues of the Wrath of the Lord. And more than five and one-half billion or two-thirds of Earth's inhabitants had died violent, painful deaths. During these plagues of the Wrath of God, the people who dwelt on Earth would cry out in terror for mercy, but as soon as the destruction stopped, they would refuse to repent and would blaspheme God (Revelation 9:20-21; 16:11).

At the end of the seven years and six sets of plagues of the Wrath of the Lord, Mesih's global kingdom was greatly decimated and devastated and, for all practical purposes, was at an end. However, God had another exercise in humiliation in store for him.

Moses and Elijah had openly walked the streets of Jerusalem every day since Mesih had stood in the Most Holy Place of the Temple and declared himself to be "god." They constantly spoke out against him, proclaiming that he was the false messiah, telling people not to take his mark or to worship his image, but to worship the true Messiah, Jesus of Nazareth. And they performed all kinds of signs and wonders, exactly as had Moses and Elijah of ancient Israel, and destroyed all who attempted to attack them. But then, three and one-half years after Mesih had stood in the Most Holy Place of the Temple and declared himself to be "Lord of the World," it seemed that the two witnesses had lost their supernatural powers! Fire no longer came from their mouths to consume those who got in their way. They were no longer calling forth the plagues that tormented their enemies. A glimmer of hope that the tide of death and destruction caused by his two nemeses was about to turn rose in Mesih's evil heart. And he, at the head of all that was left of the armies of the kings of the earth who ruled under him, came into Jerusalem and personally shot the two witnesses dead. Then, as they lay in the streets of Jerusalem for all the world to see and gloat over, and to demonstrate Mesih's power and sovereignty, the armies of the kings of the earth ransacked Jerusalem, ravished the women, and took half of the residents captive (Zechariah 14:2). But then, to the total amazement and consternation of everyone and the dismay of Mesih, three and one-half days after they had been killed, Moses and Elijah revived and ascended into Heaven! Immediately, there was an earthquake in Jerusalem, the city was divided into three parts, and 7,000 of the enemies of the Jews were killed. Mesih and his followers were terrified, but the Jews in Jerusalem recognized the hand of the Lord and glorified Him. (Revelation 11:3-13)

Then, suddenly, there was a brilliant flash of light, like lightning flashing from horizon to horizon, and the glorified Messiah, Jesus, appeared in totally white, luminous clouds, descending out of Heaven (Matthew 24:27, 30)! And there was the overwhelmingly loud sound of a great shofar (Jewish trumpet), and gleaming white angelic beings appeared and flew to every part of the sky all around the earth; and other glorified beings from all over the earth, under the earth, and even from within the seas flew up to meet them, from where they were instantly taken to meet the Messiah in the air (Matthew 24:31; 1 Thessalonians 4:16, 17). Then, the Messiah, the angels, and the "raptured" ones all vanished into Heaven.

And that seventh and final trumpet sounding also announced the third "woe"—the final set of plagues of the Wrath of God. And because the reign of Antichrist on Earth had ended, a loud chorus of voices was heard shouting from Heaven, "The kingdoms of this world have become the kingdoms of our Lord and of His [Messiah], and He shall reign forever and ever!" (Revelation 11:15)

Then, all Heaven broke forth in a series of catastrophes that, for the next ten days, demolished the whole planet: A great, global earthquake caused every island to disappear and every mountain (except the mountains in and near Jerusalem—Mount Zion, Mount Moriah and the Mount of Olives) to collapse. The earthquake shook the earth so violently that it also caused all the buildings of all the world's cities to collapse (except Jerusalem which, although it was split into three sections, remained standing). Then, a giant comet fell on the now lifeless, barren former USA and New Baby-lon (which was now inhabited only by evil spirit beings—Revelation 18:2), sinking that land and much of North America beneath the waves of the sea. Finally, hundreds of millions of 100-pound, flaming "hailstones" (comet fragments) rained down on the earth, killing virtually all of the planet's remaining inhabitants (except those supernaturally protected by the Lord and the remaining armies of the kings of the earth in and around Jerusalem). (cf. Revelation 11:15-10; 16:17-21; 18:20-21).

The Final Showdown

After that, a great multitude in Heaven was heard proclaiming with a loud voice,

> *'Alleluia! Salvation and glory and honor and power belong to the Lord our God. For true and righteous are His judgments, because He has judged the great harlot who corrupted the earth with her fornication; and He has avenged on her the blood of His servants shed by her.' Again they said, 'Allelujah! Her smoke rises up forever and ever!' And the twenty-four elders and the four living creatures fell down and worshiped God who sat on the throne, saying, 'Amen! Allelujah!' Then a voice came from the throne, saying, 'Praise our God, all you His servants and those who fear Him, both small and great!' And it was heard, as it were, the voice of a great multitude, as the sound of many waters and as the sound of mighty thundering, saying, 'Alleluia! for the Lord God Omnipotent reigns!'* (Revelation 19:1-6)

Finally, the Messiah Jesus—the King of Kings and Lord of Lords—was seen streaking through the heavens from the east, riding a great and powerful, gleaming white horse and wearing a crimson garment, followed by a great host of angels and glorified saints wearing pure white linen garments and also riding white horses. The Lord Jesus then stood at the peak of the Mount of Olives, which split from the west to the east forming a valley that ran all the way to the north end of the Dead Sea. All the Jewish inhabitants of Jerusalem who remained in the city and who had not taken the mark of the beast then fled through the valley to the east. Mesih sent his army (what was left of it after all the plagues of the Wrath of the Lord) after them like a flood, but, incredibly, the earth opened up, forming a huge crevasse that swallowed his army. Then a white light like a great laser sword came from the mouth of the

146

Messiah, slaying all the armies of the kings of the earth who had gathered against Jerusalem (cf. Revelation 16:13-14). The Messiah then took Kurturaci Mesih and his Chief of Religion and cast them alive into the Dead Sea which had filled with blazing bitumen from the great rift in the earth that had swallowed Mesih's army. (cf. Zechariah 14:3-5; Revelation 19:11-21).

The Beginning

Of course, that is not the end of the story, which, for those who understand and believe it and who believe in the One who authored it all, is thrilling indeed. Revelation goes on to describe the binding of Satan for 1,000 years; the millennial Kingdom of God; the new heavens, new earth, and New Jerusalem: who will be there, who will not, and what will happen there; the final war of Gog and Magog; the Final Judgment; and a peek at eternity in the glorious presence of the Lord God. But, hopefully, this has given you a taste of what the Revelation is all about.

And, hopefully, this narrative has whetted your appetite to get into the Scripture for yourself to get all the details and to find out what God's plan is for *"the End of the Age."*

To help you do that, the Lord has given us a detailed, crystal-clear commentary on the book of Revelation, the entire contents of which are published on our ministry website at www.RevelationUnderstoodCommentary.com, where you can find abundant Scriptural support for everything written in this book, *The Tenth Harbinger*, and much more concerning the events prophesied in the Revelation.

But meanwhile, if you are interested in knowing the role and the destiny of Christians during the soon-coming Final Seven Years, keep reading.

Chapter 9

Will Christians Escape, Survive, or Take Dominion of the Earth During the Final Seven Years?

*"Now brother will deliver up brother to death, and a father his child; and children will rise up against parents and cause them to be put to death. And you will be hated by all for My name's sake. **But he who endures to the end will be saved.** When they persecute you in this city, flee to another. For assuredly, I say to you, you will not have gone through the cities of Israel before the Son of Man comes."* (Matthew 10:21-23)

This watchman is now going to write about a subject concerning which he is passionate. And that is the role and the destiny of Christians during the soon-coming Final Seven Years. And he wants to confront the above question head-on with a resounding **NONE OF THE ABOVE!** Christians will, with perhaps very few exceptions, neither escape nor survive (physically) nor take dominion over the earth during the Final Seven Years. And he is going to explain exactly why, according to God's infallible Word, he unequivocally proclaims that answer.

Three Erroneous Views

There are three repugnant, very dangerous teachings in the Christian Church—especially the American Christian Church—concerning the *"end of the age"* that contradict and undermine the clear exhortations of our Lord concerning what the attitude and the behavior of His disciples should be during the Final Seven Years. And those are the pretribulation rapture, the survivalist, and the dominionist fallacies. All three are insipid doctrines that totally nullify what Jesus clearly told His disciples about the terrible times that were coming and what they needed to do about it (and what, by extension, the Christians today need to do about it). Those three *"doctrines of demons"* set those who espouse them up for the destruction, not only of their bodies, but very possibly their souls. And

149

that is why this watchman is so urgent about tearing down those strongholds of the enemy (2 Corinthians 10:4), before it is too late for those who take refuge in them, and he prays that those of you who read this will pay close attention, lest you perish in the coming holocaust.

The Pretribulation Rapture "Pie-in-the-Sky" Fantasy

The "pretribulation rapture" is the name given to the erroneous doctrine that Jesus Christ will return in the clouds at some unknown point in time prior to the commencement of the Final Seven Years to catch the redeemed saints up to meet Him in the sky and take them to Heaven. The pretrib eschatological doctrine was popularized by the Left Behind series of best-selling novels and films by Tim LaHaye and Jerry B. Jenkins that were published between 1995 and 2007.[1] A large proportion of Christians who believe in the coming Final Seven Years (which they call "the tribulation"), espouse the pretrib rapture teaching. That is probably because that doctrine has great appeal—who would not like to escape the terrible times coming at the "end of the age"?

However, there is a problem with the pre-trib rapture notion: It is a fantasy, no more rooted in reality than the Left Behind fiction novels based on it. There is absolutely no Scriptural support for that doctrine. But, worst of all, it is a deception of the devil that will destroy the faith and perhaps even the souls of its adherents.

The Christian ministers, "scholars," and teachers that promulgate the pretrib rapture delusion base that doctrine on a few verses of Scripture taken out of context, misinterpreted, and misapplied. For example, to allegedly prove the pretrib rapture, they connect three passages of Scripture written by the apostle Paul:

Now this I say, brethren, that flesh and blood cannot inherit the kingdom of God; nor does corruption inherit incorruption. Behold, I tell you a mystery: We shall not all sleep, but we shall all be changed—in a moment, in the twinkling of an eye, at the last trumpet. For the trumpet will sound, and the dead will be raised incorruptible, and we shall be changed. For this corruptible must put on incorruption, and this mortal must put on immortality. (1 Corinthians 15:50-53)

For if we believe that Jesus died and rose again, even so God will bring with Him those who sleep in Jesus. For this we say to you by the word of the Lord, that we

150

who are alive and remain until the coming of the Lord will by no means precede those who are asleep. For the Lord Himself will descend from heaven with a shout, with the voice of an archangel, and with the trumpet of God. And the dead in Christ will rise first. Then we who are alive and remain shall be caught up together with them in the clouds to meet the Lord in the air. And thus we shall always be with the Lord. (1 Thessalonians 4:14-17)

For God did not appoint us to wrath, but to obtain salvation through our Lord Jesus Christ, who died for us, that whether we wake or sleep, we should live to-gether with Him. (1 Thessalonians 5:9-10)

This is the pretrib rapture proponents' reasoning: At the time of the resurrection of the dead, both the redeemed who are resur-rected and those who are still alive will be instantly given new, glo-rified, incorruptible, immortal bodies (1 Corinthians 15:50-53). Both the resurrected redeemed and those who are still alive will then be *"caught up"* ("raptured") to meet the Lord in the air and be taken to Heaven (1 Thessalonians 4:14-17). The rapture must oc-cur prior to the start of the "tribulation," because that is when the Lord's wrath will be poured out on earth-dwellers, but the re-deemed are not appointed to wrath (1 Thessalonians 5:9-10).

Sounds logical, does it not? Yes, the Bible does clearly teach the resurrection and rapture of the redeemed saints of the Lord. And it clearly teaches that the Church will not be subject to the Wrath of the Lord that will come on the rest of the world. How-ever, there are at least four problems with the pretribulation rapture conjecture: (1) The teachers of that doctrine do not distinguish between the wrath of Satan and the Wrath of the Lord; (2) they do not correctly ascertain **when** the wrath of Satan (the Great Tribula-tion) will be begin and **when** the Wrath of the Lord will be poured out on the earth-dwellers; (3) they do not correctly identify **when** the resurrection and the rapture will occur; and (4) they ignore the clear teachings and exhortations of Jesus and the writers of the New Testament concerning role the Lord has given Christians to play in the Lord's end-times redemption drama.

As has already been explained in this book, the first half of the Final Seven Years will be the *"beginning of sorrows"*—the period of time during which Antichrist will be gaining control of the world. It will not be the time during which either the wrath of Satan or the Wrath of God will be poured out on Earth. The Great Tribulation (the wrath of Satan) will begin at the midpoint of the Final Seven Years. The Wrath of the Lord will not start to be poured out on Earth until the second half of the seven years (cf. Revelation 6:15-17). The resurrection and rapture will not occur until the last day of the Final Seven Years, when the seventh and final trumpet sounds (Matthew 24:31; 1 Corinthians 15:52; Revelation 11:15). The Great Tribulation will be cut short at the end of the seven years (cf. Revelation 13:5) by the return of the Lord Jesus to gather His elect (the redeemed saints) and the *"last plagues"* of the Wrath of God (the bowls of wrath) being poured out on the earth (Matthew 24:21-22; 29-31; Revelation 11:18; 15:1; 16:1).[2]

Please notice that **at no time** does Jesus or any of the writers of the New Testament promise the Church exemption or escape from tribulations, persecutions, or even martyrdom, including during the Final Seven Years. In fact, He assures us of just the opposite, if we are His true disciples. He exhorts us to *"endure to the end"* (Matthew 24:13), not to look for an easy, quick escape. And **every one** of the seven congregations to whom the Revelation of the Lord was written was exhorted to *"overcome"* whatever tribulations or death they faced, not to expect an escape (Revelation 2:7, 11, 17, 26; 3:5, 12, 21). Overcoming the suffering we face by remaining faithful to the Lord—to the death, if necessary—is one of the main ways that we witness to the world and encourage fellow believers with the reality of His presence and power in our lives, and the hope that we have of eternal life, is it not? (cf. Philippians 1:20-25; Revelation 2:10) Did not the apostles rejoice that they were counted worthy to suffer because of their faith in Jesus Christ? (Acts 5:41; 2 Thessalonians 1:5; Colossians 1:24)

So, **how dare** the charlatans in the Church contradict God's Word and hold out to the children of God that lie of the devil, that false hope, that pretribulation rapture fantasy! When they do not get the quick and easy escape that they have been promised, the faith of those poor, misguided souls will be shipwrecked when it runs aground on the terrible times soon to come. Surely, the Lord's warning to the watchman applies to those false teachers and shepherds of the Lord's flock:

If the watchman sees the sword coming and does not blow the trumpet, and the people are not warned, and the sword comes and takes any person from among them, he is taken away in his iniquity; but his blood I will require at the watch-man's hand. (Ezekiel 33:6)

The Suicidal Survivalist Mentality

Just as many in the Church entertain an escapist fantasy, others think they can hunker down in bunkers or caves, or disappear into the woods or remote locations, and survive whatever comes. So, they gather guns, buy water filters, generators and other equipment, and store non-perishable food and other supplies to make them-selves feel safe and secure. But, that survivalist mentality is just as delusional and non-Scriptural as is the pretribulation rapture fanta-sy.

Think about it: If the economy collapses or is shut down by a totalitarian government and the masses are without means of pur-chasing food, fuel and utilities, what will immediately ensue? Riots, chaos, killing and looting. Correct? Do the survivalists really think they can fight off or hide from the desperate hordes? Yes, they may … but not for long. And consider this: Antichrist, his reli-gious leader, and probably their police forces will have supernatural powers (1 Thessalonians 2:9; Revelation 13:14-15) and the most sophisticated surveillance and tracking technology at their disposal, not to mention most of the masses serving as their informants—even close relatives ratting on one another (cf. Luke 12:53). And, most important, Scripture states clearly that Antichrist will be given complete power and authority over all the people of the world, in-cluding the "saints" (the Christians), during the last half of the Fi-nal Seven Years (Revelation 13:7).

So, will anyone survive the Great Tribulation? Yes, there will be some, but very few (true) Christians. The Bible states that those of the nation of Israel who are saved but have not yet recognized that Jesus is the Messiah (cf. Romans 11:26) will flee from the wrath of the dragon (Satan) into the *"wilderness"* of the world and be supernaturally sustained and protected there during the last half of the seven years (Revelation 12:6, 14). The prophet Zechariah also foretold that on *"the day of the Lord,"* when all the nations are gath-ered against Jerusalem, and the Lord, in person, does battle against those nations (apparently Armageddon), the Lord's people in Jeru-salem will flee out of the city to the east. These are apparently also Jews who look forward in faith to the coming Messiah but have not yet recognized that He is Jesus, not Christians, because these verses also speak of the Lord returning with "all the saints" (redeemed, glorified Christians) at that time (Zechariah 14:1-5; Revelation 19:8, 14). There will also be some unredeemed Gentiles among the nations who will not perish during the Great Tribulation and the Day of the Lord (because they will not take the mark of the beast nor come up against Jerusalem at the battle of Armageddon). These Gentiles, whose lives are spared by the merciful providence of the Lord, will be brought physically, with the saved of Israel, into the millennial Kingdom of God. And their descendants will make up the Gentile *"nations"* (Hebrew: *goyim*) who will go up to Jerusalem every year during the Millennium to celebrate the Feast of Tabernacles. (Zechariah 14:16; Revelation 14:9-10; 20:8)

So, the only ones who the Bible indicates will survive the Final Seven Years and be brought into His millennial Kingdom in their physical bodies are those who He will personally protect and sustain during that terrible time. Those who arrogantly think they can survive by relying on their own wits and resources are as deluded as the pretribulation rapture adherents, and they will just as surely perish during the Final Seven Years.

The Dominionist Apostasy

In over-reaction to the above trends, the rise of pseudo-spiritual, worldly, politically correct "super" churches has occurred. Espousing a dominionist, Kingdom-now doctrine with over-emphases on positive thinking, spiritual gifts, signs, wonders and miracles, the smooth-talking, charismatic leaders of these congregations, promising professional, social and personal success—health, wealth, and prosperity—are attracting adherents faster than any other religious movement or organization in America—resulting in numerous "mega-churches" with many thousands of members.

But, an honest study and interpretation of Scripture reveals that this trend, with its denial of the coming Great Tribulation, the Wrath of God, and even the future millennial Kingdom of God, is totally contrary to the teachings and life-styles of Jesus and His disciples, and actually plays into the evil hands of the coming world ruler—Antichrist. Jesus clearly stated, "My kingdom is **not** of this world." Then, He clarified that His kingdom is not of this (present) world by stating that if it was His followers would fight for it

(John 18:36). And He warned His disciples that they would, in fact, **not** be socially accepted, financially prosperous, or emotionally or physically comfortable in this present world, but that they would, like Him and the true, faithful people of God before Him, be despised, betrayed, persecuted, impoverished and killed (Matthew 10:25-28; 24:9-10; Hebrews 11:36-38).

Jesus also warned His disciples that charlatans (false prophets, messiahs, apostles, teachers, and ministers) would come, in a spirit of covetousness, exercising supernatural powers and deceiving many (Mark 13:22 and cf. 1 Corinthians 11:13, 15; 2 Peter 2:1). And this false, materialistic, worldly form of Christianity will set the stage for the ultimate imposter who will deceive, with his supernatural powers, the whole world into following and worshiping him (2 Thessalonians 2:9-10; Revelation 13:3, 8).

And, sure enough, Jesus' prophecies are being exactly fulfilled. All of His twelve apostles suffered persecution and eleven of them died as martyrs. And down through the centuries, many millions of true followers of Jesus have suffered and died at the hands of both infidels and false (anti-) Christians (e.g., the Inquisitions). Today, although it is not (yet) apparent in "Christian" America, more Christians are being martyred, especially in Communist and Islamist nations, than at any point of time in history. In fact, statistical studies indicate that as many as two-thirds of all Christian martyrs in history died during the twentieth century.[3]   And, as has been thoroughly explained in this book, current events in the light of Bible prophecy indicate that the holocaust is coming soon to the U.S.A. Yet, the "positive confession," Kingdom Now preachers, blinded by their own arrogance, continue to insipidly misapply the promises of the spiritual and physical benefits of the coming Kingdom of Heaven (cf. Luke 6:38: 18:29, 30) to this present, corrupt, rapidly-deteriorating world, when Scripture clearly tells us that the Kingdom of God on Earth will be fully established only when the King of Kings returns **in person** to reclaim His creation from the one who usurped it from Him in the beginning (Acts 3:21; Revelation 19:11-20:6).

How should we then live?

Telling Christians that they will be raptured before the "tribulation" begins is as helpful as telling the passengers on the Titanic to relax and not worry because, at any moment, a giant blimp would pass over and take them all away before the ship sank. Telling Christians to store up provisions and protection so they can survive the coming holocaust is as effective as telling the passengers on the Titanic to grab food and guns, then to find spots on the ship where they can hole up and feed and protect themselves until the danger passes. Telling Christians that they are children of the King, so they should take dominion over their own lives, their country and this world, is like telling the passengers on the Titanic to take control of that ship in the name of Jesus and trust Him to keep it afloat while they continued enjoying the pleasures of their well-deserved, luxurious cruise. Hopefully, by now, you can see the ridiculousness of American "Christianity" in the face of the rapidly approaching "perfect storm" of Satan's fury and the Lord's wrath being poured out on those who entertain such vain and conceited fantasies.

After Jesus, in no uncertain terms, told His disciples what was coming on this world, until they saw Him coming in the clouds with the overwhelming sound of a great trumpet and a flash of brilliant light from horizon to horizon (there will be no mistaking him for the false messiah) (Matthew 24:27-30), He did not tell them to get on with life as usual, waiting patiently and not worrying because He would return and whisk them away before the really bad stuff starts; nor did He tell them to store up provisions, to arm themselves to the teeth, and to go into hiding so that they could survive the coming "great tribulation" (Matthew 24:21); nor did He tell them that they were (in the flesh, on this earth) "more than conquerors" (Romans 8:29) and "no [physical] weapon formed against [them would] prosper" (Isaiah 54:7) (favorite misapplied Scriptures of the dominionist preachers).

What did the Lord tell His disciples (including us)? He told us that His kingdom is **NOT** of this world (John 18:36). Then, Jesus clarified that declaration by stating that the earth-dwellers couldn't go where He was going (John 8:21). He gave another clue as to where He was going by stating,

In My Father's house are many mansions; if it were not so, I would have told you. I go to prepare a place for you. And if I go and prepare a place for you, I will come again and receive you to Myself; that where I am, there you may be also. (John 14:2-3)

Then, finally, God's Word states that the believers' true, ultimate home is in New Jerusalem (which will come down out of Heaven **after** the conclusion of the Final Seven Years) from which we will reign with the King of Kings for a thousand years, and in which we will dwell with Him forever (Revelation 20:6; 21:2-3).[4]

So, with what lies ahead of the redeemed people of God **following** the Final Seven Years in mind, does it not seem absurdly petty, self-centered, short-sighted and delusional for any to focus their attention on either escape from or survival or worldly success in this miserable (by comparison), rapidly deteriorating, "puff-of-smoke" life on earth? And that is the exact message of Jesus Christ to His disciples.

Jesus was constantly trying to get His listeners' minds off the things of this world and onto the World to Come. The Master's core message during His ministry on Earth was, "Repent, for the Kingdom of **Heaven** is at hand!" (Matthew 4:17) In fact, John the Baptist, the forerunner of Jesus, preached exactly the same message: "Repent, for the Kingdom of **Heaven** is at hand!" (Matthew 3:2) Yet, how often do we hear the positive-confession, Kingdom-now preachers of today preaching repentance in preparation for the coming Kingdom of Heaven? ... seldom, if ever. And Jesus told his disciples **not** to lay up their treasures on earth, but in Heaven (Matthew 6:19), and **not** to be concerned even about saving their lives, because if they lost their (physical) lives because of their faithfulness to Him, they would save their (eternal) lives (Luke 9:24). Does it really seem like our Savior was concerned about whether or not we survive the tribulations of this world? Did He tell His disciples to be concerned about surviving or prospering on this earth? No, He told them exactly the opposite: that He was sending them out like sheep among wolves, and that they would meet the same fate—suffering, persecution and martyrdom—as He did (Matthew 10:16-24). Then, after Jesus warned his disciples of the terrible times to come at *"the end of the age,"* did He tell them either to go into hiding or to fight and overcome the pagans or their oppressors and establish His kingdom on earth? No, He told them,

> *Do not fear those who kill the body but cannot kill the soul. But rather fear Him who is able to destroy both soul and body in hell,"* and, *"If My kingdom were of this world, My servants would fight, so that I should not be delivered to the Jews; but now My kingdom is not from here.* (Matthew 10:28; John 18:36)

Or, did Jesus tell his disciples to keep living their lives as usual—working, playing, taking vacations, saving up for retirement, and so forth—patiently waiting for His deliverance from whatever trials and tribulations might be coming? No, He told them that their lives must change radically if they wanted to be His disciples—that they needed to dedicate **everything**, no matter what it cost them (time, money, and so forth), to spreading the Gospel (Good News) of the Kingdom. He told them that they must always be alert, watching and waiting for His return, and to get to work going to the whole world spreading the same Good News of the coming Kingdom of Heaven that He had given them. (Luke 9:23; 12:33; Matthew 24:44-46; Mark 16:15).

So again, **how dare** any so-called Christian minister, teacher, "apostle," or "prophet" contradict and undermine the clear teachings and examples of Jesus and the writers of the New Testament by telling us that Christians will not be affected by the terrible events of the Final Seven Years because we will be raptured out of here before they begin; or that, if we will just gather guns and ammunition, store up provisions and go into hiding, the Lord will protect us and we will survive that time; or that the (human) "army of the Lord" is going to fight and overcome the anti-Christ and his evil forces before the King of Kings returns with the armies of Heaven to do that (Revelation 19:11-16); or, most deceptive of all, that there will be no future Final Seven Years because the Church is going to establish the Kingdom of Heaven on earth through the supernatural power of Christ that is already in it. (That is the *"strong delusion,"* the *"lie,"* that the Lord will allow those who choose to follow the false messiah rather than the true Messiah to believe—2 Thessalonians 2:11).

And again, it is not those who escape or survive the tribulations of this life or achieve dominion over the earth who will enter the (eternal) Kingdom of Heaven. It is those who *"endure to the end,"* maintaining a faithful witness to the Lord, who will be saved (Matthew 24:13). Not one of the writers of the New Testament spoke of escaping from, hiding from, or fighting those who persecuted them, or of being exempt from trials, tribulations and suffering. In fact, the apostle Paul said that he rejoiced in the sufferings that were involved in his ministry to the Christians (Colossians 1:24). And Paul considered the patience and faith of the believers when they endured persecutions and tribulations for the sake of the Kingdom of God a glorious thing and evidence of their worthiness to inherit the Kingdom (cf. 2 Thessalonians 1:4-5).

So, we must beware of those who attempt to steal our inheritance in the wonderful World to Come **following** the Final Seven Years by deceiving us into thinking the Church will not even enter that time of testing and tribulation, or into thinking that the Church will be able to hide from and not be affected by it, or into thinking that time will not even come, because it will be the Church who will establish the Kingdom of God on Earth **before** Christ returns in person to rule over it.

The Church's true mission on Earth is to keep the light of the Good News of the coming Kingdom of Heaven shining as brightly as we can—to the death, if necessary—no matter who or what tries to extinguish it. Then, when the King of Kings does come, with the armies of Heaven, to vanquish His foes and establish His millennial Kingdom on Earth, He will consider those of us who have faithfully kept the commission He gave us to the end worthy to take our places as royalty in His Kingdom (Revelation 19:11-20:6).

To get a little preview of how incomparably more wonderful dwelling with the Lord in His Kingdom will be, when it is established in its fullness on Earth, than residing in any kingdom or "paradise" in this present world, read the next chapter—"In The End, there is GOOD NEWS!"

Chapter 10

In The End, there is GOOD NEWS!

"Eye has not seen, nor ear heard, nor have entered into the heart of man the things which God has prepared for those who love Him."
(1 Corinthians 2:9)

So far, much of the content that has been shared in this book has been pretty negative, hasn't it?—mankind wallowing in sin, phony "Christianity," the annihilation of America-Babylon, horrible times to come on the whole world. But, we have to understand what is really happening in the world before we can fully appreciate what I am going to share with you now. And I am really glad that you have come to this page, because now I get to tell you the end of the story. And it is fantastic!—far beyond what you or I have ever imagined. It is even more wonderful than any fantasy-world movie we have ever seen, book we have ever read, or story we have ever heard or imagined, because, according God's *"sure word of prophecy"* (2 Peter 1:19), the *Bible*, it is absolutely true!

In The Beginning

As I trust is clear by now, to fully understand the present and the future, we must first understand the past. So, let us go back to the beginning—to God's original plan for his creation, particularly man (the *Bible's* generic term for human beings).

In the beginning (of creation) God created the world (the whole cosmos—universe), all that is in it, and man in His own image (Genesis 1:27). Now, what do you think that means—created in the image of God? How does that make man different from the rest of God's creation—plants, animals, and inanimate matter? The *Bible* gives us some clues. It states, *"God is spirit"* (John 4:24). It also states, *"God is love"* (1 John 4:8). And Jesus said that *"God is good"* (Mark 10:18). So, man was created a good, loving, spiritual being, in the image of God. "Well, how does that make man any different from my pet dog—a good, loving, spirited animal?" someone might ask. The difference is that, in the core of his being—his spirit—man was created to commune with and, indeed, to be united with the Spirit of God forever. The *Bible* says that, "*He who is united with the Lord is one spirit with Him.*" (1 Corinthians 6:17) One spirit with God—that's an amazing reality to try to comprehend, isn't it? But, that's the way it was in the Garden of Eden: Adam and Eve walked with God and talked with God, in perfect spiritual union with Him. But, they blew it by sinning against God and thus separating themselves from God's life-giving Spirit, bringing immediate spiritual death and eventual physical death on themselves and physical death on every other living thing (cf. Genesis 3:22). Death is simply separation from God, who is the source of all life. So, although our physical bodies die and decay (cease to exist), our souls (including our spirits) will continue to exist "forever" (either united with God in eternal life, or separate from Him in "eternal" death), after the rest of creation, including the plants and animals of this present world (which are not spiritual beings), have ceased to exist altogether (cf. Revelation 20:11; 21:1). Also, the goodness and love of God, which, in union with Him, man was created to manifest, are drastically and categorically different from the "goodness" and "love" of animals. Pet dogs, for example, just act out of instinct in natural affection for and loyalty to their owners. But, we probably won't see a dog voluntarily giving its life to save someone who has abused it or someone it perceives as a threat or an enemy, will we? Yet, isn't that what Jesus did? Isn't that what we would do if we were united with God in His love? Wouldn't we, if we had God's special goodness and unselfish love in our hearts, be kind to someone we saw in need and hurting, even if they had been hateful and cruel to us? See the difference between the totally unselfish God-kind of love and the "love" and "goodness" of those who are not one with God, which are no different from the "goodness" and the natural affection of animals?

So, in the beginning, God created man in His own image—categorically different from and transcending the rest of His creation. He also placed man in a position of benevolent dominion over His creation. Man was given the job of naming all the animals and taking care of the creation (cf. Genesis 1:28)! Now imagine that, if you can: what knowledge! what intelligence! what wisdom! what skill! what power! man must have had to be assigned a perfect, beautiful, wonderful creation to care for! What a fantastic life!

But, tragically, Adam and Eve believed the Lie of the Devil, who told them, "*You shall be as gods*" (Genesis 3:6). In other words, Satan was implying that Adam and Eve could do on their own, apart from God's Spirit in union with theirs, as "gods" themselves, the superhuman job that God had given them to do. They also believed that they could get away with doing as they pleased (eat the forbidden fruit), regardless of what God had said. But what a terrible mistake, because it allowed Satan to get a foothold in God's creation and immediately take Adam's place as the prince (ruler) of this World (John 12:31)! And it has been downhill for all of God's creation, including man, since that time; the whole creation has been subject to futility, corruption, and decay (cf. Ecclesiates 2:17); which will continue until God destroys the present deteriorating world and its inhabitants who oppose Him. And, so far, that's what most of this book has been about.

But, that's not the end of the story; there's incredible Good News! God's original plan for man has not changed, except that it is even more fantastic now than it was in the beginning! Grasp, if you can, what God's Word tells us:

Paradise Restored!

Acts 3:19-21 states that God will send Jesus Christ when it comes time (after the seven years of tribulation and the Wrath of God) to restore all things to their Edenic state. The period of time when conditions on Earth will again be wonderful beyond our comprehension was foretold numerous times by Old Testament prophets (Isaiah 65, Jeremiah 23, Joel 2, et al.). It will begin when the Lord returns with the armies of Heaven to destroy the armies of Antichrist (Revelation 19:11-21). He will then establish His kingdom on the renewed Earth, and will rule over the nations of people who are on Earth at that time (Revelation 19:15), maintaining perfect peace as the "last Adam" (1 Corinthians 15:45) during His millennial reign (Revelation 20).

But, that's just the beginning of the Good News! All those who belong to the Lord Jesus—who have trusted Him as their Savior and God and are united in spirit with Him—will get to reign with Him, not just on Earth, but over His entire earthly and heavenly creation, including the angels! The Lord Jesus said, speaking of His faithful Followers,

> *To him who wins the victory and does what I want until the goal is reached, I will give him authority over the nations . . . just as I have received authority from my Father. I will also give him the morning star"* (meaning Himself—cf. Revelation 22:16). (Revelation 2:26-27)

And the apostle Paul asked his fellow Believers, *"Don't you know that we are to judge angels?"* (1 Corinthians 6:3) To me, that sounds like we Believers in the Lord Jesus the Messiah are going to be totally indwelled by Him, one with Him, having exactly the same power and authority He has to reign with Him, in Him, and He in us over His creation—with even more power and authority than the first Adam had (over just the Earth) in the beginning. Try to wrap your mind around that!

To more fully appreciate how wonderful it will be to be a child of God in His Millennial Kingdom, read the following astonishing statement from His Word (paraphrased):

> *It was in keeping with His pleasure and purpose, for His own praise and glory, that God determined before the creation of the universe that through His Son, Jesus Christ, we would be His spiritual children. In Christ, God our Father chose us in love in advance to be spiritually pure, without defect, in His presence. In union with Christ through His sacrifice on the cross, we are set free—our sins are forgiven. And in union with Him, commensurate with His grace which the Lord has lavished on us, we were given an inheritance: the Lord has blessed us with every spiritual blessing in Heaven. His ultimate plan, which was a secret until it was revealed by and in Christ, is to place everything in Heaven and on Earth under Christ's headship. And we, the children of God, are to reign with our Lord and Christ over all creation for a thousand years! This is the Lord's will, purpose, and pleasure for our lives.* (Ephesians 1:3-14; Revelation 20:4)

So, there it is, my friend—God's ultimate purpose for your life. Incomprehensibly wonderful, isn't it? Please, please, please, don't miss out by believing Satan's Lie (*"You shall be as gods."*), by putting any stock in the things of this world, by following a false messiah, or by denying your Lord and Savior before His return. Stay faithful until The End and you will receive your awesome, glorious, "eternal" inheritance in The World to Come! I hope to see you there.

For complete documentation or Scriptural support for
anything you have read in this book, visit
RevelationUnderstoodCommentary.com
or contact Watchman Bob at watchmanbob@gmail.com.

Appendices

Appendix 1

Scriptural Evidence that America is Modern Babylon the Great

This watchman realizes that probably the most difficult part of this book for most American Christians to swallow is the assertion that The United States of America is prophesied modern Babylon the Great. However, there are over 200 verses of Scripture and over 60 indicators in the Bible of who modern Babylon the Great is. And, when all those verses of Scripture and all those indicators are taken into consideration, it is crystal clear that no other nation than the U.S.A., with its *"great city"* New York City, especially after it is taken over by the Middle Eastern Islamists, could possibly fit the description. As partial evidence of this fact, please read the following commentary on Revelation 17 and 18 and ask yourself honestly, "Which other modern city-state/empire could possibly be Babylon the Great?" Also, remember that Jonathan Cahn's *The Harbinger* and James Fitzgerald's *The 9/11 Prophecy* state that the World Trade Center towers were destroyed in the same way that Babylon the Great is prophesied to be destroyed in these two chapters, and James Fitzgerald asserts that the 9/11 destruction was a foreshadowing of the destruction of the entire nation (although, in overlooking the Tenth Harbinger, he does not understand the full extent of that destruction).

Revelation Chapters 17 and 18 are parenthetical chapters inserted to give more details about the destruction of modern, prophetic Babylon—the kingdom of Satan on Earth (cf. Isaiah 14:4)—immediately before and during the Final Seven Years of world history. Chapter 17 focuses on spiritual, religious Babylon and Chapter 18 focuses on material, secular Babylon. But, as we will clearly see, the two are inextricably intertwined in one, great, modern city-state (nation). In the original Greek, there were not two separate chapters describing Babylon; the description was of two different aspects of the same city-state/nation/empire. And understanding the identity and destiny of *"Babylon the Great"* is a major key to un-

169

derstanding the sequence of events of the Revelation. But Chapters 17 and 18 are highly symbolic—in the form of a riddle. Let us see if we, by the enlightenment of the Holy Spirit, can solve the riddle.

Chapter 17—Spiritual, Religious Babylon

17:1-5   *Then* (a) *one of the seven angels who had the seven bowls came and talked with me, saying to me, "Come, I will show you the judgment of* (b) *the great harlot* (c) *who sits on many waters,* (d) *with whom the kings of the earth committed fornication, and the inhabitants of the earth were made drunk with the wine of her fornication." So he carried me away in the Spirit into* (e) *the wilderness. And I saw a woman* (f) *sitting on a scarlet beast which was full of names of blasphemy, having seven heads and ten horns. The woman was* (g) *arrayed in purple and scarlet, and adorned with gold and precious stones and pearls, having in her hand a golden cup full of abominations and the filthiness of her fornication. And on her forehead a name was written:* (h) *MYS-TERY, BABYLON THE GREAT, THE MOTHER OF HAR-LOTS AND OF THE ABOMINATIONS OF THE EARTH.*

a.   This angel is probably the seventh, as it was during the pouring out of his bowl that *"Babylon was remembered before God, to give her the cup of the wine of the fierceness of His wrath"* (16:19).   In this chapter and in Chapter 18, he is giving John more details about the identity, characteristics, and destiny of modern, prophetic Babylon.

b.   In both Chapters 17 and 18 (18:3), Babylon is described as a harlot—one who gives herself to others, not because she loves them or is interested in their welfare, but to gain their favors, which ultimately results in their destruction as well as hers.   In this chapter the emphasis is on her spiritual/religious harlotry; in Chapter 18 the emphasis is on her political/commercial harlotry.

c.   She sits on (dominates and controls) the earth dwellers (cf. verse 15).

d.   Her seductive enticements entangle all classes of earth dwellers, nobility as well as the masses.

e.   The *"wilderness"* in this verse is a symbol of the unsaved world.

f. The harlot is supported by and empowered by Satan. She is his spiritual kingdom on earth (cf. Isaiah 14:4, 12; Revelation 12:3).

g. Her attractions—riches, beauty, and intoxicating drink—appeal to the flesh, not to the spirit.

h. And, she *is* Babylon. The fact that, in this chapter, her identification is a mystery—not obvious—and her real power over the earth dwellers is spiritual—not physical—indicates that this is Babylonian spirituality or religion. The religion of ancient Babylon was centered on sex rites involving thousands of temple prostitutes. It was the religious duty of every Babylonian woman to serve as a temple prostitute at least once in her life. Ishtar was called "the mother of [temple] prostitutes." When Israel was worshiping pagan gods, she was referred to as a harlot (e.g., Hosea 4:15). Some say that the whore of Revelation 17 is the apostate Christian Church or the Roman Catholic Church, but she is much more than that. Babylonian religion was very eclectic, consolidating the worship of many gods, not only Babylonian but of the surrounding nations. The eclectic religion of modern, prophetic Babylon will be centered in Babylon, the city-state/nation/empire, but it will ultimately consolidate all the religions of the world into a global religion led by the False Prophet (cf. 13:11-15; 19:20). It may resemble Christianity because it will consist of the worship of the false Christ and his "father," Satan (13:4), but it will also resemble Islam and other religions of the world which also anticipate a coming god-man or messiah.

17:6-11 *I saw* (a) *the woman, drunk with the blood of the saints and with the blood of the martyrs of Jesus. And when I saw her,* (b) *I marveled with great amazement. But* (c) *the angel said to me, "Why did you marvel? I will tell you the mystery of the woman and of the beast that carries her, which has the seven heads and the ten horns. The beast that you saw was, and is not, and will ascend out of the bottomless pit and go to perdition. And* (d) *those who dwell on the earth will marvel, whose names are not written in the Book of Life from the foundation of the world, when they see the beast that was, and is not, and yet is. Here is the mind which has wisdom:* (e) *The seven heads are seven mountains on which the woman sits. There are also* (f) *seven kings. Five have fallen, one is, and the other has not yet come.* (g) *And when he comes, he must continue a short time.* (h) *And the beast that was, and is not, is himself also the eighth, and is of the seven, and is going to perdition.*

a.   The religion of Babylon, which is energized and controlled by the spirit of the devil, is responsible for the death of the saints and martyrs of Jesus.

b.   John is amazed by the incongruity of the religion of Babylon being responsible for the death of members of the true Community of believers in Jesus.

c.   The angel explains that the religious spirit of Babylon gets her power from Satan and his incarnation, Antichrist. Notice that both Satan and Antichrist have seven heads and ten horns, but here they are not distinguished by the crowns being on their heads or their horns as they are in 12:3 and 13:1. So, the scarlet beast, Satan, and the beast that *"was, and is not, and will ascend out of the bottomless pit and go to perdition,"* Antichrist, are spiritually one, just as God the Father and God the Son are One.

d.   The earth dwellers marvel at Antichrist because of his *"head"* (kingdom) that was destroyed but then revived and the signs and wonders performed in his name (cf. 13:3, 13).

e.   Some have reasoned, because of her garments of purple and red (the colors of the Roman Catholic Church) and the seven *"mountains"* (Rome is the "city of seven hills"), that the woman, Babylon, is the Roman Catholic Church or Rome. However, the Greek word (*oros*) translated *"mountains"* here really means, just as it is translated, *"mountains"* or large land masses, not "hills." The Greek word (*buonos*) for "hills" (actually a Latin word, borrowed by the Greeks, which commonly referred to Rome) is not used here. (See Luke 3:5 where both terms are used.) In Scripture, mountains also symbolize large areas of political power and dominion. So, the harlot Babylon holds religious/spiritual sway over large realms of the earth—perhaps continents or large administrative areas. It would seem that Rome and its dominating religion, the Roman Catholic Church, is a prototype of modern Babylon, but Rome does not come close in her religious influence (or, as in Chapter 18, in political or economic influence) to the total global dominance of the eclectic, pseudo-messianic, Babylonian religion described in this chapter.

f.   The seven kings that manifest the spirit of Satan and Antichrist on Earth apparently represent rulers of the seven empires that ruled over and persecuted God's people Israel and the rulers that will persecute God's People the Christians during the Great Tribulation period of the Final Seven Years. Those seven kingdoms or empires were: Egypt, Assyria, Babylonia, Medo-Persia, and Greece (the five that "*have fallen*"), Rome (the one that "*is*" at the time Revelation was written), and modern, prophetic Babylon (the one that "*has not yet come*"). Modern religious and secular Babylon will be annihilated by fire, as we will see in 17:16 and 18:8, but will then be replaced by the global kingdom of Antichrist (17:17), the Revived Roman/Ottoman Empire (cf. Daniel 7:7, 23).[1]

g.   The seventh "king"—the ruler or president of modern Babylon— will rule a short time.

h.   Antichrist, the ultimate counterfeit of the true Messiah, "*is of the seven*" previous kings (embodies the spirit of all seven) and is the eighth and final worldly king. An intriguing possible interpretation of this description, when it is combined with the prophecy of 13:3 and the rather curious prophecy that the seventh king will rule a short time, is that, before it is destroyed by fire, the kingdom over which he rules (modern religious and secular Babylon) will be destroyed by war, but will then be "miraculously" revived, and he will become the eighth king after whom the whole world will follow in wonder and awe.

17:12-15 (a) *The ten horns which you saw are ten kings who have received no kingdom as yet, but they receive authority for one hour as kings with the beast. These are of one mind, and they will give their power and authority to the beast.* (b) *These will make war with the Lamb, and the Lamb will overcome them, for He is Lord of lords and King of kings; and those who are with Him are called, chosen, and faithful."* Then he said to me, (c) *"The waters which you saw, where the harlot sits, are peoples, multitudes, nations, and tongues."*

a.   After Antichrist takes over at the midpoint of the Final Seven Years, for the short time (signified by "*one hour*") that he is in control, the world will be ruled by ten "*kings*" under him, who yield their authority and power to rule to him. Verses 3, 7 and 9 indicate that Earth will be divided up into seven "kingdoms" or administrative areas *("heads"* or *"mountains")* that will be ruled by ten *"kings"* under the *"beast"* or Antichrist. This is exactly the same scenario prophesied by Daniel, except that he provides the additional detail that three of the ten kings will be "subdued" (brought down) by the anti-Christ (Daniel 7:24).

b. This is a reference to 16:14-16 and 19:11-21, when the King of Kings and Lord of Lords returns with the armies of Heaven at "Armageddon" to defeat and destroy *"the kings of the earth and of the whole world . . . who are gathered . . . to the battle of that great day of God Almighty."*

c. The waters where Babylon sits (17:1) are explained as *"peoples* (Greek: *laos*—tribes or nations), *multitudes, nations* (Greek: *ethnos*—ethnic groups), *and tongues"* (people who speak various languages)—in other words, all the earth dwellers of the world.

17:16-18 (a) *"And the ten horns which you saw on the beast, these will hate the harlot, make her desolate and naked, eat her flesh and burn her with fire.* (b) *For God has put it into their hearts to fulfill His purpose, to be of one mind, and to give their kingdom to the beast, until the words of God are fulfilled.* (c) *And the woman whom you saw is that great city which reigns over the kings of the earth."* (d)

a. Verse 16 may be one of the most poorly translated and misleading verses in the *Bible.* Virtually every translation, following the lead of the KJV, states that the ten kings are the ones who burn Babylon. But the structure of the Greek is somewhat ambiguous. When correctly translated, it indicates that *"fire"* is the subject of the sentence rather than the ten kings, who may be passive. In other words, it is the fire that does the burning of Babylon, not the ten kings, who may be just passive onlookers.[2] That they "hate" the harlot does not necessarily mean that they are involved in her destruction. To this commentator, that makes more sense than the way this verse is commonly translated, because it is difficult to conceptualize how the ten kings, who will not even receive their kingdoms until *after* Babylon is destroyed, could destroy in *"one hour"* (cf. 18:10, 17, 19) the most powerful, world-dominating kingdom (nation or empire) in the history of the world. Also, Old Testament prophecy indicates that Babylon will be destroyed in the same way that

Sodom and Gomorrah were destroyed—by fire from Heaven—after which no human will dwell there, only demons and unclean spirits, which seems to fit the scenario of Chapters 17 and 18 (cf. Jeremiah 50:32, 39, 40; 51:25, 30, 58; Revelation 18:2, 8). Most *Bible* expositors, because of the confusion caused by the mistranslation of this verse, state that the harlot of Chapter 17 (religious Babylon) is destroyed at a different point in time than is secular Babylon of Chapter 18. But that is a false distinction and a forced interpretation that over-allegorizes and mutilates the meaning of the text. It is impossible to conceive how spiritual, religious Babylon could be separated from the secular state and destroyed without destroying the government with whom she is inextricably intertwined and supports (cf. 13:11-18).

b. And here is another indication that the annihilation of all natural life in Babylon will be caused by the Lord rather than by her human enemies: The reason for the burning of Babylon is because God has put it in the hearts of the ten kings to give their kingdom (singular), which they have not yet received (verse 12), to Antichrist. The ten kings may indeed hate Babylon because she, under her present ruler (the seventh king) and system of government, is dominating the world, making it impossible for them to receive and consolidate their domains into the global kingdom of Antichrist. But they are powerless to do anything about it until the Lord intervenes and destroys her by fire.

c. So, the woman who rides the beast is *"that great city"* which reigns over the kings of the earth. This *"great city"* is Babylon, because the *"great city"* Jerusalem (11:8) has never reigned over the kings of the earth. Notice that here she is not just the harlot—religious, spiritual Babylon—but a physical place—a *"city"*—the same Babylon as in Chapter 18.

d. Again, notice that the ten kings and Antichrist will not receive their kingdom until **after** all natural life in Babylon is destroyed by fire. That means that, although Babylon is the spiritual "headquarters" of Satan, she is not the ultimate global kingdom ruled by Antichrist—the "Revived Roman Empire." It also means that Babylon must be burned **before** the midpoint of the Final Seven Years because that is when Antichrist takes over as world ruler. But that presents a problem because the details of Babylon's destruction are placed here, in Chapter 17, and in 18, just before the celebration of her destruction in Chapter 19, which appears to be at the end of the seven years, just before the Lord returns with the armies of Heaven to defeat and destroy His enemies at "Armageddon." However, as will be seen as we continue through Chapter 18, that apparent dilemma is easily and clearly resolved. Remember that the details of Chapters 17 and 18 are parenthetical—not in strict chronological sequence.

Chapter 18—Material, Secular Babylon

18:1-3 (a) *After these things I saw another angel coming down from heaven, having great authority, and the earth was illuminated with his glory. And he cried mightily with a loud voice, saying,* (b) *"Babylon the great is fallen, is fallen, and has become* (c) *a dwelling place of demons, a prison for every foul spirit, and a cage for every unclean and hated bird! For* (d) *all the nations have drunk of the wine of the wrath of her fornication, the kings of the earth have committed fornication with her, and the merchants of the earth have become rich through the abundance of her luxury."*

a. *"After these things I saw"* indicates a change in perspective, but not in time. As we will clearly see, the Babylon of Chapter 18 is exactly the same as the Babylon of Chapter 17. The only difference is that Chapter 18 focuses on the material, secular aspect of Babylon whereas Chapter 17 focuses on the spiritual, religious aspect of Babylon. But, in actuality, although Babylonian spirituality is universal, religious and secular Babylon cannot be separated; they are indissolubly married, just as was religion and state in ancient Babylon. In fact, modern physical Babylon (the city-state/nation/empire) is the main purveyor of Babylonian spirituality/religion throughout the world.

b. Exactly the same name, *"Babylon the Great,"* is used here as in 17:5. Chapter 18 just takes up where Chapter 17 left off, with the fall (burning) of *"that great city,"* Babylon the Great.

c. This is total annihilation of all natural life![3] After Babylon is destroyed by fire (her first destruction), resulting in desolate desert conditions, no human can dwell there, only demons and evil spirits (cf. the commentary on 17:16; also Isaiah 13:19-21).

After she is burned, Babylon is uninhabited by natural living things, but is still the kingdom and base of operations, so to speak, of Satan and his evil spiritual horde.

d. As in Chapter 17, Babylon is the whore of Earth, but Chapter 18 focuses on her political whoredom with the rulers of the earth and her material whoredom with the merchants of the earth.

18:4-8 *And I heard* (a) *another voice from heaven saying,* (b) *"Come out of her, my people, lest you share in her sins, and lest you receive of her plagues. For her sins have reached to heaven, and (c) God has remembered her iniquities. (d) Render to her just as she rendered to you, and repay her double according to her works; in the cup which she has mixed, mix double for her. In the measure that (e) she glorified herself and lived luxuriously, in the same measure give her torment and sorrow; for she says in her heart, (f) `I sit as queen, and am no widow, and will not see sorrow.' Therefore her plagues (g) will come in one day—death and mourning and famine. And she will be utterly burned with fire, for (h) strong is the Lord God who judges her."*

a. The voice of the Lord
b. As the Revelation is written to both the Jews and to the Followers of Jesus, *"come out of her"* would seem to apply in a literal sense to God's physical People the Jews who have not yet accepted Jesus as their Redeemer and who remain on the earth throughout the Final Seven Years and into the Millennium, and in a spiritual sense to His People the Community of Believers in Jesus who are taken to Heaven at the sounding of the *"Last Trump"* (1 Corinthians 15:52) on Yom Teruah at the end of the seven years, because the believers in Jesus are promised that,as long as they remain faithful, they will not have to endure the *"last plagues"*—the plagues of the Wrath of God (cf. 1 Thessalonians 5:9; Revelation 15:1) or be subjected to His judgment (cf. John 5:24). But those *"last plagues,"* as well as the preceding *"Great Tribulation"* (Matthew 24:21; Revelation 7:14)—the wrath of Satan (12:12)—will the time of *"Jacob's trouble"* (Jeremiah 30:7) for those of God's People who have not yet recognized that Jesus is their Messiah, separating the *"sheep"* from the *"goats"*—"true Israel" (cf. Romans 9:6) from those who do not really believe in God or in the coming Messiah Jesus. For

proof that this command is directed to both God's Old Testament people the Jews and His New Testament people the Christians, see the parallel commands in Jeremiah 50:8; 51:6, 45 and 2 Corinthians 6:17.

c. Cf. 16:19

d. Babylon will reap what she has sowed—double: two separate judgments—the judgment by fire (destroying all natural life) and total physical annihilation (destroying Satan's spiritual base of operations—verse 21).

e. She sees herself as a queen of those nations to whom she is illicitly married. A title of Ishtar, chief goddess of Babylon, was "Queen of Heaven."

f. She is a proud, wealthy, luxurious nation. She will be utterly destroyed by fire in a very short period of time, indicated by *"one day"* in this verse and by *"one hour"* in verses 10, 17 and 19.

g. Confirming that it is because of the judgment of the Lord and by His power, not by the power of the ten kings, that Babylon is destroyed.

18:9-17a [The prophecy of the voice from Heaven continues:] (a) *"The kings of the earth who committed fornication and lived luxuriously with her will weep and lament for her, when they see the smoke of her burning, standing at a distance for fear of her torment, saying, `Alas, alas, that great city Babylon, that mighty city! For in one hour your judgment has come.' And* (b) *the merchants of the earth will weep and mourn over her, for no one buys their merchandise anymore: merchandise of gold and silver, precious stones and pearls, fine linen and purple, silk and scarlet, every kind of citron wood, every kind of object of ivory, every kind of object of most precious wood, bronze, iron, and marble; and cinnamon and incense, fragrant oil and frankincense, wine and oil, fine flour and wheat, cattle and sheep, horses and chariots, and bodies and souls of men. The fruit that your soul longed for has gone from you, and all the things which are rich and splendid have gone from you, and you shall find them no more at all. The merchants of these things, who became rich by her, will stand at a distance for fear of her torment, weeping and wailing, and saying, `Alas, alas, that great city that was clothed in fine linen, purple, and scarlet, and adorned with gold and precious stones and pearls! (c) For in one hour such great riches came to nothing.'"*

a.   This confirms that Babylon is the political center of Earth: The kings of Earth weep and lament when their wealth is destroyed when Babylon is destroyed.   Apparently, all the nations of Earth are actually client-states of Babylon and their rulers are kept in luxurious power by Babylon.
b.   Babylon is also the commercial center of the world; she is the main importer of the world's commodities, making the merchants of the earth wealthy.
c.   But the source of their wealth is destroyed in *"one hour."*

18:17b-19   [The prophecy is fulfilled in John's vision:] (a) *Every shipmaster, all who travel by ship, sailors, and as many as trade on the sea, stood at a distance and cried out when they saw* (b) *the smoke of her burning, saying, "What is like this great city?" They threw dust on their heads and cried out, weeping and wailing, and saying, "Alas, alas, that great city, in which all who had ships on the sea became rich by her wealth! For in* (c) *one hour she is made desolate."*

a.   Babylon is a land of major seaports.
b.   The sailors see, from a distance, the smoke of Babylon burning. This confirms that Babylon's destruction by fire is a literal event.
c.   This is the third time in this chapter that *"one hour"* is mentioned. Apparently, the Lord is making a point: The destruction of Babylon occurs in literally one hour.

18:20-24   (a) *"Rejoice over her, O heaven, and you holy apostles and prophets, for God has avenged you on her!"* (b) *Then a mighty angel took up a stone like a great millstone and threw it into the sea, saying, "Thus with violence the great city Babylon shall be thrown down, and shall not be found anymore. The sound of harpists, musicians, flutists, and trumpeters shall not be heard in you anymore. No craftsman of any craft shall be found in you anymore, and the sound of a millstone shall not be heard in you anymore. The light of a lamp shall not shine in you anymore, and the voice of bridegroom and bride shall not be heard in you anymore. For your merchants were the great men of the earth, for (c) by your sorcery all the nations were deceived. And (d) in her was found the blood of prophets and saints, and of all who were slain on the earth."*

a. Let the celebration over the annihilation of all living things including the human inhabitants of Babylon begin!

b. But now, there is a second destruction! And the dilemma (cf. the commentary on 17:18) as to how Babylon can be destroyed both prior to the midpoint of the Final Seven Years and at the end of the seven years is solved: There are two destructions: (1) the destruction by fire of all natural life in Babylon prior to the midpoint of the seven years, which sets the stage for the ten kings and Antichrist to take over the world, and (2) the physical destruction of Babylon by a giant millstone-like object, sinking her beneath the waves of the sea, never to be found anymore (cf. Jeremiah 51: 42, 55, 64), here at the end of the seven years. This apparently also alludes to the fact that revived Babylon ("the Revived Roman Empire"), the global kingdom of Antichrist, of which the modern nation Babylon the Great is the precursor and prototype, is totally destroyed at the end of the Final Seven Years.

c. Satanic spiritual power, as in sorcery (witchcraft), is the reason for Babylon's success, as the headquarters of Satan's horde of evil spirit-beings, in dominating the world religiously, politically, and commercially, even after her destruction by fire. It is revealing that the Greek word translated *"sorcery"* in this verse is *pharmakeia*, from which the English word "pharmacy" is derived. The occult is heavily involved in drug use. Prescribed drugs, drugs in vaccinations, drugs in our food, and illegal drugs are perhaps the main means for opening the doors of our souls to evil Babylonian spiritual influences.

d. Of course, Babylon herself did not literally kill all the prophets, saints, and others murdered on Earth. But, figuratively speaking, as the "throne of Satan," the same spirit of the devil (specifically, Ishtar) who animates and energizes Babylon, even before and after her destruction by fire, has been responsible for their deaths throughout history.

Appendix 2

Be Saved from the Wrath of God

Most Bible expositors variously teach that Christians will be caught up ("raptured") to Heaven before the events of the Great Tribulation and the Day and the Wrath of the Lord commence, or that they will be supernaturally protected from those events, or that those events have already occurred in the past and the Church is, at the present time, establishing the Kingdom of Heaven on Earth. But, an honest exposition of the Biblical text reveals that none of those views is correct.

The Great Tribulation, the Day of the Lord and the Wrath of God are not synonymous terms. Many Bible expositors and teachers label the entire Final Seven Years as *"the* tribulation" and make no distinction between that period of time and its events and the Day (and the Wrath) of the Lord. But an honest examination of the text reveals that The Great Tribulation (cf. Matthew 24:21; Revelation 7:14) is totally different from the Day (and the Wrath) of the Lord. The Great Tribulation is the wrath of Satan (Revelation 12:12) being poured out on all who oppose him and begins at the midpoint of the Final Seven Years when his incarnation Antichrist declares himself to be *"god"* (2 Thessalonians 2:4; Revelation 13:5). However, the Day of the Lord occurs later, on the last day of the Final Seven Years, when the *"last plagues"* of the Wrath of the Lord are poured out on the followers of the anti-messiah (Revelation 6:15-17; 15:1).

Nowhere in Scripture are the Followers of Jesus (the "Church") promised exemption from any of the physical suffering, tribulations, persecutions and death that are the lot of all human beings as long as we are in our corrupt, human flesh and subject to sin. Our complete exemption from suffering will occur only when we are in our new, glorified bodies in the presence of our Redeemer in His millennial kingdom. Jesus Himself told his disciples that they would suffer persecution and tribulation (cf. Matthew 24:21; Mark 10:30). And the apostle Paul frequently spoke of his infirmities, reproaches, needs, persecutions, distresses and so forth (e.g., 2 Corinthians 12:10).

There are two extremes in interpreting what the Bible states about suffering. One is the "word of faith," "health, wealth and prosperity," "name it and claim it," "believe it and receive it" doctrine that no suffering in this life is necessary for the Believer whose faith is intact. The other is that true Believers in the Messiah will escape to Heaven in the Rapture before the real suffering of the Great Tribulation and the Wrath of the Lord begin. Both views are flawed, unscriptural and potentially tragic, resulting in the destruction of the faith of those who cling to either doctrine when they find themselves in the midst of the wrath of either Satan (the Great Tribulation) or the Lord (the Wrath of God).

So, let us look briefly at what it really means to be saved from the Wrath of God.

What is the Day of the Lord?

In the *Bible*, the Day of the Lord is a very prominent and important prophetic theme. The explicit term, *"Day of the Lord,"* occurs over 20 times in Scripture. It is used in both the Old Testament and the New Testament. It is described by eight Old Testament prophets, mentioned by three New Testament writers, and alluded to many other times as *"that day," "the Day of Christ,"* and by other terms. Here is the prophet Zephaniah's description of that Day:

The great Day the LORD is near, near and coming very quickly. Hear the sound of the Day of the LORD! When it's here, even a warrior will cry bitterly. That Day is a Day of fury, a Day of trouble and distress, a Day of waste and desolation, a Day of darkness and gloom, a Day of clouds and thick fog, a Day of the trumpet and battle-cry against the fortified cities and against the high towers [on the city walls].

I will bring such distress on people that they will grope their way like the blind, because they have sinned against the LORD. Their blood will be poured out like dust and their bowels like dung. Neither their silver nor their gold will be able to save them. On the Day of the LORD's fury, the whole land will be destroyed in the fire of His jealousy, for He will make an end, a horrible end, of all those living in the land. (Zephaniah 1:14-18)

As prophesied in the Revelation (6:12-14), the Day of the Lord will be announced by the most awesome catastrophes in world history, including cataclysmic worldwide natural and/or human-caused disasters. Then it will include the period of time of a few years during which the initial plagues of God's judgments announced by the seven trumpets is poured out on those who have rejected and rebelled against Him. Then, at the blast of the seventh and *"last trumpet"* on Yom Teruah (the "Feast of Trumpets") at the end of the Final Seven Years, the resurrection of the righteous will occur and Christ Jesus will return and *"catch away"* the redeemed of God to Heaven (Mark 13:26-27; 1 Corinthians 15:52; 1 Thessalonians 4:14-17). Next, while the marriage and wedding feast of the Lamb and His Bride are being celebrated in Heaven (Revelation 19:7-9), the *"last plagues"* of the judgments of God (cf. Revelation 11:18; 15:1) will be poured out on Earth (Revelation 16:1). Then, on Yom Kippur (the "Day of Atonement"), the newly-crowned King of Kings and Lord of Lords (the Messiah Jesus) will descend with the armies of Heaven (the glorified saints and angels) to destroy His enemies at the battle of "Armageddon," cast Antimessiah and the false prophet into the Lake of Fire, and cleanse the earth of all unregenerate earth dwellers (19:11-21). Then, after binding and imprisoning Satan, the Messiah will bring His People Israel out of the *"wilderness"* into which they have fled from the persecution of the anti-messiah and establish the glorious millennial Kingdom of Heaven on Earth (Isaiah 11:12; Zechariah 14:1-11; Revelation 12:6, 14). At this time, the heavens and earth will be renewed and New Jerusalem will descend from Heaven (cf. Isaiah 65:17, 18; Revelation 21:1) , the tribes of Israel will occupy the Land (Ezekiel 40-48), and the surrounding nations will be formed by Gentiles on whom the Lord had mercy and allowed to enter His millennial kingdom (Zechariah 14:16). Finally, the Day of the Lord will end with the Final Judgment when the redeemed of God will be ushered into eternity in His glorious presence and the damned (including Satan) will be cast into the Lake of Fire (Revelation 20:11-15).[1]

So basically, the Day of the Lord will begin with the biggest showdown in world history—a period of time (not a literal 24-hour day) during which the Lord will take back the wonderful, perfect Creation that Satan usurped from Him 6,000 years ago. The Lord will first set Satan up—giving his incarnation, Antichrist, a short time after proclaiming himself to be *"god"* to (in his deluded mind) establish his dominion on Earth. But then, through a series of ever-intensifying, supernatural disasters, culminating in the bowls of God's Wrath being poured out at the end of the seven years, Antichrist's global kingdom will be totally demolished.

But, the point is, we don't want to be on Earth during the time when the *"last plagues"* of God's Wrath are being poured out here! It is going to be a wonderful, glorious time from the perspective of those who are already in Heaven, as we celebrate with all the heavenly hosts the destruction of the Lord's enemies and the redemption of His Creation, but a horrible, horrible time, like the world has never before seen, for those still on Earth. The Remnant of God's physical people the Jews, who have not given in to the incredible deception or agonizing oppression of that time, and some God-fearing Gentiles, who have not taken the mark of the beast, will be supernaturally protected and saved, but all others who have been suckered or pressured into following Antimessiah as their (false) messiah will find themselves in unimaginably horrible, hopeless straits.

When will the Day of the Lord occur?

As with other future End-Times events, the timing and sequence of the Day the Lord is a matter of great debate among Bible scholars and prophecy teachers. A few things are clear in Scripture: (1) there will be a seven-year period of time in the near future—a time called in the *Bible* the *"Birth Pains of the Messiah"* or the *"Time of Jacob's Trouble"*—when the history of the world, as you and I have known it all our lives, will be brought to a terrifyingly tumultuous close, (2) the last half of that seven years, immediately following the midpoint, will be a time of *"great tribulation"*—a time when the wrath of Satan (Revelation 12:12) will be poured out on all who oppose him, especially believers in Jesus as the true Messiah who are on Earth at that time. God's people the Jews who are looking forward in faith to the coming Messiah but have not yet recognized that He is Jesus will be hidden and protected in the *"wilderness"* during the Great Tribulation—Revelation 12:14), and (3) the last part of that seven years will be progressively overshadowed by the judgments and the Wrath of God (cf. Revelation 6:17) being poured out on all who oppose Him, including Antichrist.

Virtually all scholars and teachers who believe in the literal seven-year scenario agree about the Great Tribulation (the wrath of Satan), the Day of the Lord, and the Wrath of God being part of it. The disagreement is over the timing and sequence of events within the seven years. Joseph Good (www.hatikva.org), for example, believes that the Day of the Lord, the Great Tribulation, and the Wrath of God all run concurrently throughout the seven years. The prewrath rapture people—Robert Van Kampen [deceased], Marvin Rosenthal, Charles Cooper, et al. (cf. www.prewrath rapture.com)—believe that the Great Tribulation comprises a short period of time immediately following the midpoint of the seven years, after which the Day of the Lord, which includes the Wrath of God, will occur during the last year or two of the seven. S. R. Shearer (www.antipasministries.com) believes that the tribulation comprises the entire seven years, with the Day of the Lord being a literal 24-hour day that occurs on the last day of the seven years.

This commentator has been studying the Scripture and all these teachings for many years, and tends, to an extent, to go along with the prewrath view because it seems to be the most natural, literal, common-sense interpretation which best harmonizes all the prophetic Scripture. However, if one holds to a literal prophetic fulfillment of the Spring and Fall feasts of the Lord, then, just as the Messiah's first coming, death and resurrection, and the pouring out of His Spirit were exactly, to the day and hour, foreshadowed by the Spring Feasts, His second coming, the resurrection and rapture of His Bride (the Church), the pouring out of the last plagues of the Wrath of the Lord (the plagues of the bowls of wrath following the sounding of the seventh and final trumpet), the "sheep and goat" judgment (Matthew 25:32-33), and the establishment of His millennial kingdom must all occur within the 15-day period of the Fall Feasts following the sounding of the final trumpet blast on Yom Teruah (the "Feast of Trumpets").

But, guess what?—when it comes down to where "the rubber meets the road"—to how I need to be living my life in the present moment—I do not know and I do not care about the exact timing and sequence of these events. All that I know and care about is that **they will occur**, and I need to be doing my best to be warning everyone I can to be prepared, regardless of when in the sequence of events, they occur. There also will be other specific events during the seven years that people need to be warned about or prepared for, whether they occur at the beginning, middle, or end of the seven years. The timing of some events (e.g., Antimessiah standing in the Temple declaring himself to be *"god"* at the midpoint of the seven years) are clearly specified. So, I believe that God has made clear, at least to those who study prophetic Scripture diligently and sincerely want to know the Truth, the sequence and timing of certain events. The sequence and timing of other events—the annihilation of Babylon the Great, the beginning point of the Day of the Lord, and so forth—are not so clear. And all that the endless debate over controversial times and sequences accomplish is to distract us from living each day in total self-denial for the good of others and the glory of God, and so, I believe, are nothing more than devices of Satan to distract us from the work of God on Earth at the present time. I doubt that the untold millions around the world who are in agonizing suffering, starving to death, freezing to death, being oppressed or persecuted, or being killed every day are very concerned about when the rapture will occur or when their oppressors (and God's enemies) will be destroyed, do you? They just need to know that **it will happen**, and that **it will happen soon**, and what they need to do about it. They need salvation and hope, not debatable details.

And there are several indications that the implications of the events of the Final Seven Years pertain just as much to the Jews as to the Followers of Jesus. For example, the seven years are called *"the Time of Jacob's* [Israel's] *Trouble"* (Jeremiah 30:7). And this will be especially true during the Great Tribulation. Because Revelation gives the details of how the *Tanakh* prophecies will be fulfilled, when these things do occur just as was prophesied by Israel's prophets and by Jesus to His disciples and in the Revelation, their eyes will be opened to see that He is the Messiah for whom they have been looking. And that is why it is just as important to preach the Gospel according to the Revelation to the Jews as to the Gentiles: They may not immediately accept it, but when these events unfold, their eyes will be opened to the Truth, and they will be saved (Romans 11:26)!

But meanwhile, are **you** ready for all these wonderful or terrifying (depending on your point of view) *". . . things which must shortly* [in rapid succession] *come to pass"* (Revelation 1:1)?

Where will you be on the Day of the Lord?

The Bible indicates that the Christians, whether or not they enter the seven years, will not have to endure at least the *"last plagues"* of the Wrath of God. Also, there are some indications that only the unsaved earth dwellers who have taken the mark of the beast will be affected by the trumpet and bowl plagues (cf. Revelation 9:4, 20). It tells us that the redeemed will be *"caught up"* (from the Latin, *rapio*) in our newly-acquired, glorified bodies, to meet the Messiah in the sky, then taken to a place he has prepared for us (in Heaven) (cf. 1 Corinthians 15:52; 1 Thessalonians 4:17; John 14:2-3) before the Lord's wrath is poured out (cf. 1 Thessalonians 5:9).

Nevertheless, it is difficult to see, if believers are present on Earth at all during the last half of the Final Seven Years, how they can avoid being affected by the plagues of the Lord that affect virtually the whole earth. One possible explanation is that the believers (those who survive the Great Tribulation) will be present on Earth during the entire Final Seven Years, but will be raptured on the last day, before the *"last plagues"* of the wrath of God are poured out. Another possible solution is that the "wrath" of the Lord to which 1 Thessalonians 5:9 refers is His wrath that destroys everyone and everything opposed to Him on the final Day of Judgment (Revelation 20:11-15). So this commentator will not be dogmatic about when, in the sequence of events, the Rapture will occur, except that it **will not** occur prior to the Final Seven Years.

But, regardless of whether or not the Saints are present during the Day of the Lord, they **will** have to patiently endure the Great Tribulation if they are present during that time (cf. the commentary on 12:7-17g; 13:6-10b; 14:6-13d; and 16:15). And **if** they endure whatever trials and tribulations come their way (cf. 2 Timothy 2:12), overcome whatever obstacles Satan places in their path, and keep doing what God has given them to do until The End, they will be saved (cf. Revelation 2:26).

Of course, I am not teaching a work-your-way-to-Heaven salvation here. Good works and grace are **not** mutually exclusive (contrary to what many Christians believe and teach). I acknowledge that it is only by God's grace and Spirit that we can do anything right and keep the commandments of the Lord. But I just wanted to point out that endurance and good works (by God's enabling Spirit) are necessary confirmations of a saving faith (cf. James 2:17). In other words, if the Holy Spirit does not dwell in us, enabling us to live a good life and do good works, then our "faith" is phony and will not get us to Heaven. Just because we believe in our heads that Jesus is the Lord does not make us eligible for citizenship in the Kingdom of Heaven. Only if God the Holy Spirit dwells in us, enabling us to ". . . *deny* [ourselves], *take up* [our] *cross*[es] daily, *and follow* [Him]" with our whole heart, soul, strength, time, and all of our possessions, can we be sure of escaping the Wrath of God, and ultimately, "eternity" in Hell.

As I've mentioned on other pages of this book, most American "Christians" are deceived. They have a strong tendency to think that they are okay with the Lord when they are not. How about you? Have you really surrendered your life—"lock, stock, and barrel"—to the Lord, in the name of Jesus the true Messiah, and do you know that the Holy Spirit is in you, enabling you to do everything that you do (cf. Romans 8:9)? If you are not sure, you'd better make sure, before you find yourself right in the midst of the worst nightmare (but real) that you have ever conceived—the awesome, terrible Wrath of God.

If you have any doubt about where you stand with the Lord, please let me encourage you to go back and read Chapter 4—"Is the United States of America a True Christian Nation."

Meanwhile, if you have any questions, comments, or suggestions about anything you've read in *The Tenth Harbinger*, if you want someone to pray with or for you, if you just want to discuss these things, or if you would like to get involved in Last Trump Ministries, please visit our website at www.RevelationUnderstoodCommentary.com or contact me at: WatchmanBob@gmail.com.

Notes & References

Notes & References

Introduction

1. Jonathan Cahn, *The Harbinger* (Lake Mary, FL: FrontLine, 2011).
2. Israel's prophesied response to the first attack by the Assyrians (732 B.C.) and defiantly proclaimed by America's leaders after the 9/11 attack on the World Trade Center, http://www.politijim.com/2011/09/monday-freak-out-tom-daschle-and-john.html (accessed September 11, 2013).
3. Watchman Bob, *The Revelation of Yahushua the Messiah* (self published, 2010), available through http://www.revelationunderstoodcommentary.com or Amazon.com.
4. *Revelation Understood! Commentary*, http://www.revelationunderstoodcommentary.com
5. "Prophecy Being Fulfilled in Current Events," http://www.revelationunderstoodcommentary.com/revelation-commentary-blog.html
6. James F. Fitzgerald, *The 9/11 Prophecy* (Washington, D.C.: WND Books, 2013).

Chapter 1—*The Harbinger.* Insightful but Incomplete

1. Robert Jamieson, A.R. Fausset and David Brown, *Commentary on the Whole Bible* (Grand Rapids, MI: Zondervan Publishing House, 1961), 503.
2. Details and dates of the history of Israel (other than those recorded in the *Bible*) are based on Yohanan Aharoni and Michael Avi-Yonah, *The MacMillan Bible Atlas,* 3rd ed. (Jerusalem: Carta, 1993), 90-113.
3. Research has shown that Pul, identified as the king of Assyria in 2 Kings 15:19, was Tiglath-pilezer III, http://www.bible-history.com/archaeology/assyria/Tiglath-Pileser-III.html (accessed September 16, 2013).

4. Numerous articles and books, e.g., "NORAD Standdown," http://911research.wtc7.net/ planes/analysis/norad (accessed September 16, 2013), have documented how inexplicable it is that each of four commercial airliners were allowed to fly off-course for from 16 to 52 minutes, especially in the area of the nation's largest city and its capital, without being intercepted by North American Air Defense (NORAD) fighter jets, when standard operating procedure (SOP) is to scramble those jets within two minutes of notification that communication has been lost with an aircraft or radar indicates that it is off-course. This would seem, however, to be just another example of the inevitability of the occurrence of an event prophesied in the *Bible*.

5. Kenneth W. Michael Wills, "Assyrian Empire Military Tactics," http://www.ehow.com/ info_8709839_ assyrian-empire-military-tactics.html (accessed September 18, 2013).

6. Kim Benzel, Sarah B. Graff, Yelena Rakic and Edith W. Watts, *Art of the Ancient Near East*, http://www.metmuseum.org/~/media/Files/Learn/For%20Educators/Publications %20for%20Educators/Art%20of%20the%20Ancient%20Near%20East.pdf (accessed September 18, 2013), 48.

7. Alan Boyle, "Ancient wall in Israel matches up with Bible's tale of Assyrian attack," http://www.nbcnews.com/science/ancient-wall-israel-matches-bibles-tale-assyrian-attack-6C10953508 (accessed September 18, 2013).

8. The sources of all quotations in the preceding two paragraphs are cited in *The Harbinger*, pages 62-63.

9. CT Forum, "How Christian Leaders Have Changed Since 9/11," http://www.christianitytoday.com/ct/2011/september/howleaderschanged.html?start=2 (accessed September 20, 2013).

10. "hewn stones <01496>" (from *Strong's Concordance*), cited in *BibleWorks for Windows*, Version 8.0.005s.1 (Norfolk, VA: Bibleworks LLC, 2009).

11. "Remarks, Governor George E. Pataki, Laying of the Cornerstone for Freedom Tower, July 4, 2004," http://renewnyc.com/content/speeches/Gov_speech_Freedom_Tower.pdf.

12. "Zacchaeus: Up a (Sycamore) Tree (Luke 19:4),"
http://trivialdevotion.blogspot.com/ 2013/02/zacchaeus-up-
sycamore-tree-luke-194.html (accessed September 22, 2013).

13. "The Cedars of God,"
http://en.wikipedia.org/wiki/Cedars_of_God (accessed September 22, 2013).

14. Randy Kennedy, "Uprooted in the Attacks, Now Planted in
Bronze," The New York Times,
http://www.nytimes.com/2005/07/06/arts/design/06chur.html?p
agewanted=all (accessed September 22, 2013).

15. Elliott Nesch, "Prophetic Word in 9/11,"
http://www.holybibleprophecy.org/ 2011/09/11/911-10th-
anniversary-the-lords-word-in-september-11th-by-elliott-nesch (accessed Septermber 22, 2013).

16. John T. Woolley and Gerhard Peters, "John Edwards: Remarks to the Congressional Black Caucus Prayer Breakfast, September 11, 2004," http://www.presidency.ucsb.edu/ws/
index.php?pid=84922#axzz1M02bgo9D (accessed September 24,
2013).

17. Washington File, "Senate Majority Leader Daschle Express-
es Sorrow, Resolve," September 12, 2001,
http://wfile.ait.org.tw/wf-archive/2001/010913/epf407.htm (accessed September 25, 2013).

18. In *The Harbinger* (page 155), Jonathan Cahn explains that the
Hebrew term *Schemitah* means *"the release, the remission, the letting rest."*

19. Donna Danna, "How Close are Stock Market Crashes to
Jewish Feast or Fast Days,"
http://www.fivedoves.com/letters/sep2012/donnad927-1.htm
(accessed September 26, 2013).

20. WhiteHouse.gov, "Remarks of President Obama—as Prepared for Delivery, Address to Joint Session of Congress, Tuesday,
February 24, 2009,"
http://www.whitehouse.gov/the_press_office/ Remarks-of-
President-Barack-Obama-Address-to-Joint-Session-of-Congress
(accessed September 26, 2013).

Chapter 2—A Second Witness: *The 9/11 Prophecy*

1. Unless otherwise noted, all descriptions of James F. Fitzgerald's experiences in this chapter are based on his account in *The 9/11 Prophecy* (Washington, DC: World Net Daily, 2013).
2. James F. Fitzgerald, *The WatchWORD Bible* (video book), distributed by World Net Daily, www.wnd.com.
3. *The 9/11 Prophecy*, page 22.
4. *The 9/11 Prophecy*, page 24.
5. *The 9/11 Prophecy*, pages 24-28.
6. For the identity of the first "horseman of the Apocalypse," read the commentary on Revelation 6:2 at http://www.revelationunderstoodcom- mentary.com/beginning-of-sorrows.html (accessed November 21, 2013).
7. For identification of *"the one who restrains,"* see Alan Kurschner, *Antichrist, Before the Day of the Lord* (Pompton Lakes, NJ: Eschatos Publishing, 2013), 36-39.
8. *The 9/11 Prophecy*, page 157.
9. *The Harbinger*, pages 221-223.
10. *The 9/11 Prophecy*, page 187.

Chapter 3—A Third Witness is Called

1. Watchman Bob, "Who are the People of Yahuah ('God')?" http://www.revelationunderstood commentary.com/people-of-Yahuah.html (accessed October 9, 2013).
2. "American Exceptionalism," http://en.wikipedia.org/wiki/American_exceptionalism (accessed October 9, 2013).
3. Dave Gifford, "Eight interesting facts about Revelation's use of the Old Testament," *Gifmex's Bog of Apoca-Lists*, http://www.revelation.giffmex.org/?p=17 (accessed October 10, 2013).
4. Watchman Bob, *The Revelation of Yahushua the Messiah* (self-published, 2010), printed by CreateSpace, http://www.createspace.com, and distributed through http://www.revelationunderstood commentary.com and http://www.amazon.com.

Chapter 4—Is the United States of America a True Christian Nation?

1. Pride also motivates anti-Semitism. Even though Christians may say that they are pro-Israel and even that the Jews are the people of God, they usually consider Jews second-class citizens in the Kingdom of God, or not really the people of God at all. The apostle Paul wrote the entire eleventh chapter of Romans to refute and warn against that view, explaining that the Jews are the original People of God who have been temporarily put "on hold"—blinded to the fact that Jesus is their Messiah—so that the Gentiles who are branches of the "wild olive tree" who come to faith in Jesus, could be "grafted into" the "natural olive tree" (Israel). So, the grafted-in believers in Jesus should certainly not look down their noses at the Jews, because if the natural branches could be cut off but later grafted back in, how much easier would it be to cut off arrogant, anti-Semitic, anti-Zionist grafted-in branches? (cf. Romans 11:1, 13-25) Paul further explains the relationship between the Jews and the grafted-in believers by calling them "fellow citizens" in the "commonwealth of Israel" (Ephesians 2:12, 19). So, it is actually more correct to say that Gentiles who have come to faith in Jesus are Israelites than it is to say that Jews who have come to faith in Jesus are Christians.

2. Matthew Mead, *The Almost Christian Discovered; or, the False Professor Tried and Cast*, http://www.jesuseveryday.com/free_christian_books/Matthew_Mead- The_Almost_Christian_ Discovered.pdf (accessed October 11, 2013).

Chapter 5—The True Spiritual Roots of America

1. "Founding Fathers of the United States of America," http://en.wikipedia.org/wiki/ Founding_ Fathers_of_the_United_States (accessed October 11, 2013).

2. For a few of the many Scriptures that state or imply that Jesus is God, see "Some Bible verses that say, 'Jesus is God,'" http://www.bugman123.com/Bible/JesusIsGod.html (accessed October 12, 2013).

3. "Deism," http://en.wikipedia.org/wiki/Deism (accessed October 14, 2013).

4. Unless otherwise indicated, the information in this section on Thomas Jefferson is derived from "Thomas Jefferson," http://en.wikipedia.org/wiki/Thomas_Jefferson (accessed October 14, 2013).

5. "Jefferson's Religious Beliefs," http://www.monticello.org/site/research-and-collections/jeffersons-religious-beliefs (accessed October 14, 2013).

6. "Jefferson's Religious Beliefs"

7. "Thomas Jefferson and Slavery," http://www.monticello.org/site/plantation-and-slavery/thomas-jefferson-and-slavery (accessed October 15, 2013).

8. Unless otherwise indicated, the information in this section on Benjamin Franklin is derived from "Benjamin Franklin," http://en.wikipedia.org/wiki/Benjamin_Franklin (accessed October 15, 2013).

9. Walter Isaacson, editor, *A Benjamin Franklin Reader* (New York: Simon & Schuster, 2003), 492.

10. Darren Staloff, "Deism and the Founding of the United States," http://nationalhumanities center.org/tserve/eighteen/ekeyinfo/deism.htm (accessed October 17, 2013).

11. Unless otherwise indicated, information in this section on Alexander Hamilton is derived from "Alexander Hamilton," http://en.wikipedia.org/wiki/Alexander_Hamilton (accessed October 20, 2013).

12. Douglas Adair & Marvin Harvey (1955). "Was Alexander Hamilton a Christian Statesman?". William and Mary Quarterly 12 (2): 308–329, as referenced at http://en.wikipedia.org/wiki/ Alexander_Hamilton (accessed October 20, 2013).

13. Information in this section on James Madison is derived from http://en.wikipedia.org/wiki/ James_Madison (accessed October 20, 2013).

14. Information in this section on Unitarianism is derived from http://en.wikipedia.org/wiki/ Unitarianism (accessed October 20, 2013).

15. Unless otherwise indicated, information in this section on John Adams is derived from http://en.wikipedia.org/wiki/ John_Adams (accessed on October 20, 2013).

16. "United First Parish Church," http://www.ufpc.org/historyvisitorprogram/history.html (accessed October 21, 2013).

17. "John Adams," http://www25.uua.org/uuhs/duub/articles/johnadams.html (accessed October 21, 2013).

18. Charles I. Bevans, editor, *Treaties and Other International Agreements of the United States of America 1776-1949, Vol. 11: Philippines-United Arab Republic* (Washington D.C.: Department of State Publications, 1974), 1072.

19. Unless otherwise indicated, information in this section is derived from Cutting Edge Ministries, "Masonry Proven Conclusively to be Worship of Lucifer, Satan!" http://www.cuttingedge.org/free11.html (accessed October 21, 2013).

20. "Masons (Freemasonry), Christian or Anti-Christian?" http://www.rapidnet.com/~jbeard/bdm/Cults/masons.htm (accessed October 21, 2013).

21. Unless otherwise indicated, information from this section on George Washington is derived from "George Washington," http://en.wikipedia.org/wiki/George_Washington (accessed October 22, 2013).

22. The Ignorant Fisherman Blog, "Christian Quotes from President George Washington," http://www.theignorantfishermen.com/2009/06/few-quotes-from-george-washington.html (accessed October 22, 2013).

23. "Bad News about the Washington Prayer," http://www.redstate.com/qbart/2011/04/28/bad-news-about-the-washington-prayer/ (accessed October 22, 2013).

24. The term "religious" in referring to Masonic observances is quoted from the George Washington Masonic National Memorial website at http://gwmemorial.org/WashingtonTheMason.php (accessed October 22, 2013).

25. The information in this paragraph is derived from the George Washington Masonic National Memorial website.

26. Information on John Jay, the public servant, derived from "John Jay," http://en.wikipedia.org/wiki/John_Jay (accessed October 22, 2013).

27. Information and quotes on John Jay, the Christian, derived from "The Jays and Religion,"

http://www.johnjayhomestead.org/images/The_Jays_and_Religio
n_for_website.pdf (accessed October 23, 2013).

28. "Religious affiliations of Presidents of the United States,"
http://en.wikipedia.org/
wiki/Religious_affiliations_of_Presidents_of_the_United_States
(accessed October 26, 2013).

29. "Famous Freemasons," http://whale.to/b/33.html (accessed October 26, 2013).

Chapter 6—The Identity and Destiny of America in *Bible* Prophecy

1. Unless otherwise indicated, the information on ancient Babylon is derived from two sources: "Ancient Babylonia – History of Babylonia," http://www.bible-history.com/babylonia/Babylonia History_of_Babylonia.htm (accessed October 30, 2013) and Jeffrey Goodman, *The Comets of God* (Tucson, Arizona: Archaeological Research Books, 2011).

2. "Barack Obama: The Man Who Would Be God?" http://www.conservativecrusader.com/ articles/barack-obama-the-man-who-would-be-god (accessed October 30, 2013).

3. "The American Empire and the U.S. System of Client States," http://www.antipasministries. com/html/file0000133.htm (accessed October 30, 2013).

4. In spite of the USA's deadline to withdraw military forces from there by the end of 2011, she still maintains a very powerful training, advisory, support, and mercenary presence in Iraq. Obviously, the USA intends to maintain controlling influence in that part of the world, because she has just completed and moved into her new, fantastic, sprawling embassy in Iraq—the largest in the world—located just 50 miles from the site of the ancient city of Babylon! Ironic, isn't it? "U.S. Embassy in Iraq Largest, Most Expensive Ever," http://www.foxnews.com/story/2009/01/05/us-embassy-in-iraq-largest-most-expensive-ever (accessed October 30, 2013).

5. "New World Order—President Bush's Speech to Congress," http://www.al-bab.com/arab/ docs/pal/pal10.htm (accessed October 30, 2013).

6. R.A. Coombes, *America, the Babylon—America's Destiny Foretold in Biblical Prophecy*, on CD Rom at http://americathebabylon.com (last accessed October 4, 2013). However, Coombes passed away in 2013, and the americathebabylon.com site has been removed from the Internet. *America, the Babylon* is now available in condensed book form through Amazon.

Chapter 7—The Tenth Harbinger

1. The photo of the Genesis 11 page and Suson's description of his discovery may be viewed at "september11.net," http://www.septembereleven.net/page141.htm (accessed October 4, 2013).
2. *The Comets of God*, 298-302.
3. *The Comets of God*, 299.
4. *The Comets of God*, 289-291, 308-309.
5. See the commentary on Revelation 6:2 in *The Revelation of Yahushua the Messiah*, 91-92.
6. *America the Babylon.*
7. *The Comets of God*, 184.
8. The comet fragment just 100 meters in diameter that exploded over the Tunguska River Basin in Siberia in 1908 flattened more than a half million acres of forest, *The Comets of God*, 161.
9. *The Comets of God*, 77.

Chapter 8—The Final Seven Years

1. The term *"one week"* in Daniel 9:27 is translated from a Hebrew term *(shabuwa')* which can mean seven days or years, depending on the context. In the context of other Scriptures (e.g., Daniel 12:11), it is clear that the *"one week"* of Daniel 9:27 is one week of years (seven years), as is clarified in the *Complete Jewish Bible* and the *New International Version* of the *Bible*.
2. See the commentary on Revelation 6:2 at http://www.revelationunderstoodcommentary. com/beginning-of-sorrows.html (accessed November 6, 2013).

3. Notice that the events of Matthew 24:4-8 (the *"beginning of sorrows"*) perfectly parallel the events of Revelation 6:2-8 (the conquering of the world by Satan).

4. "Abomination of Desolation," http://en.wikipedia.org/wiki/Abomination_of_desolation (accessed November 6, 2013).

5. For thorough, detailed, Scriptural support for this watchman's understanding of the Final Seven Years, read his commentary, especially on Revelation 6-19, at http://www.revelation understoodcommentary.com/commentary-on-revelation.html (accessed November 6, 2013).

6. For Coombes' excellent analysis of Revelation 17:16, see *America the Babylon*, available through Amazon.

7. Daniel 11:36-37 prophesies that the coming king (Antichrist) *"shall exalt and magnify himself above every god, shall speak blasphemies against the God of gods, and shall prosper till the wrath has been accomplished.... [and] He shall regard neither the God of his fathers nor the desire of women, nor regard any god; for he shall exalt himself above them all."* This means that, if Antichrist is a Muslim (as this commentator believes), when he declares himself to be "god," he will have no more regard for *"the God of his fathers"* (Allah) and will establish his own global religion in which he will be worshiped as "god." (According to the Qur'an, it is blasphemy for anyone to consider himself equal with Allah or even to be Allah's son.)

Chapter 9—Will Christians Escape, Survive, or Take Dominion of the Earth During The Final Seven Years?

1. "Left Behind," http://en.wikipedia.org/wiki/Left_Behind (accessed November 9, 2013).

2. For a detailed explanation of the sequence of events of the Final Seven Years, see the commentary on Revelation 6-19 beginning at http://www.revelationunderstoodcommentary.com/ beginning-of-sorrows.html (accessed November 12, 2013).

3. "Martyrs Today," http://www.fatherpius.littleway.ca/ref46.html (accessed October 29, 2013).

4. For complete details and Scriptural support of this interpretation, see the commentary on Revelation Chapters 20 and 21 beginning at http://www.revelationunderstoodcommentary.com/millennial-kingdom.html (accessed November 11, 2013).

Appendix 1—Scriptural Evidence that America is Babylon the Great

1. Current events are rapidly confirming the fulfillment of the prophecies concerning the rise of the revived Roman/Ottoman Empire and its ruler, the anti-messiah.

The capital of the ancient Roman Empire under Constantine (a type of the anti-messiah) was Constantinople (now Istanbul, Turkey). The Roman Empire was then divided into the Western Empire with Rome as its capital and the Eastern Empire with its capital still Constantinople. After the destruction of the Western Empire, the Eastern Roman Empire became the Byzantine Empire, which later became the Islamic Ottoman Empire in 1299 CE. The Ottoman Empire had a long history, finally falling in 1923 CE. However, Islam, with its goal of establishing a new Caliphate (empire ruled by *Sharia*—Islamic—law) is, by far, the world's fastest-growing religion and Muslims are, by far, the fastest-growing religious population group world-wide, literally invading the nations of the world, particularly the Western nations. And Turkey, a Muslim-dominated nation, is considered a "Eurasian" nation because of its location as a land-bridge between Europe and Asia and its strong economic and political ties with both Eastern and Western nations. So, it is not too difficult to see that Turkey, which is also the primary location of the peoples who will come against Israel in the Last Days (cf. Ezekiel 38), may very well be the location of the capital of the Revived Roman Empire just as it was the location of the capital of the ancient Roman Empire. Is it not interesting that Turkey recently cut off diplomatic ties with Israel and has sided with other Arabic nations in their determination to destroy Israel?

Also, it seems clear from Obadiah's prophecies (e.g., Obadiah 4) vis-à-vis other Bible prophecies (e.g., Isaiah 14:13; Daniel 8:10; 11:37) that the anti-messiah will be an Arabic Muslim—specifically a descendant of Jacob's twin brother Esau.

The descendants of Abraham's son and Isaac's outcast half-brother Ishmael (the Arabs) mirror Israel in many ways, including being descendants of twelve patriarchs (the sons of Ishmael), their belief in one god (Allah), and looking forward to a messiah (the Mahdi). And they have always been the rivals of Israel, coveting Israel's inheritance from God through Abraham (the Promised Land, its capital Jerusalem, and dominion over the world).

When Edom, the nation formed by the descendants of Esau (Ishmael's nephew)—Judea's treacherous kinsman-neighbor to the south—was conquered by Nebuchadnezzar, although she remained an identifiable province of Babylon, many of her inhabitants migrated into the surrounding areas, including what is now Saudi Arabia and into Israel. In the absence of the Judeans, who had been carried away into captivity into Babylon, the Edomites were permitted to occupy Jerusalem. But then, the Jews were permitted to return to their homeland by Cyrus, King of Persia, in 536 BCE. And, in 130 BCE, when Jerusalem and Judea were again occupied and controlled by the Jews, the ruler of Judea at that time, John Hyrcanus, forced the Edomites to convert to Judaism. Nominally, they complied, but maintained a treacherous presence in Jerusalem and Judea. The Jews remained suspicious of them, calling them "half-Jews." Then, when the Romans subjugated Judea, they made Herod I ("the Great"), an Edomite (Latin: *Idumean*) "Jew," King of the Jews. And it was Herod the Great who, in his maniacal determination to get rid of the newborn Messiah Jesus, had all baby boys under the age of two in and around Bethlehem killed.

Get the picture: the "King of the Jews," a descendant of Israel's displaced twin brother Esau, in a diabolical frenzy trying to kill the true King of the Jews. What clearer type of the false messiah could there be?

Then, exactly as prophesied (Jeremiah 49:10 and numerous other passages), the Edomites seem to have disappeared after the destruction of the Temple by the Romans in 70 CE. Apparently, they were absorbed into the surrounding, now Arabic/Muslim nations, especially into what is now Turkey.

But, at the End of the Age, one of their descendants will again ascend to the throne of David, and, having no regard for the god of his fathers (Allah) (Daniel 11:37), he shall claim to be not only King of the Jews, but Lord of the World.

2. For an excellent technical analysis of 17:16 (which is beyond the competency of this commentator), *America the Babylon: America's Destiny Foretold in Biblical Prophecy*, available through Amazon.

3. As scientist and scholar Jeffrey Goodman has pointed out in his well researched and thoroughly documented book *The Comets of God*, it would be impossible for even thousands of simultaneously detonated nuclear bombs to annihilate all natural life in an area the size of the U.S.A. But a comet less than a mile in diameter exploding in the atmosphere above a 10,000 square mile area would very quickly incinerate all living plants, animals and humans in that area, rendering it uninhabitable. Scientific studies of the sites of Sodom and Gomorrah have proven that those cities were destroyed by a comet fragment exploding in the atmosphere above them. Likewise, on June 30, 1908, at 7:15 a.m., a relatively small comet fragment approximately 100 meters (the length of a football field) in diameter exploded in the atmosphere above the Tunguska River Basin in Siberia, incinerating a 1,000 square mile forested area and several herds of reindeer below, and scorched the skin of eye witnesses 40 miles away (*The Comets of God*, pages 54-57 and 143-152). Also, computer simulations have shown that a comet just two miles in diameter exploding in Earth's atmosphere will engulf the entire planet in flames. So, it is easy to see, is it not, how a comet exploding above modern Babylon the Great will very quickly annihilate all living plants and animals in that city-state/nation?

Appendix 2—Be Saved from the Wrath of God

1. For an overview of the Feasts of the Lord and their relevance to the events of the Day and the Wrath of the Lord see the commentary on Revelation 19 at http://www.revelationunderstood commentary.com/armageddon-prophecy.html (accessed on November 14, 2013).

Made in the USA
Lexington, KY
21 November 2014